BRIDE'S

WEDDING PLANNER

BRIDE'S

WEDDING PLANNER

By the Editors of BRIDE'S Magazine

Fawcett Columbine · New York

Acknowledgments

BRIDE'S Magazine gratefully acknowledges the inspiration and guidance of Barbara D. Tober, its Editor-in-Chief, and Andrea Feld, Managing Editor. We would also like to thank writer Sarah T. Boyle, for her diligent effort to update this book for the '90s. Thanks also to tireless staff editors Tamara Eberlein, Heather Twidale, Julia Martin, and Robyn Liverant, and to free-lancers Miriam Arond and June Rogoznica.

For their insights in each of their areas of expertise, thanks to staff members Sally Kilbridge, Cynthia Penney, Rachel Leonard, Denise O'Donoghue, Elizabeth Rundlett, Donna Ferrari, Alecia Beldegreen, Jo-Ann Bloomberg, and Connie Keller.

And for their contributions to the aesthetic appearance of the book, BRIDE'S thanks Art Director Phyllis Richmond Cox and Anne Marie Mennillo.

A Fawcett Columbine Book
Published by Ballantine Books
Copyright © 1977, 1980, 1989 by The Condé Nast Publications, Inc.

Library of Congress Catalog Card Number: 89-91941

ISBN: 0-449-90467-9

Design by Holly Johnson

Illustrations by Maryann Berté
and Rollin McGrail

Manufactured in the United States of America

Revised Edition: January 1990
10 9 8 7 6 5 4 3 2 1

Contents

Congratulations!

What excitement lies in store for both of you. Planning and enjoying your wedding and the home you'll both share as a married couple can be among the most rewarding of life's activities. But, you've got to be organized. Chances are, you're both working . . . with precious few hours for comparison shopping, double-checking and staying home to receive deliveries and phone calls. That's why the editors of *BRIDE'S* Magazine have compiled this wedding planner: to make life easier not only in the months before your wedding, but after you return from your honeymoon, too.

Because we know you want your wedding celebration and all the accompanying festivities to reflect your special style, we've created pages of charts and checklists, budget sheets and diagrams to take the guesswork out of the months ahead. You and your groom can save time and energy by spending a few hours together now, making decisions and planning strategies. Examine all the options before you choose the type of wedding that reflects your personalities, the guests you'll invite to share your joy, the attendants you'll want in your wedding party, the perfect spot for a romantic honeymoon.

Included in this essential book are: tips for selecting the *ultimate wedding dress* as well as charming bridesmaids' dresses that attendants of all shapes and sizes will *really* wear again . . . suggestions for planning a Long Weekend Wedding that brings guests from thousands of miles away, or a Progressive Wedding that takes *you* on a trip to visit and party with both families and mutual friends . . . guidelines for selecting home furnishings and entertaining equipment that will turn even the most sterile four walls into a "private world" that welcomes you home each day.

Just in time for the 1990s, we've added the most up-to-date information on how to get: the results you want from a professional photographer and/or videographer; breathtakingly beautiful bouquets and table arrangements from your florist; and sumptuous cakes that will *taste* as good as they look. Included, too, is an extensive section on everything you, your fiancé *and* your family need to know about choosing food, wine and liquor for a gala reception, as well as all those other parties that surround "the big day": the rehearsal dinner, showers, bridesmaids' and ushers' events, the engagement party.

The editors of *BRIDE'S* Magazine have

thought long and hard about how to make your wedding, honeymoon, and first year of marriage as trouble free as possible, and we have put all our experience and expertise to work in preparing this invaluable book—especially for the two of you. We want to help you organize all the details well in advance so you can both be relaxed and comfortable on your wedding day. We've tried to answer all your questions, and anticipate problems even before they need to be solved. Our goal is for you and your groom, your family and friends to enjoy a wedding day that will live in your memory as nothing less than a moment to treasure . . . forever.

With all good wishes to you and your fiancé for a lifetime of happiness as friends and partners.

Barbara Tober
Editor-in-Chief
BRIDE'S Magazine

Section 1:

GETTING STARTED

YOUR ENGAGEMENT

Congratulations—you've decided to get married! There are so many exciting moments ahead—making wedding arrangements and planning a life together. But first, you'll probably want to spread the good news.

Tell your parents first. It's preferable to share the news of your engagement in person. If your parents live far away and you announce your plans over the phone, schedule a visit with them soon after.

The groom may want to speak privately with his future father-in-law. Some grooms feel comfortable with the old tradition of "asking for your hand"; others enjoy the opportunity of chatting privately about upcoming plans.

Tell children immediately. If either of you has children, tell them the news as soon as possible. Be prepared for questions about living arrangements, stepsiblings, rules and discipline, and wedding plans.

Inform supervisors and co-workers. Assure them that you plan to maintain the quality of your work and notify them, in advance, of any days off that you'll need for wedding planning and the honeymoon.

Call your other friends and relatives. If you've selected your attendants, you might tell them about your choice when you announce the news of your engagement. Or you can ask them to be in your wedding at some later date—just be sure they'll have enough time to arrange their schedules.

HOW TO BUY ENGAGEMENT AND WEDDING RINGS

Engagement and wedding rings are age-old symbols of love and commitment. Most brides and grooms today choose diamonds for engagement rings, according to the Diamond Information Center in New York, N.Y. About 90 percent of all men marrying now purchase wedding bands. Here are some tips on making these important wedding purchases.

To Shop or to Pop the Question

Some couples shop for the bride's engagement ring together (which, in most instances, the groom still pays for entirely), after discussing and deciding upon marriage. They feel that since the ring is a major purchase that will be worn for a lifetime, the bride who wears it should be

1

sure she loves it. Other couples prefer the romantic surprise of the husband-to-be "popping the question" with a ring in hand. And others prefer to window-shop together when discussing marriage, so the groom gets an idea of what the bride likes, then surprises her with the actual engagement ring.

Financing the Stone

Many financial experts recommend that you not spend more than three weeks' salary, or six percent of your income, on your engagement ring. Today many jewelry stores offer credit or layaway plans for easier financing.

Where to Shop

Engagement and wedding rings are sold by chain stores, catalog showrooms, department stores, independent jewelers, and so-called wholesalers. You may want to visit several types of stores to compare. Look for reputable companies, preferably ones that friends have recommended. Another way to determine if stores or dealers are dependable is to find out if they are members of the *American Gem Society* (AGS), an organization that sets high ethical standards and provides advanced education for jewelers. A store may display an *American Gem Society* logo on its windows, on business cards, in advertisements, on plaques, or on appraisal forms.

When to Shop

You will probably want to wear your engagement ring as soon as you announce your engagement, so shop right away, particularly if you want a customized design. If you're running short on time, however, you can buy the engagement ring any time (even after the wedding). Wedding rings should be ordered about three months before the wedding.

Style Considerations

• Choose a ring that goes well with your hand size—perhaps a narrow band, a single stone for small hands; a wider band and bolder style for large hands.

• Will you wear your engagement ring and wedding ring on the same finger? Many engagement/wedding rings come in matched sets. If you are buying them separately, try them on together to see how they look and fit.

Ring Materials

The most common choices for stone settings are gold, white gold, silver, and platinum. Platinum is the strongest; a platinum head is often used to hold stones on a ring of any metal. Gold is a popular choice—most rings are 14K or 18K alloys of gold and stronger metals for durability.

Many brides now select gemstones along with diamonds for engagement rings. You might choose sapphires to flank either side of a diamond, or a gemstone in the center, encircled with diamonds. Rubies and sapphires (as opposed to opals and emeralds) are most resistant to chipping and cracking.

Shapes

The round diamond—or the solitaire—is the most popular, perhaps because its brilliant cut reflects light so well. Other shapes include the marquise (pointed at both ends), oval, pear, and emerald (square or rectangular).

The Four Cs of Diamond Quality

Carat is the unit of weight used to measure diamonds. There are 100 points to a carat, and a stone weighing less than a carat may be referred to by its points, such as 23 points or .23. Diamonds may also be classified by terms such as ⅕ or ¼ carat, but these classifications can be misleading. For example, a ¼ carat can actually weigh anywhere between 23 and 28 points. It's better to find out the weight in points.

Cut refers to the shape of the stone and the arrangement of the facets—the polished flat planes. The better the cut, the more the diamond reflects light and the more it sparkles.

Color can vary greatly, although at first glance, all diamonds appear colorless. The Gemological Institute of America grades color in diamonds with letters, starting with D as the clearest, going down to Z. D, E, and F diamonds are quite rare—you will find most diamonds in the H range.

Clarity is a diamond's degree of freedom from internal flaws such as carbon spots and bubbles. Most of these flaws are not visible to the naked eye and must be detected by trained personnel using a microscope. Flawless stones are very rare. Since most flaws are not visible, color and cut are more important criteria when selecting your diamond.

Men's Wedding Rings

• Plain gold bands are still the most popular. Other trends: innovative designs with interlocking bands in white, yellow, or rose gold; or a black finish integrated with the gold.

• Bands with a few small diamonds are also popular. Most men prefer rings with recessed stones for a cleaner look.

• Although the groom may select his own ring, the bride traditionally pays for it.

• Some men choose to wear an engagement ring as well as a wedding ring. Styles are similar to wedding rings, and matched sets are available.

Shopping Tips

• Know approximately how much you want to spend.

• Beware of shops that only show you one ring at a time and pressure you to buy on the spot. You should be able to compare several rings side by side. Bring a notepad and pencil.

• Get an outside appraisal once you've chosen a stone. After purchase (but as a condition of final sale), take the stone to an independent, qualified appraiser to ensure the quality of the stone and the setting is as represented.

• Ask about warranties and guarantees. If you find a discrepancy in the grading of the stone, can you get all your money back? If the ring is bought by the groom and the setting style is not acceptable to the bride, will the store allow an exchange of settings? Is there an unconditional money-back guarantee if the stone is returned in 5–7 days?

• Find out about repair policies. Sizing, cleaning, and tightening of the stone, if needed during the first six months, should be done free of charge.

• Your receipt should describe the engagement ring in detail—the stone's weight, shape, and color—for insurance purposes.

Insurance

Be sure to protect your rings. They can be insured on your basic homeowner's policy, or by a floater on your parents' policy, until you get your own insurance. Precious stones increase in value over the years, so have your jewelry reappraised every three to five years, and adjust your insurance accordingly.

Sources: Diamond Information Center, New York, N.Y.; Kay Jewelers, Inc., Alexandria, Va.; ArtCarved, New York, N.Y.; I.B. Goodman, New York, N.Y., and Cincinnati, Ohio; Tiffany & Co., New York, N.Y.; Cartier, New York, N.Y.; American Gem Society, Los Angeles, Calif.

NEWSPAPER ENGAGEMENT ANNOUNCEMENTS

News of your engagement may appear in the newspapers of the town where your parents and your fiancé's parents live, or in the town where you and your fiancé live and work. The announcement can be timed to fall on or near the date of an engagement party, or appear a few months to a year before the wedding.

To get an engagement announcement published, call the newspaper (ask for the life-style editor) and ask about the requirements. Be sure to ask about fees and deadlines. If you wish to print a photograph, find out what's needed; most require a black-and-white glossy.

The customary announcement wording is: *"Mr. and Mrs. James Baxter of Deerfield Drive announce the engagement of their daughter, Alison Anne, to Joe Smith, the son of Mr. and Mrs. Alan Smith of Detroit. A May wedding is planned."*

Are your parents divorced? The engagement announcement is made by the parent with whom you've lived; your other parent is mentioned. Sometimes, if divorced parents remain friendly, they announce the engagement together. A deceased parent is mentioned as the *"late Mr. (or Mrs.) Baxter."* If both parents are deceased, the announcement may come from another relative, or close friend. Sometimes a couple sponsor a wedding themselves, and the announcement is made by them: *"Susan Mary Jones is to be married in June to James Quinn Johnson."* The groom's parents shouldn't make the engagement announcement, even if it is appearing in their local newspaper.

If you're marrying again, it's perfectly appropriate to announce the engagement in the newspaper. Word the remarriage announcement the usual way, using the bride's legal name: *"Mr. and Mrs. John K. Jones announce the engagement of their daughter, Susan Jones Wilson, to Mr. Joseph Quinn Johnson. . . ."* Publish just the news of the wedding if you or the groom is recently widowed or divorced.

ENGAGEMENT PARTIES

Traditionally the bride's parents host the first engagement party, which may coincide with the publication of your announcement in the newspaper. During the party, the bride's father may announce the engagement with a toast, since the news may be a surprise to some party guests.

Subsequent engagement parties may also be hosted by friends, the groom's parents, relatives, or even the bride and groom themselves.

Engagement Party Planning Tips:

• Any type of party (cocktails, brunch, dinner, luncheon) is appropriate.

• Gifts are not expected, although some people will want to celebrate the occasion with presents.

• To avoid hurt feelings, invite only those guests you will invite to the wedding.

• If formal party invitations are sent, they should invite guests to a party *"in honor of Jane Wilson and Joe Smith."* Guests can also be invited by phone or informal written invitation.

• Traditionally, the bride's father toasts the couple, and the groom responds with a toast to his bride, and if appropriate, her family.

• Thank the hosts of your engagement party with a note and a small gift.

NEWSPAPER ENGAGEMENT WORKSHEET

To appear: _____   _____
　　　　　　　　　(date)   (bride's parents' names)

_____
(street address)

_____
(city, state, zip code)

_____
(area code, telephone number)

Mr. and Mrs. _____ of _____ announce the engagement
　　　　　　(bride's parents' names)　　(their city, if out of town)

of their daughter, _____ , to _____ ,
　　　　　　　(bride's first and middle names)　　(groom's first and last names)

the son of Mr. and Mrs. _____ of _____ .
　　　　　　　　　(groom's parents' names)　　　(groom's parents' city)

The bride is _____ .
　　　　　　　　(career/place of employment/title)

Her father is _____ .
　　　　　　　　(career/place of employment/title)

Her mother is _____ .
　　　　　　　　(career/place of employment/title)

The groom is _____ .
　　　　　　　　(career/place of employment/title)

His father is _____ .
　　　　　　　　(career/place of employment/title)

His mother is _____ .
　　　　　　　　(career/place of employment/title)

Other information _____ .

A _____ wedding is planned.
　　(month/season)

SETTING THE DATE

How do you choose a wedding date?

• Contact churches or synagogues, reception sites. They may be booked for a year or two in advance; other items and services (dress, flowers, photographer, music) may have to be ordered or reserved six or more months in advance of the wedding.

• Think about which season you prefer or dates (such as Valentine's Day, your parents' anniversary) which may have a special meaning for you or your groom.

• Check availability of key family members and close friends. Will vacation plans, events such as graduations, conflict?

• Determine the best times to take off from work, school, or military service.

• Decide whether you need extra time to discuss issues such as children and money.

BRIDE'S CALENDAR

You will need six months to two years to arrange a large wedding in an urban area at a popular site or during the favorite wedding months of June, August, September, October, and December. On the other hand, you can plan a wedding in a much shorter time span than the one given below (although you may not get your first choice of reception site, dress, musicians, etc.).

Six Months or More Before

☐ Select a wedding date and time.

☐ Think about your wedding style. Buy bridal magazines for ideas. Start discussing priorities. For example, would you rather have many guests and a simple meal, or fewer guests and a gourmet seated dinner?

☐ Discuss wedding budget with your parents; if you're sharing expenses, include the groom and his parents.

☐ Decide how many guests may attend, then let the groom's family know how many they may invite, and by what date you need their guest list.

☐ Choose a location for the ceremony and reception.

☐ Visit the clergymember or other ceremony officiant together to start planning the ceremony.

☐ Hire a wedding consultant or party planner, if you want to use one.

☐ Begin choosing caterer, wedding cake baker, photographer, videographer, musicians, florist. Make appointments to taste, see, or hear their work; ask questions about costs. Make your decisions and sign contracts.

☐ Schedule engagement portrait (with or without your fiancé).

☐ Plan your wedding color scheme.

☐ Choose and order a wedding dress, headpiece, and accessories. Remember that dresses often require fittings and adjustments. If you want your wedding portrait to appear in newspapers, your dress will have to be ready about a month before the wedding date—check with newspapers and your photographer on timing.

☐ Pick out your engagement ring together with your fiancé.

☐ Discuss ideas for your new home with your fiancé and begin household shopping.

☐ Select your china, crystal, silver, linens, and other household needs and register your preferences with wedding gift registries at a variety of stores.

☐ Choose your wedding attendants (maid

or matron of honor, bridesmaids, flower girls, ring bearer).

☐ Set a date to order the attendants' dresses and accessories.

☐ Discuss honeymoon plans together. If you plan to travel outside the country, make sure your passports, visas, and inoculations will be in order.

☐ Announce your engagement in the newspaper.

☐ Reserve rooms for out-of-town guests and attendants.

☐ Order thank-you note stationery with and without married names.

Three Months Before

☐ If you're sending engraved invitations, order them so they will be ready to send six to eight weeks before the wedding. (Engraving may take six weeks.)

☐ Think about and begin to plan parties surrounding your wedding—such as a gathering for out-of-town guests who arrive the night before and activities for guests before and after the wedding. Close friends can host these events. When plans become firm, prepare a schedule for guests.

☐ Finalize arrangements with caterer, wedding cake baker, florist, musicians, photographer, videographer. Sign contracts for each. Compile lists of songs to be played, photographs to be taken.

☐ Firm up ceremony plans. Decide on personal touches such as readings and songs; begin writing vows, if desired.

☐ Complete guest list. Decide who will get invitations and who will get announcements.

☐ Order invitations, announcements, and other wedding-related stationery, such as at-home cards. Begin addressing the envelopes on receipt.

☐ Order wedding rings.

☐ Check requirements for wedding license.

☐ Shop for any new clothes you may need for a trousseau.

☐ Let your mother and your fiancé's mother know the wedding color scheme so they may start to shop for dresses in harmonizing colors.

☐ Confirm the delivery date of your wedding dress; make final selection of attendants' dresses, your accessories.

☐ Schedule your bridal portrait appointment to coincide with the delivery of wedding dress.

☐ Choose other wedding participants and helpers—such as ceremony reader, guest book attendant, someone to look after gifts, babysitter for guests' young children.

☐ Start planning transportation. Contact limousine companies. Consider the needs of out-of-town guests. Can friends drive them to wedding events? Should you rent mini-vans, hire extra drivers?

☐ Schedule physical examination with family doctor or gynecologist to get blood tests necessary for obtaining marriage license, to discuss birth control options, to get any inoculations for a trip abroad. Make appointments with dentist, eye doctor, dermatologist too, if necessary.

☐ Complete honeymoon plans. Make all reservations.

Six to Eight Weeks Before

☐ Mail wedding invitations.

☐ Meet with caterer and/or other person in charge of reception to go over all details, such as timing, menu, and table placement.

☐ Finalize lists of songs, poses—for musicians, photographer, videographer.

☐ Make appointments with hairstylist, manicurist, for about two weeks before the wedding, and if desired, on wedding day.

☐ Have the final fitting of wedding dress, headpiece, and accessories.

☐ Have formal bridal portrait taken.

☐ Find out requirements for newspaper announcement of your wedding from the life-style editor. Write up and send in information according to deadlines.

☐ Choose a wedding present for groom if you have both decided to exchange gifts. (It's optional.)

☐ Choose attendants' gifts. Bridesmaids' presents may be identical; the maid and matron of honor may receive a different gift.

☐ Pick up wedding rings; check engraving.

☐ Plan bridesmaids' party or other gathering with attendants.

☐ Discuss plans for wedding-related parties such as rehearsal dinner or Sunday morning brunch. (Others may be hosting these.) Keep guests informed of schedule of events.

☐ Complete shopping for honeymoon, trousseau.

☐ Write thank-you notes for gifts promptly—a few a day.

☐ Update health and life insurance to reflect married status.

☐ Think about gift protection on wedding day. Purchase a "floater" on insurance policy; find a safe place for gifts brought to the reception site. If you haven't already done so, ask a friend, or hire someone, to watch over gifts during the festivities.

☐ Complete arrangements for out-of-town guests. Do they have schedules and maps for all events? Who will need to be picked up at the airport, driven to wedding events? Arrange to have welcome gifts—such as baskets of fruit or bottles of wine—placed in guests' rooms.

Two Weeks Before

☐ Go with your fiancé to obtain your marriage license.

☐ Finalize guest list. Have your mother or attendants call guests you haven't heard from. Work on reception seating plan.

☐ If changing your name and address, begin to make arrangements to have records—such as bank, Social Security card, personnel forms, driver's license, changed.

☐ Prepare toasts for the rehearsal dinner, the reception.

☐ Confirm honeymoon reservations and pick up tickets.

One Week Before

☐ Call all wedding service personnel—musicians, photographer, videographer, caterer, rental company, florist, baker, drivers—and reconfirm date, times, duties, guest number.

☐ Make a list of small details to remember: tips for rest room and parking attendants, bartenders; clergy fee; favors and place cards to be delivered to reception site.

☐ Present gifts to attendants at bridesmaids' party or rehearsal dinner.

☐ Remind attendants and other participants of wedding day duties, timing.

☐ Be sure the wedding announcements (if any) are addressed, stamped, and ready for your parents or a friend to mail immediately after the wedding.

☐ Keep up with thank-you notes.

☐ Give or go to bridesmaids' party.

☐ Hold wedding rehearsal, rehearsal dinner (usually hosted by groom's parents).

☐ Practice wedding day hairstyle and makeup and determine how long it takes to complete, or confirm hair and makeup appointment for wedding day.

☐ Make an "emergency kit" of safety pins, comb, tissue, cosmetics, etc., for wedding day.

☐ Begin packing for your honeymoon. Buy traveler's checks.

☐ Arrange to move belongings to your new home.

☐ Try to relax! If possible, schedule a day of pampering with a facial, massage, manicure, and pedicure.

GROOM'S CALENDAR

The groom will be included in many aspects of wedding planning. Together you will interview caterers, audition bands, select items for your new home—and make many decisions about your wedding and your new life. Here is a checklist of some of the things he will take care of on his own.

Six Months or More Before

☐ Find out from your fiancée how many guests you and your family may invite, then sit down with your family and plan your guest list.

☐ Talk to your family about what wedding expenses they will cover. Traditionally the groom or his family pays for engagement and wedding rings, marriage license, ceremony officiant's fees, rehearsal dinner, ceremony flowers, and honeymoon. A new option is to share other wedding costs with the bride's family—and pay for items such as the reception flowers or liquor.

☐ With your fiancée, visit the clergymember or other official who will perform your wedding ceremony.

☐ Discuss with your fiancée the number of ushers you will need (traditionally one for every 50 guests to be seated); decide which friends and relatives to ask.

☐ Purchase your fiancée's engagement ring. If she wants a matching set, order her wedding ring now. If not, it may be ordered later.

☐ Discuss and decide upon honeymoon plans with your fiancée, and start making arrangements. If you plan to travel outside the country, make sure passports, visas, and inoculations will be in order.

☐ With your fiancée, decide what you will need for your home. Choose silver, china, glassware, linens, etc., and list choices with wedding gift registries at a variety of stores.

Three Months Before

☐ Finish your guest list and give it to your fiancée, making sure that all names are spelled correctly and that addresses are complete.

☐ Consult with fiancée about wedding attire. Order attire for yourself, best man, ushers, fathers. (Out-of-town attendants can send measurements to your local formalwear store.)

☐ Order wedding rings.

☐ Complete honeymoon reservations. Buy and pick up tickets.

☐ Make an appointment with your doctor for a physical, any needed blood tests or inoculations. Arrange for check-ups at the dentist, eye doctor, if necessary.

☐ Go over your wardrobe to make sure it's in good shape. Buy any new clothes you'll need for the honeymoon.

☐ Make arrangements to pay for the bride's bouquet, boutonnieres for the men, and corsages for mothers.

Six to Eight Weeks Before

☐ Make arrangements for the rehearsal dinner if you or your parents are hosting it.

☐ Give or attend bachelors' party.

☐ Pick up wedding rings; check engraving.

☐ Check to see if your health insurance will cover your wife or if hers will cover you. Make necessary changes. Update life insurance to make her the beneficiary. Discuss a will.

☐ Select a gift for your bride if you've decided to exchange them.

☐ Buy gifts for your best man and ushers. While ushers' presents may be identical, the best man often receives a special gift.

☐ Make sure all legal, medical, and religious documents are in order.

☐ Help your fiancée write thank-you notes.

☐ Consult with fiancée about arrangements for out-of-town ushers, relatives, and friends. Help reserve hotel rooms and coordinate transportation.

Two Weeks Before

☐ Make a date with your fiancée to get the marriage license. (Celebrate the occasion with a special lunch!)

☐ Ask the best man to drive you and your bride from the reception to the airport, station, or dock; or hire a limousine. Consider a creative departure—such as by boat or horse-drawn carriage. If you're driving yourself, give the best man an extra set of car keys in case you misplace yours on wedding day.

☐ Double-check honeymoon reservations.

One Week Before

☐ Present gifts to best man and ushers at the rehearsal dinner.

☐ Remind best man and ushers of times and details for rehearsal, rehearsal dinner, and wedding. Brief the head usher on ceremony seating arrangements. The bride's relatives and friends usually sit on the left, the groom's on the right (in a Christian ceremony; the reverse, in a Jewish ceremony). Explain where family members should sit and outline any special arrangements for disabled guests.

☐ Put the clergymember or ceremony official's fee in a sealed envelope and give it to the best man, who will deliver it after the ceremony. Check with your fiancée about any other tips you'll be responsible for, such as one for the limousine driver.

☐ Get a going-away outfit ready so you can change after the reception.

☐ Start honeymoon packing. Purchase traveler's checks.

☐ Have your hair trimmed.

☐ Arrange to move belongings to your new home.

YOUR WEDDING STYLE

What kind of wedding do you want? Today the options are innumerable—from a week-long round of festivities for a crowd to a simple ceremony and gourmet luncheon for a few close friends. More and more brides and grooms see a wedding as a personal statement, a reflection of their tastes and interests. For example, they might wear formal attire, but hold the wedding in a loft, and participate in ethnic dances learned from their grandparents. They'll include a champagne toast, but the cake will be dark chocolate and decorated with white, gold, and black Art Deco trim.

Below are the traditional guidelines for wedding styles. Your wedding may not fit exactly into any of the categories, but the definitions may be useful when planning and working with wedding professionals.

Very Formal

Held in church, synagogue, hotel ballroom
200 or more guests
Engraved or printed invitations with traditional wording

Bride wears a gown with a cathedral or chapel train and veil.

Four to twelve bridesmaids in floor-length dresses; other attendants such as flower girls, ring bearer, pages

Groom, guests, ushers, in formal attire (white tie and tails, if after 6 P.M.)

Elaborate reception, usually with seated meal

Formal

Can take place at church, synagogue, hotel, club, or home

At least 100 guests

Engraved or printed invitations with traditional or personalized wording

Bride wears long gown with a chapel or sweep train, headpiece and veil, or veiled hat.

Two or six bridesmaids in long or tea-length dresses

Groom and his attendants in formal attire (black tie for evening)

Reception with food and beverages, depending on time of wedding

Semiformal

Can take place at church, synagogue, home, hotel living room, or other location

Fewer than 100 guests

Engraved or printed invitations

Bride wears a floor-length or street-length dress in white or pastel color; a hat, hair flowers, or simple headpiece with or without a short veil.

One or two bridal attendants in street-length or cocktail-length dresses

Groom and his attendants wear dark suits and ties, dinner jackets, or contemporary formal suits.

A reception with light refreshments

Informal

A daytime ceremony anywhere, including city hall

Fifty or fewer guests

Handwritten or personal invitations

Bride wears a suit or cocktail-length dress.

One honor attendant in cocktail-length dress or suit

Groom and best man in business suits

Reception at home or restaurant

Military Wedding

Often held at military chapel, but other locations are acceptable

Invitations list groom's (and/or bride's) rank and service.

Bride wears a formal, floor-length wedding gown with train and veil. If she is in the service, she may wear full-dress uniform or a wedding gown.

Bridesmaids may wear uniforms if in the service; otherwise, dresses they would wear in any formal wedding ceremony.

Groom wears full-dress uniform. Attendants who are in the service wear full-dress uniform; those who are not wear traditional formal attire.

The recession ends with the arch of swords. Ushers in military attire form two lines facing each other; at the command, they raise their swords or sabers to form an arch under which the bride and groom will pass.

At the reception there may be regimental decorations and music.

Guests are seated by rank.

Double Wedding

Two sisters, close relatives, or good friends may share their wedding day.

Invitations are usually issued jointly.

Brides wear different dresses with trains and veils of about the same length.

Two groups of attendants in the same or harmonizing colors

The older bride (if they are sisters) goes first in the procession and recession.

Reception follows the style of the wedding

NEW WAYS TO WED

Not long ago, the bride, groom, their families, and most of their guests came from the same area. Now it's more likely that the bride comes from one coast, the groom from the other, with relatives and friends scattered in between. Since guests have to travel long distances to attend a wedding, brides and grooms have come up with some innovative ways to get everyone together for a memorable good time.

Perhaps the most common of these ways to wed is the **Weekend Wedding.** The celebrating begins with a welcome party/rehearsal dinner on Friday, a day of activities (team sports, sightseeing, a barbecue or pool party), the wedding late Saturday afternoon or evening, a farewell brunch on Sunday.

The Progressive Wedding is one in which the bride and groom travel to the guests, rather than have the guests travel to them. The celebration might begin with the wedding ceremony in the bride's hometown in Los Angeles, California, progress to his grandparents' brunch in Omaha, Nebraska, a few days later, continue to a friend's cocktail party in Chicago, Illinois, and conclude at his parents' home in Boston, Massachusetts, for a dinner dance reception after the honeymoon.

The Honeymoon Wedding invites guests to travel to a romantic vacation locale. There, they enjoy a few days with the bride and groom. After the ceremony (on a Caribbean beach, in a French country chapel), the couple continue their honeymoon there—or at a different hotel.

A Day on the Water Wedding takes place on a boat—floating on a lake, bay, river, or ocean. The couple (or hosts) rent a boat large enough for guests, clergy, musicians, caterers, and crew. Plan a wedding on a summer afternoon, or in the evening—along city shores, with sparkling lights as a backdrop.

A Day in the Country Wedding is held in a rural setting at a quaint chapel, charming inn, or family home. The bride and groom may arrive and leave in a flower-bedecked horse and carriage, or on horseback. Flowers and food reflect a country mood: wildflowers in baskets, locally grown vegetables, homemade cake.

A Sentimental Journey is made by a couple who return to marry at a place with nostalgic meaning: the college campus where they met, a family vacation spot.

An Ethnic Wedding highlights the couple's backgrounds with traditional costumes, music, dances, food.

A Winter Holiday Wedding has seasonal accents: candlelight; decorations of holly, mistletoe, evergreen; velvet dresses trimmed with fur; carol singing.

A Period or **History Wedding** highlights a past era: Renaissance, medieval, Victorian, Edwardian, with costumes and decor. The wedding can be part of a Renaissance fair, a town event.

An All-Night Blow-out Wedding features merrymaking till dawn. Plan an hors d'oeuvres buffet, a seated dinner, a dessert buffet, a cake cutting, and finally a breakfast with dancing and other activities.

A Whole-Clan Celebration includes the entire family. It might coincide with other occasions such as anniversaries, birthdays, or marriage reaffirmations.

A Bi-Cultural Wedding combines the cultures of two disparate backgrounds into one joyous celebration. For example, a Mexican bride might salute her heritage by following the traditions of draping a white silk cord around her shoulders and those of her groom. They could lead the guests in traditional Mexican marriage dances. The groom, in turn, could recognize his Chinese background by drinking with his bride from goblets of honey and wine, which are joined with a red ribbon.

The Small Family Wedding includes only close friends and relatives. The setting is intimate—a chapel, country inn, home—and the reception is simple.

The Surprise Wedding invites guests to a party. Only when they arrive do they realize they're actually at a wedding!

WEDDING STYLE WORKSHEET

Now that you have some ideas about wedding styles, it's time to envision your wedding. Sit down together and discuss the many aspects of a wedding, listed below. In each case, write down what you want most, even if you're not sure it's available. Don't think about budget yet—the worksheet will help you set priorities so you can then adjust your budget.

Preferred date: _____

Alternate dates: _____

Time of day: _____

Location of ceremony: _____

Invitations and announcements (engraved, printed, or a unique design): _____

Officiant: _____

What should the ceremony include? Readings? Personalized vows? _____

_____

Ceremony musical selections: _____

_____

_____

Floral decorations: _____

_____

_____

Bridal gown ideas: _____

_____

_____

Number of attendants: _____

Names of attendants: _____

_____

_____

_____

Attendants' attire (ideas): _____

_____

_____

Flowers for bride and attendants: _____

_____

_____

Rough estimate of number of guests—Hers: _____ His: _____

Reception site: _____

Floral decorations: _____

_____

_____

_____

Music: _____

_____

_____

Beverages *When guests arrive:* _____

With meal: _____

For toasts: _____

Food *Hors d'oeuvres:* _____

Main meal—seated or buffet: _____

_____

Desserts *(in addition to cake):* _____

Other ideas (food stations, make your own sundae): _____

_____

Wedding cake (flavor, decorations): _____

Her ideas: _____

_____

His ideas: _____

_____

Other reception needs: (tent, getaway vehicle): _____

_____

_____

Other ideas for personalizing ceremony and reception (programs, ethnic traditions, etc.): _____

_____

_____

Honeymoon ideas: _____

_____

_____

THE OLDER BRIDE

The age at which women get married for the first time has been steadily increasing, from 20.8 in 1968 to 23.6 in 1988. While women once got married as soon as they finished high school or college, they now graduate from high school, college, *and* want to work for a few years before marriage. Today, many women get married for the first time when they are in their thirties.

An older bride may have the same large, formal wedding in a traditional gown that she would have had if she'd married earlier. However, there may be some differences in the way she plans the wedding.

Budget/sponsors. While their parents may be facing retirement, the bride and groom may be earning good incomes and want to pay for all or part of their wedding themselves. The bride's parents may, or may not, be wedding hosts. Their names could appear on invitations and announcements, or the couple may do the inviting and announcing themselves: *The honor of your presence is requested at the wedding of Mary Kate Smith to John Quinn Jones.*

Pre-Wedding Parties. An older bride may prefer a coed cocktail or dinner party with her fiancé, mutual friends, and *their* partners, rather than a traditional shower. Since the couple's friends are likely to be older and further along in their careers—and with more disposable income—than younger couples, there may be more parties held in the couple's honor.

Gifts. An older bride who has lived on her own already may have many of the household essentials. However, she may still wish to register for a more elegant pattern of dinnerware, additional wine glasses, or other luxury items that go beyond the basics needed by someone who is just setting up a household. (Never write a preference for monetary gifts on invitations. Close friends can spread the word.)

Dress. If an older bride chooses *not* to wear a traditional gown with a long train and elaborate headpiece, how can she find the right look? Check bridal salons; they carry wedding dresses in a variety of styles, lengths, and colors. (For example, consider a bridesmaid's dress in white.)

Guests. The older bride and groom may have cultivated a large number of friends and business associates, and so their wedding guest list may be quite long, especially if they also include relatives and friends of their parents.

MARRYING AGAIN

The number of remarriages increases each year. No longer is a second wedding an unusual affair. It is viewed by participants and guests as the celebration of a happy new beginning. Many first-time traditions can be included in a remarriage—it's up to both of you to choose the ones that make you feel comfortable.

Here are some guidelines:

Telling the family. Children from either partner's previous marriage should be told first, then parents, friends, and relatives.

Newspaper announcements. You may announce your remarriage in the newspaper. If the bride or groom was recently widowed or divorced, however, it is best to wait and publish only the news of the wedding.

Pre-wedding parties. Friends—rather than family—often hold pre-wedding parties for second marriages. These might be cocktail or dinner parties to honor the engaged couple, rather than traditional showers.

Gifts. Guests are not obligated to give wedding gifts for second marriages, but many will want to do so. You can list your gift preferences at wedding gift registries at many different types of stores. As always, send thank-you notes as soon as possible.

Planning and budget. Partners may choose to make this celebration completely different from their first wedding, or they may want to repeat first wedding traditions they enjoyed. Smaller ceremonies and receptions are common. Although the bride and groom often pay for the second wedding, one or both parents may wish to contribute, or in some cases, may pay for the entire event.

Visiting your clergy. If you want a religious ceremony, meet with a clergymember as soon as you can. You may have to participate in counseling, get special dispensations, or meet other requirements.

Attendants. It is appropriate and joyful, but not necessary, to have attendants, although you must have two legal witnesses. Children from a previous marriage who are old enough should definitely be included. Boys can be ushers, acolytes, or ring bearers. Girls can be bridesmaids or flower girls. Or children can escort their mother down the aisle.

Invitations and announcements. The bride and groom may issue the invitations and announcements. If there are more than 50 guests, the invitations can be printed or engraved. The bride's parents may "have the honour" of announcing your marriage, or the bride and groom may send their own announcements.

Dress. Many remarrying brides wear dresses of white, ivory, or pastel in any length or style, according to the formality of the ceremony, but forego veils and trains (age-old symbols of virginity which create the larger-than-life aura of a first-time bride). The groom and his attendants may wear formalwear or suits that are appropriate to the wedding style.

Ceremony procedures. Anyone the bride loves may escort her down the aisle: her father may do the honors again, a brother, or her children. If there is no center aisle at a small wedding, the bride and groom may enter together through a side door. All ways of personalizing your ceremony through readings, songs, vows, are fine—as long as they meet with your clergymember's approval. (See Section 2 for ideas.)

Reception traditions. Include any and all reception traditions such as the receiving line, first dance, cake cutting, bouquet toss, rice throwing.

Honeymoon. A honeymoon is just as important for a remarriage as for a first marriage. Consider a two-part trip if you have children: a few days for bride and groom alone; a family vacation afterward with the children.

WHO PAYS FOR WHAT?

Traditionally the bride's family pays for most of the ceremony and reception costs. Now, however, the groom's family may want to share expenses as a symbol of unity, or to help you two have the wedding of your dreams. The bride and groom often contribute to expenses as well, or may even choose to pay for the whole wedding themselves.

The Bride (or Her Family) Usually Pays These Wedding Expenses:

Invitations, announcements, enclosures
Wedding dress, veil, accessories
Trousseau of clothes and lingerie
Bouquets or corsages for honor attendant, bridesmaids, and flower girl

Flowers for the church and reception

Engagement and wedding photographs

Rental fee (if any) for the church, synagogue

Fees for the sexton, organist, soloist

Rental of aisle carpet, marquee, other equipment for wedding site

Transportation of bridal party to ceremony and reception sites

Reception, including food, drinks, music, other entertainment, decorations, professional services (unless the groom's family offers to pay a part of these expenses)

Groom's ring (for a double ring ceremony)

Wedding gift for the groom

Gifts for bride's attendants

Hotel lodging (if necessary) for any bridesmaids from out of town

Bride's engraved personal stationery

The Groom (or His Family) Usually Pays These Wedding Expenses:

Bride's engagement and wedding rings

Marriage license

Clergymember's or judge's fee (it can range from $10 to $100; ask in advance)

Bride's flowers, including going-away corsage and bouquet (see below)

Wedding gift for the bride

Boutonnieres for men in wedding party

Corsages for mothers (see below)

Complete wedding trip

Gifts for the best man and ushers

Lodging (if necessary) for out-of-town ushers

Expenses That Are Optional or Determined by Local Custom:

Bride's bouquet, traditionally a gift from the groom, may be purchased by bride's family as part of the outfit.

Corsages for mothers and grandmothers are provided by the groom, but the bride may buy those for her own mother, grandmother.

Bachelors' party is given by the groom in some areas of the country, by his attendants or his male friends in other places.

Rehearsal dinner is given by groom's family in many areas, but may be given by the bride's family or friends.

Attendants' dresses are usually bought by each person, or bride may buy them.

Bridesmaids' party is usually given by the bride, but may be given by her attendants or her family in some communities.

YOUR FAMILIES AND YOUR WEDDING

A wedding is a momentous occasion for the parents of the bride and groom, too. Ideally, both sets of parents will get along, become friends—and enjoy the wedding and its planning. Here are some guidelines:

Get your parents acquainted after you announce your engagement. Traditionally the groom's mother makes the first move with a phone call or note to the bride's mother and an invitation to get together—for cocktails, dinner, or brunch—if they live nearby. If the bride's parents haven't heard from the groom's parents, they can call them. Their first meeting can be at a restaurant or home, preferably with the bridal couple. If possible, they should meet sometime before the wedding, even if they have to travel to the wedding site a day or two early.

Start discussing wedding priorities. You

two should discuss your wedding style with your parents *before* you discuss finances. Does one family feel they have to invite every cousin plus all their neighbors? Or do they think it's not a wedding if there isn't a seated dinner and dancing? While the bride's and groom's ideas for a wedding style should come first, in the interest of family harmony, compromises may have to be made. For example, you could have a small ceremony and let the groom's parents invite all their guests to a large reception. Discuss what is most important to you and your parents. Food *is* love, and families may feel strongly about the choice of crepes or fresh shrimp, prime ribs or fish, and how the reception meal is served.

The groom's family can offer to share expenses. They may make this offer during a gathering with the bride's parents, or the groom may pass their offer on to the bride's parents. If his parents don't know that it is acceptable to share expenses, the *groom*, never the bride, should raise the subject with his parents.

The bride's parents may decline their offer. The bride's parents may have saved and planned for a wedding for years. Even if the groom's parents want to make the wedding larger and more lavish, the bride's parents can politely decline their offer, saying they prefer a more intimate party. The bride and groom should make their wishes known too—preferably at a gathering with both sets of parents.

If the bride's parents accept their help, figure out ways to split costs. There are several ways to divide wedding costs. The couple and each set of parents can each pay one-third of the expenses. Or the bride's parents may pay for the ceremony costs, his the reception costs. Another option is to specify certain costs that each family will cover. The groom's family might agree to pay for all flowers, liquor, and transportation. Arrange to have bills sent directly to each party involved.

Have the bride's mother fill his mother in on other wedding plans. The bride's mother should tell his mother how many guests her family may invite and when you will need the names and addresses (with zip codes). Traditionally the bride's mother may choose the dress she will be wearing to the wedding first, then discuss her decision with the groom's mother—who buys a dress in a similar length and complementary (not necessarily the same) color. However, the two mothers may prefer to discuss dress styles before shopping, or shop together. If the groom's mother already has a dress she hopes to wear, the bride's mother might select a dress to complement it. When choosing wedding day attire, mothers should consider: time of day and formality of the wedding; color scheme of decorations and attendants' attire; how the mothers will look standing next to each other in photographs.

Consider ways to include the groom's parents in the wedding. You may want to list the groom's parents on the wedding invitation, ask both sets of parents to participate in the wedding procession, include them in lighting a Unity Candle, or have them read poetry or prose during the ceremony—or all of the above.

WEDDING BUDGET CHART

	Estimated Costs	Actual Costs	Deposit Paid	Balance Due	Who Pays*
Stationery					
Invitations					
Announcements					
Notepaper for thank-yous					
Reception napkins					
Matches					
Cake boxes					
Other (at-home cards, maps)					
Total					
Ceremony					
Site rental fee					
Clergymember, officiant fee					
Other fees (sexton, cantor)					
Musicians (organist, soloist)					
Total					
Wedding consultant/party planner					
Reception					
Rental for hall, club, hotel					
Food					
Liquor					
Waiters, bartenders					
Equipment (tent, linens, etc.)					
Wedding Cake					
Music					
Total					
Flowers					
For Wedding					
Ceremony site decoration					
Bride's bouquet					
Attendants' flowers					
Corsages for mothers					
Boutonnieres					

*bride's family, groom's family, couple

	Estimated Costs	Actual Costs	Deposit Paid	Balance Due	Who Pays*
Flowers, continued					
For Reception					
Buffet decorations					
Table centerpieces					
Cake table					
Other (bandstand, receiving line)					
Total					
Photography					
Formal engagement portrait					
Formal wedding portrait					
Candids at wedding					
Proofs					
Videotape					
Other (extra prints, albums, or tapes)					
Total					
Bride's outfit					
Dress					
Headpiece					
Accessories (slip, shoes, hosiery, etc.)					
Trousseau or honeymoon clothes					
Total					
Groom's attire					
Formalwear					
Honeymoon clothes					
Total					
Gifts					
Attendants					
Groom (optional)					
Bride (optional)					
Rings					
Friends who hosted parties, helped					
Parents					
Total					

*bride's family, groom's family, couple

	Estimated Costs	Actual Costs	Deposit Paid	Balance Due	Who Pays*
Transportation					
Limousines					
Chauffeur tip					
Parking					
Gas for friends who drive					
Car wash for friends who drive					
Total					
Extras					
Table favors (almonds, rice bags)					
Hotel accommodations (guests, attendants)					
Other					
Total					
Honeymoon					
Total					
Other parties					
Engagement					
Bridesmaids'					
Bachelors' (if groom is hosting)					
Rehearsal dinner (if bride is sponsoring)					
Weekend Wedding parties					
Total					
TOTAL WEDDING COSTS TOTAL $_____					

*bride's family, groom's family, couple

MONEY-SAVING TIPS

Aim for *value* when considering costs. Materials or services that are merely inexpensive may be that way for a reason—a wedding is one time when you need vendors to be reliable, products such as flowers or photographs to be of high quality. Here, some money-saving tips:

Invitations

• Consider thermography, a printing process that looks like engraving but can be much less expensive.

• Think about mail-order invitations or pre-packaged cards in which you will handwrite the information.

• Order invitations that will require only one stamp.

Wedding Attire

• Consider wearing a bridesmaid's dress in white or a formal, ready-to-wear dress in an appropriate shade.

• Look into wedding dress sales, the availability of sample dresses or discontinued lines.

• Look through designer dress catalogs for attendants' dresses.

• Select shoes that can be dyed another color for later use.

• Make accessories such as garter, ring pillow, bridal purse. Include personal touches—such as lace trimmings from your mother's wedding gown.

Flowers

• Ask your clergymember if another bride will be married at your church or synagogue that day (before or after your wedding). If so, contact her and find out if she would like to share the cost of ceremony decorations.

• Use ceremony floral arrangements and greenery to decorate reception areas. For example, have an usher move the large bouquets that flank the altar to your reception site, where the flowers can brighten up a hallway where the receiving line stands.

• Carry one or two dramatic flowers rather than a bouquet, and have your bridesmaids do the same.

• Use flowers that are in season.

• Consider a wedding in a garden—and give nature a chance to decorate.

• Use garlands of ivy or evergreen—less expensive than flowers.

• Borrow or rent potted plants from a florist for reception decorating.

Reception

• Plan your reception for morning or early afternoon. A breakfast or brunch is less expensive than a luncheon or dinner; at an afternoon reception, you can serve hors d'ouevres and cake, rather than a full meal.

• Look for less expensive sites—such as church meeting halls, community centers, parks, private homes.

• Have friends or family make some or all of the food. Check gourmet cooking magazines for creative menus.

• Check local culinary and bakery schools. They may prepare food for cost.

• Borrow rather than rent if you need items like punch bowls, linens, dishes.

• Ask friends to help with bartending, set-up, and clean-up.

• Try to rent tables, dinnerware, serving pieces, directly from a rental store, rather than have the caterer do it and then charge you an extra fee.

• Research the many ways to save on liquor; it may be much cheaper to buy bottles rather than have a caterer charge per drink. Purchase bottles at discount liquor stores. Serve a punch or wine only, rather than a full bar.

Music

• Hire a disc jockey with tapes—usually less expensive than a live band, and guaranteed continuous music.

• Hire musicians for a minimum amount of time (i.e., for two hours starting with the first dance, ending after the cake cutting).

• Hire music students to play at the ceremony, reception.

• Have friends provide ceremony music (organ, piano, guitar, harp) or sing songs.

Photography

• Have a professional photographer take only the minimum wedding photographs, such as shots of family and attendants. Have friends take candids of wedding activities.

• Compare photographers' packages. Make sure that extra prints for relatives and friends are included, or can be purchased later at reasonable prices.

THE GUEST LIST

How do we arrive at a number? There are several considerations:

• Space. How many will the church, synagogue, or other ceremony site hold? How many can fit into the reception site? If you are planning an outdoor wedding, will there be room indoors in case of rain?

• Budget. How many can you afford to serve at a reception? You and your families may have to decide what's most important to you—a seated dinner and open bar for fewer guests, or the ability to invite everyone you want—to a party that's less elaborate.

• Mood. You both may prefer a gathering of a few close friends to a big bash, or vice versa.

How many does each family get to invite? The fairest way to handle this part of guest list etiquette is to set a total number and let the groom's family invite half, the bride's family half. Or divide it in thirds—a third for the bride's and groom's friends, a third for each of the families. If one of the families lives far away from the wedding site and won't have many friends traveling the distance, they will have fewer guests than the number allotted. Look for duplicates on the lists. As a general rule, about three-quarters of those invited will be able to attend. As you receive regrets, you can send invitations to others—it is acceptable to mail them up to two and a half weeks before the wedding. (Call guests you *really* want to come!)

Who gets invited? Invite relatives, friends, your wedding officiant and spouse, members of the wedding party and spouses (and, if appropriate, their parents). It's not necessary to invite companions for single friends, but if you do, send them separate invitations, at their addresses, rather than writing "and Guest" on an invitation. If there's room, you might also invite business associates and children of guests.

Send wedding announcements to people you feel should know about your marriage, but are not inviting to the wedding. (Neither a wedding invitation or announcement requires the recipient to send a gift.)

How do we cut down the guest list? Start by eliminating certain categories of people—such as business associates, club acquaintances. You might also not invite children of guests. (Instead of writing "No children" on invitations, leave their names off envelopes. Your mother and friends can mention to those who ask that you prefer children to stay at home.) If you seem to have a lot of disappointed friends, consider planning an additional reception (perhaps a party in the groom's hometown after your honeymoon, or a restaurant luncheon for friends at the office).

OUT-OF-TOWN GUESTS

Many guests today travel long distances to come to a wedding. Brides and grooms often live across the state or across the country from where they grew up, or went to colleges far from their hometowns.

Since these guests are going to a lot of trouble to be with you, do *whatever* you can to make their visit enjoyable. They, like you, will be getting together with dear friends and relatives they see only every few years, and will appreciate opportunities for comfortable chats.

Here are planning tips for welcoming out-of-town guests:

Inquire about group rates. Many hotels

GUEST/ANNOUNCEMENT LIST

Names _____ Phone _____   GIFT DESCRIPTIONS

_____   _____   1)

Children _____   2)

Address _____   3)

City: _____ State _____ Zip _____   DATE THANK-YOU NOTE SENT

1) Wedding Invitation _____ 2) Party Invitation _____   engagement _____

Announcement _____ Number Attending 1) _____ 2) _____   shower _____

wedding _____

Names _____ Phone _____   GIFT DESCRIPTIONS

_____   _____   1)

Children _____   2)

Address _____   3)

City: _____ State _____ Zip _____   DATE THANK-YOU NOTE SENT

1) Wedding Invitation _____ 2) Party Invitation _____   engagement _____

Announcement _____ Number Attending 1) _____ 2) _____   shower _____

wedding _____

Names _____ Phone _____   GIFT DESCRIPTIONS

_____   _____   1)

Children _____   2)

Address _____   3)

City: _____ State _____ Zip _____   DATE THANK-YOU NOTE SENT

1) Wedding Invitation _____ 2) Party Invitation _____   engagement _____

Announcement _____ Number Attending 1) _____ 2) _____   shower _____

wedding _____

Names _____ Phone _____

      _____   _____

Children _____

Address _____

City: _____ State _____ Zip _____

1) Wedding Invitation ____ 2) Party Invitation ____

Announcement ___ Number Attending 1) ____ 2) ____

GIFT DESCRIPTIONS

1)

2)

3)

DATE THANK-YOU NOTE SENT

engagement _____

shower _____

wedding _____

Names _____ Phone _____

      _____   _____

Children _____

Address _____

City: _____ State _____ Zip _____

1) Wedding Invitation ____ 2) Party Invitation ____

Announcement ___ Number Attending 1) ____ 2) ____

GIFT DESCRIPTIONS

1)

2)

3)

DATE THANK-YOU NOTE SENT

engagement _____

shower _____

wedding _____

Names _____ Phone _____

      _____   _____

Children _____

Address _____

City: _____ State _____ Zip _____

1) Wedding Invitation ____ 2) Party Invitation ____

Announcement ___ Number Attending 1) ____ 2) ____

GIFT DESCRIPTIONS

1)

2)

3)

DATE THANK-YOU NOTE SENT

engagement _____

shower _____

wedding _____

and motels will reserve a block of rooms at a discount. Ask a travel agent about finding the lowest airfares—group rates are sometimes available, and fares are less expensive if booked in advance. Normally guests pay for their own transportation and lodging, even if hosts make the reservations. Enclose a reservation form with a price list in your invitations. Neighbors may also house close relatives or bridesmaids.

Plan activities for guests and let them know about the events. Since guests usually arrive the night before the wedding, invite them to the rehearsal dinner or sponsor an informal gathering at their hotel. If the wedding will be held late on a Saturday, friends or relatives could host a brunch, pool party, picnic, or other group activity during the day. Consider a farewell breakfast, too, the morning after the wedding. Some brides reserve a hospitality suite at the hotel where guests are staying. Guests can visit this room whenever they like for spontaneous get-togethers.

Let guests know about these gatherings as soon as possible, preferably when you send invitations. (Have your stationer print up a schedule that looks as nice as your wedding invitations, or photocopy a beautifully typed list.) Closer to the wedding date, give them more exact information: times, addresses, names and telephone numbers of hosts.

Provide additional information. In advance, send guests practical travel information, including plane and train schedules, names of nearest airports, train stations, and bus depots. Provide rental car information, as well. Since they will need to know what clothes to pack, list the style of each party planned, and the climate. You might want to write all this information in a series of wedding newsletters.

Coordinate wedding site travel arrangements. It's a nice gesture to have someone meet and drive guests from the airport, train station, or bus depot to their lodgings. Bridesmaids, ushers, or friends can help with the driving. You may need to rent a van or even a bus to take a group of guests from their hotel to the wedding and back. Find out what guests prefer—some will want to rent cars and be on their own. (Use the following chart.)

Assign a guest liaison. A close friend or relative could take responsibility for out-of-town guests. This person would see that guests get to and from the wedding festivities and act as a source of information about your area. He or she could also handle any unexpected crises—such as finding a baby-sitter or filling a prescription.

Consider the needs of guests' children. If guests are traveling long distances, they may be reluctant to leave young children behind. Decide whether you want children at the wedding or not. There are several options for making sure that parents and children have a good time—without distracting other guests. One: You could provide a list of local baby-sitters for parents to call and set up their own arrangements. Two: Hire the baby-sitters yourself and set up playrooms for children. Churches and synagogues often have classrooms that may be available; ask friends with children if you could "borrow" their yards or play areas. Three: Set up special tables for them at the reception with favors they can play with—such as small puzzles or coloring books; consider hiring a clown or other entertainer they would enjoy. Give parents a list of local childrens' attractions—such as museums, playgrounds, nature centers—so they will have something to do during the times they are not at the wedding.

Have a welcome gift waiting in guests' rooms. This present could be homemade cookies, a bottle of champagne, a basket of fruit, or a box of essentials like maps, cologne, toothbrush, even antacid. Or personalize the gifts—a guide to museums for art lovers, maps of jogging and bike trails for athletes. Another idea for welcome gifts: Give something that reflects the weekend's activities, such as a baseball cap, or T-shirt with your names and wedding date. Include any updated information on the schedule of events, and maps.

LOGISTICS CHART FOR OUT-OF-TOWN GUESTS

Photocopy this chart so you have one for each family attending.

I. Name of Guest _____ Number in family _____

Address _____

_____

Telephone _____

Date and time of arrival _____

How arriving (airplane flight number, train, etc.) _____

_____

Transportation from airport, train, or bus station _____

_____

Place where they are staying (name, address, telephone) _____

_____

_____

Transportation from lodging back to airport, train, or bus station _____

_____

Baby-sitting needs: _____

_____

_____

Any other special needs (e.g., wheelchair access, dietary restrictions) _____

_____

_____

THE WEDDING PARTY

Part of your treasured wedding memories are the good times you share with those closest to you, especially those you include in the wedding party. Asking someone to be a wedding attendant is an honor—he or she becomes a participant in the wedding drama, rather than just a spectator.

Let bridal party members know you've selected them as soon as possible, so they can make travel and work plans. When making your decisions, use the list of attendants' duties on the following pages and these guidelines:

Honor Attendant

• The maid or matron of honor is usually a very close friend or sister. An honor attendant could also be a mother or grandmother. Or have a best person: a brother, male cousin, or other person who's especially close to you.

• You may have two honor attendants and split their duties. For example, one could hold your bouquet during the ceremony, one could hand you the groom's ring. One could stand beside the groom in the receiving line, one could sit at his left at the bridal table.

• The honor attendant usually signs the marriage certificate as a witness, and therefore needs to be old enough to sign a legal document. If you want a person who is not of legal age to be your honor attendant (your daughter, young sister), an older bridesmaid could sign the marriage certificate.

Bridesmaids

• The number of bridesmaids depends on the size and style of the wedding: from none, at the smallest ceremony, to 12, at a large, formal one.

• The number of bridesmaids does not have to match the number of ushers. At the wedding rehearsal you can find ways to create an attractive procession and recession, no matter how many bridesmaids and ushers you choose.

• It's a good idea to include the groom's sisters or sisters-in-law to emphasize that the marriage is a merging of two families.

• You don't have to include a friend simply because you were in her wedding, or include a cousin or sister-in-law simply because you are related. You might limit your bridesmaids to relatives only, or college friends only. But if there will be hurt feelings or family bitterness if certain women are excluded, ask them to join the wedding party.

• Think of ways to honor and include friends not chosen to be bridesmaids. Someone could read a psalm or poem during the ceremony, another could preside over the guest book, pass out programs or rice bags.

• Junior bridesmaids are between 9 and 14 years of age, and may have fewer responsibilities, or slightly different (less mature) dresses, than the bridesmaids.

Best Man

• Traditionally he's a brother, cousin, close friend, or father of the groom. A sister or other close friend or relative could also be a best woman.

Ushers

• As a rule of thumb, you will need one usher for every 50 guests (to assist in ceremony seating), but you may have more.

• Ushers are generally the groom's brothers, cousins, future brothers-in-law, and friends.

• Junior ushers (ages 9–14) may be assigned to stand near the entrance to the church or synagogue to seat late-arriving guests.

• The groom may also appoint a head usher to supervise special arrangements, such as seating divorced parents or handicapped guests.

Child Attendants

• Flower girls carry a basket of flowers (often rose petals or a nosegay) to strew in the bride's path, as a symbol of ensuring a beautiful path ahead.

• The ring bearer (traditionally a boy) carries a satin pillow with a ring tied or sewn onto it. Usually this is a symbolic ring—the honor attendants hold the actual rings.

• Pages or train bearers may be appointed at a very formal wedding to carry your train down the aisle. Traditionally two boys of about the same height are chosen, but you may also have two girls.

• Candle lighters are often two boys from either family who light candles just before the mother of the bride is seated.

• In Europe the tradition is to select all child attendants. To observe this custom, appoint a maid of honor who is between 9 and 14 years of age.

• In general, child attendants are between 4 and 8 years old. While younger ones can look adorable, they often can't be expected to perform predictably in front of a crowd, or to sit or stand quietly during the ceremony.

• Invite child attendants' parents to the rehearsal dinner and wedding. (Children should come only if it is not a late evening.)

ATTENDANTS' DUTIES

After using the following lists to help choose your attendants, you might make photocopies to distribute to members of the wedding party.

The Honor Attendant (Maid or Matron of Honor):

• helps you with pre-wedding duties such as addressing envelopes, shopping, or setting up a gift display.

• supervises the bridesmaids, making sure their dresses get fitted, they have all accessories ready, and get to the wedding rehearsal and ceremony on time.

• usually pays for her own wedding outfit (except flowers), as well as travel expenses. (You can help with some of these costs, perhaps by housing her with a friend or neighbor.)

• attends all pre-wedding parties; perhaps gives one herself.

• arranges your train and veil at the ceremony and holds your bouquet.

• keeps the groom's ring and passes it to you at the appropriate moment.

• signs the marriage certificate as a legal witness.

• stands next to the groom in the receiving line and is seated in a place of honor at the reception (usually at the groom's left).

• helps you change from wedding gown to going-away clothes at the end of the reception.

• makes sure your wedding dress is safely stored and helps in other ways while you are on your honeymoon—depositing gift checks or looking after presents.

The Bridesmaids:

• have no definite pre-wedding responsibilities, but may also help with tasks such as addressing envelopes, transporting out-of-town guests, or running errands.

• pay for their own wedding outfits (except flowers), as well as transportation—unless you decide to pay for all or part of these costs.

• attend pre-wedding parties, and alone or together, have a shower for the bride.

• attend the wedding rehearsal and rehearsal dinner.

• walk in the procession and stand next to the bride at the ceremony.

• stand in the receiving line (optional).

• sit alternately with ushers at the bridal table.

The Best Man:

• supervises ushers' fittings and makes sure they are properly attired and on time on wedding day.

• pays for his own wedding attire and travel expenses.

• attends pre-wedding parties and rehearsal and may host bachelors' party or his/her shower.

• makes sure the ushers know their duties on wedding day.

• takes charge of the marriage license and bride's ring and presents them at the appropriate times.

• sees that the ceremony official is paid. (He presents a sealed envelope from the groom after the ceremony.)

• normally does not stand in the receiving line, but mingles with guests and dances.

• proposes the first toast to the new couple at the reception; collects any congratulatory telegrams and reads them.

• sits to the right of the bride at the bridal table.

• assists the groom in changing into going-away clothes.

• helps the newlyweds get off on their honeymoon by putting luggage in honeymoon car, holding tickets and keys during the wedding; may drive the bride and groom to the airport or other destination.

• organizes the return of all rented men's formalwear after the wedding and deposits wedding gift checks.

The Ushers:

• attend pre-wedding parties and the rehearsal, and may singly or jointly host a bachelors' party or other pre-wedding party.

• arrive at the ceremony site 45 minutes to an hour before the ceremony.

• seat guests by offering right arm to each woman and asking if she is on the bride's side or the groom's. Traditionally the bride's guests are on the left, the groom's on the right (the opposite in Jewish services). A man alone may also be accompanied to his seat by an usher.

• seat the groom's parents in the right front pew and the bride's mother in the left front row. If one of the ushers is a brother of the bride or groom, he would escort his own mother; otherwise, a head usher would do so.

• may perform other pre-ceremony functions such as rolling out an aisle runner or distributing programs.

• return to the front of the church after the ceremony and escort mothers, honored elderly, or disabled guests.

• loosen pew ribbons or otherwise signal guests to file out, row by row, from front to back. Ushers see that all guests have a ride to the reception site and are prepared to give directions.

• need not stand in the receiving line, but mingle with guests and dance later with single female guests.

• decorate the going-away car—in a safe way—with streamers, flowers, signs (optional).

WEDDING PARTY CHART

My maid of honor _____

Address _____

_____

Phone _____

My matron of honor _____

Address _____

_____

Phone _____

1. **Bridesmaid** _____

   Address _____

   _____

   Phone _____

2. **Bridesmaid** _____

   Address _____

   _____

   Phone _____

3. **Bridesmaid** _____

   Address _____

   _____

   Phone _____

4. **Bridesmaid** _____

   Address _____

   _____

   Phone _____

The best man _____

Address _____

_____

Phone _____

The head usher _____

Address _____

_____

Phone _____

1. **Usher** _____

   Address _____

   _____

   Phone _____

2. **Usher** _____

   Address _____

   _____

   Phone _____

3. **Usher** _____

   Address _____

   _____

   Phone _____

4. **Usher** _____

   Address _____

   _____

   Phone _____

5. **Bridesmaid** _____

    Address _____

    _____

    Phone _____

6. **Bridesmaid** _____

    Address _____

    _____

    Phone _____

7. **Flower girl** _____

    Address _____

    _____

    Phone _____

Other helper _____

Address _____

_____

Phone _____

Special helper _____

Address _____

_____

Phone _____

5. **Usher** _____

    Address _____

    _____

    Phone _____

6. **Usher** _____

    Address _____

    _____

    Phone _____

7. **Ring bearer** _____

    Address _____

    _____

    Phone _____

Other helper _____

Address _____

_____

Phone _____

Special helper _____

Address _____

_____

Phone _____

Section 2:

CEREMONY GUIDE

MEETING WITH YOUR CLERGYMEMBER

Once you've decided you want a religious ceremony, and have chosen a date for the wedding (and some alternate dates), it's time for you both to meet with the clergymember who will perform your wedding.

Remember that a clergymember is looking at your wedding from a religious perspective and needs to make sure you are committed to marriage in a spiritual context. Thus, you may be asked questions about why you want to marry, your feelings on important issues like money and children, and the extent of your religious participation.

You may also be asked for certain papers,

including:

• Certificates of baptism or confirmation, or a letter attesting to the marital or religious status of each of you.

• A special dispensation, or instruction, if you are of different faiths.

• A signed "Letter of Intention to Marry" or similar document, which usually states that you will participate in pre-marital counseling with a clergymember. In some cases, it's recommended that you attend Engaged Encounter or other counseling groups that give couples a chance to discuss their feelings about many aspects of marriage.

QUESTIONS FOR YOUR CLERGYMEMBER

In order to plan your ceremony, you will have many questions to ask your clergymember. You may want to meet with several to find the one whose beliefs best match yours.

Checklist For Your Initial Meeting

☐ Is the date we have chosen available? The

time? If not, what alternate dates and times are available?

☐ Must we be members of this church or synagogue, or know members? If we are not members, must we pay special fees?

☐ During which religious holidays, liturgical seasons, are weddings prohibited (Lent, Days of Awe)? Is any time of day inappropriate? (Judaism prohibits weddings before sundown on the sabbath; some pastors encourage Saturday morning nuptials.)

☐ Will you marry us if one of us is divorced? What special arrangements does a remarriage require? (Permission from a religious authority, proof of divorce?)

☐ Will you marry us if we are of different faiths? On what conditions? Must one partner convert? Will you perform the ceremony with a clergymember of a different faith? How do you usually share officiating duties?

☐ Do you require premarital counseling, or that we be congregation members?

☐ What are the fees for using the synagogue or church, your services, the organist, and services of staff? Who is usually tipped? How much? When?

☐ Will you marry us at a nonreligious site (such as a hotel, country club)?

☐ Can we hold a small wedding in your study or chambers, a small chapel?

☐ Are there any restrictions on ceremony dress? (yarmulkes, that a bride's or maids' shoulders be covered?) Must a bride wear white, a veil?

☐ Can we write our vows, personalize our ceremony? What are the parameters?

☐ Must readings be religious? At which point will they be performed?

☐ Is a kiss permitted at the end of the marriage ceremony?

☐ Are other weddings scheduled on our date? How much time will we have? Is there leeway, so we won't feel rushed? Can we share flowers with another bride?

☐ What is the seating capacity of the sanctuary? How big a wedding party fits comfortably in front of the altar, on the stage? If there's a center aisle, how many can walk down it abreast? If not, how does the procession work with side aisles?

☐ Are there ramps, parking, aisles wide enough for a wheelchair?

☐ Is there a changing room for the bride and her wedding party?

☐ Is the synagogue or church available for receptions? Are there any food requirements (kosher)? Can alcohol be served?

☐ Are there parking facilities on the premises, nearby? Will guests be charged?

☐ Is there adequate air-conditioning in summer, heat in winter?

Checklist For Your Second Meeting

☐ How and when do we get our marriage license? When do we give it to you? How many witnesses do we need? Can we include signing in the ceremony?

☐ Are photographers permitted to use flash attachments during the ceremony? How close to the altar may they stand?

☐ Are there any restrictions on throwing rice, flower petals?

☐ When can we gain entry to the synagogue, church, on wedding day?

☐ Is there a recommended area to position the receiving line?

☐ Must we use the staff organist, cantor? Are instrumentalists permitted? Must musical selections be approved? Is there an approved list?

☐ Do you have samples of wedding programs? How are programs passed out?

☐ Will you explain the symbolism of the ceremony? How long will it last? Will you be giving a homily, making a speech? Can we preview it in advance (no surprises)?

☐ Can we preview the wording of the service, update old-fashioned language?

☐ Can we reserve family-member seats?

☐ Which accessories are provided (huppah, candelabra, aisle runner)?

☐ Can you suggest ceremony roles for children from a previous marriage? May young relatives from a different congregation serve as altar boys, candle lighters?

☐ How can we include a wine ceremony, communion, or ethnic traditions?

☐ Who should be invited to the rehearsal? What if an out-of-town wedding party member cannot attend? Will there be music? Will you coordinate the processional, recessional?

☐ When is the rehearsal held?

☐ Will you and your spouse attend the rehearsal dinner?

☐ Will you (and your spouse) attend the reception? Will you bless the meal?

☐ Will you arbitrate between divorced parents, feuding in-laws?

CEREMONY MUSIC

What you'll need and when: For a traditional religious ceremony, the music usually begins about a half hour before the ceremony with a **prelude.** After the bride's mother has been seated, a **soloist** or **choir** may perform. You and your wedding party walk down the aisle to the sounds of a majestic **processional.** There may be additional solos or choral numbers during the ceremony, or all guests may join in singing a **hymn.** You and your wedding party leave the ceremony to the strains of a triumphant **recessional;** the organist or other musician may continue playing a **postlude** as guests file out.

How to plan your ceremony music: Start by talking to your clergymember. Ask:

• What is available at that church or synagogue—organist, choir? Are other types of music allowed (trumpet, harp, flutes)? Does he or she know of musicians to play other instruments, if it's desired?

• Are there restrictions on the types of songs that can be sung or played? (Some denominations prohibit non-religious songs.)

• What fee does the organist charge?

Discuss with your fiancé what mood you want—the traditional solemnity of a religious service or the contemporary atmosphere created by show tunes.

If you would like to use different instruments—such as flutes, woodwinds, harps, classical guitar—locate musicians through friends, local schools, or symphonies.

Consider using friends or relatives as soloists or musicians, if they are professional musicians or gifted amateurs. Less-experienced performers may simply want to play or sing an impromptu song at the reception.

Be sure to thank the friends or relatives you've asked to perform with a small gift; pay professionals.

Prepare a list for musicians of songs you want played. Be sure to provide sheet music early if musicians must learn something new. Perhaps invite relatives who will perform and the organist to the rehearsal. (Professionals will most likely *not* attend.)

Totally unfamiliar with music and appropriate songs for weddings? The organist at your church or synagogue may help by suggesting favorite tunes and playing them so you can decide. You can also purchase tapes and records of wedding music, to help in making selections.

CEREMONY MUSIC CHECKLIST

Ceremony Moment	Performance Time	Selections
Prelude	_____	_____
		_____
		_____
		_____
		_____
First solo	_____	_____
Second solo	_____	_____
Processional	_____	_____
Other	_____	_____
Recessional	_____	_____
Postlude	_____	_____
		_____
		_____
		_____
		_____

Organist (or main instrumentalist) _____ Cost $ _____

Soloist _____ Cost $ _____

Ensemble or choir leader _____

Ensemble members _____

_____

_____

_____

Ensemble cost $ _____

Total ceremony music cost $ _____

CEREMONY MUSIC SUGGESTIONS

Processional and Recessional

"Bridal Chorus from Lohengrin" ("Here Comes the Bride"), by Wagner

"Trumpet Voluntary," by Clarke

"Fanfare" from The Triumphant, by Couperin

"Trumpet Tune," by Purcell

"Apotheosis" from Sleeping Beauty, by Tchaikovsky

"Sarabande" from Suite No. 11, by Handel

"Canon in D Minor," by Pachelbel

"Water Music," by Handel

"Nadia's Theme" ("The Young and the Restless"), performed by Barry De Vorzon and Perry Botkin, Jr.

"Wedding March" from A Midsummer Night's Dream, by Mendelssohn

"Theme from Chariots of Fire," by Vangelis

"Rondo" theme from Masterpiece Theatre, by Mouret

"Benedictus," by Simon and Garfunkel

"Spring" from The Four Seasons, by Vivaldi

During the Ceremony

"Wedding" ("There Is Love"), by Stookey

"First Organ Sonata," by Mendelssohn

"Jesu, Joy of Man's Desiring," by Bach

"Sheep May Safely Graze," by Bach

"Ave Maria," by Schubert

"Evergreen," sung by Barbra Streisand

"Hallelujah Chorus" from The Messiah, by Handel

"One Hand, One Heart" from West Side Story, by Bernstein and Sondheim

"Sunrise, Sunset" from Fiddler on the Roof, by Harnick, Bock

"Heart Full of Love" from Les Miserables, by Boubil, Schonberg, and Kretzmer

"Ode to Joy," by Beethoven

PERSONALIZING YOUR CEREMONY

Pledging your love to each other—it's the most important moment of the entire wedding. Yet you both may feel that standard ceremony procedures do not reflect your individual tastes and feelings. Here are ways to express your commitment and create a celebration that reflects your uniqueness as a couple.

• **Talk to your clergymember.** Find out what parts of the traditional ceremony must be included. Your clergymember has probably helped many other couples personalize their ceremonies, and is an excellent source of ideas.

• **Analyze the traditional ceremony.** You may discover that wedding ceremonies have changed recently. For example, in Protestant and Catholic ceremonies, the bride is no longer asked to "obey" her husband. Look at the customs and words, think about the meanings be-hind them, and update or change them according to your desires. For example, having your father "give you away" may seem outdated, but you would like to include a gesture that shows your parents support the union. One way is to acknowledge them with a kiss just before you join your groom at the altar.

• **Use other sources for inspiration.** Poems, songs, or popular psychology may give you ideas for readings and vows. (See the following sections on specific ideas for personalizing ceremonies and writing vows.)

• **Give a written copy of the additions to your ceremony to the clergymember.** He or she will then be able to conduct the ceremony, direct others, and prompt you if you forget the vows you've written or the gestures you've planned.

IDEAS FOR A CREATIVE CEREMONY

Consider incorporating any of these ideas into your ceremony:

Setting

• Select an outdoor or at-home setting.
• Reverse positions with the clergymember—so that you face the guests.
• Eliminate seats at a small wedding and gather everyone in a semi-circle around bride and groom.

Arrivals

• Have honor attendants or close friends welcome guests as they arrive. (It is an Oriental custom for bride and groom to make this gracious gesture.)
• Have ushers hand guests flowers, candles, rice bags, or yarmulkes.
• Have special musicians—such as bagpipers, classical guitarists—outside the church.
• Distribute wedding programs that list names and relationships of all participants; musical, poetry, and prose selections; ceremony schedule; thank-you messages to your parents; perhaps your thoughts on marriage.

Processional

• Include both sets of parents in the processional (a Jewish custom).
• Have the groom walk with you or meet you halfway down the aisle.
• Give each mother a kiss, flower, or handkerchief embroidered with your names and wedding date when you reach the first pew.

Giving the Bride Away

• Instead of asking, "Who gives this woman in marriage?" have your clergymember ask, "Who blesses this marriage?" or "Who rejoices in this union?" All parents can answer, "We do."
• The bride should part with her father as they reach his seat, kiss him on the cheek, then walk alone to meet her groom.
• Include a Unity Candle ceremony: Have three candles on the altar—one in the center, two smaller ones on either side. The bride, her parents, or her whole family walk up and light the candle on the left; the groom's family lights the right candle. After exchanging your vows, you two light the center candle together, from the two family candles.

Before the Vows

• Read lines from a favorite song or poem.
• Have special people perform readings—a brother or sister could offer a quote on the meaning of families; attendants might talk about the importance of friends.
• Create your own prayer for everyone to say in unison.

During the Vows

(See the following section, "Writing Your Own Vows.")
• Give each bridal party member a candle, dim the lights, then light the candles in succession, and have attendants form a semi-circle around the two of you.

CEREMONY WORKSHEET

Site reserved _____ Cost, if any _____

Date _____ Ceremony time _____ to _____

Name and telephone of clergymember _____

Name and telephone of other church official (secretary, etc.) _____

_____

Procession (names of participants, order): _____

_____

_____

_____

Call to Worship or Welcome—readings or ideas: _____

_____

_____

_____

Giving Away or family gesture: ____ _____

_____

_____

Prayers or readings/Names of readers: _____

_____

_____

_____

• Exchange two sets of vows—first the traditional ones, followed by ones you've written yourselves.

• Have parents reaffirm their wedding vows after you say yours.

After the Vows

• Kiss your parents and grandparents after kissing your new spouse, to reaffirm family ties.

• Include a short period of silence, when any guest may add a prayer of his or her own.

• Have a "Sign of Peace"—a handshake or kiss passed from clergymember to you, to attendants, to guests.

The Recessional

• Stop at each pew to greet guests.

• Have attendants release helium balloons.

• Walk to your reception site, if it's nearby. Attendants and guests will follow, creating a wedding parade.

• Consider unique transportation to the reception site: a horse-drawn carriage or sleigh, a vintage car.

Bride's Vows: _____

_____

_____

Groom's Vows: _____

_____

_____

Exchange of Rings: _____

_____

Pronouncement of Marriage: _____

_____

Benediction and Blessing: _____

_____

Recessional (names and order): _____

_____

Other ideas—programs, Unity Candle, etc.: _____

_____

Clergymember's fee, if any: _____

WRITING YOUR OWN VOWS

Reciting vows is the part of the ceremony when the bride and groom make promises to each other. (In a standard Christian ceremony, the couple usually promises to "have and to hold . . . love and cherish . . . until parted by death.") You two may decide that these words don't fully reflect your commitment to each other. Perhaps you also want to mention friendship, trust, personal growth, or other values important to your relationship. When writing your own vows, consider the following:

• Although there are no legal requirements for wedding vows (all it takes to be legally married is a marriage license signed by a licensed officiant), religious groups have guidelines, so consult your clergymember first.

• Look at traditional vows and decide what concepts are important to you: love, fidelity, caring, for example.

• Consider other sources for inspiration: songs, poems, novels, popular psychology, children's books. "On Marriage," from *The Prophet*, by Kahlil Gibran, and "The Song of Songs by Solomon," in the Old Testament of the Bible, are popular choices.

• Think about what marriage means to you. Then pledge, promise, or commit to those things. For example, the bride and groom could say in unison, "I pledge to share with you life's sorrows and joys. I will always respect you and forgive you. I promise to always accept and love who you are and support your spiritual growth. I promise these things until the end of my life." You can also include references to your religious faith or goals, such as having children.

• If either partner was previously married, you may consider acknowledging this in your statements, especially if there are children from the prior union.

• Keep the solemnity of the occasion in mind. Any specific references to money, sex, housekeeping, and the like, can be written in a prenuptial agreement.

• The vows themselves should take about one to three minutes. Any additional thoughts you have on marriage can be expressed elsewhere in the ceremony, perhaps in a spiritual reading or prayer.

• The bride's vows need not be identical to the groom's—in fact, some couples prefer to keep the promises secret until wedding day. In any case, your clergymember will want to approve the vows before the ceremony and have a copy on hand. (Even if you decide to recite your vows from memory, have him hold a copy as a back-up.)

CIVIL CEREMONIES

Civil ceremonies can be of various sizes and degrees of formality. Traditionally they are small and informal occasions with only a few witnesses. But if both of you want a big wedding without religious overtones, you can have a judge or justice of the peace marry you in a grand hotel ballroom before hundreds of guests. Or you could be married at a traditional, small, civil ceremony during the day; then plan a big, formal party to celebrate that night.

How do we find someone to perform a civil ceremony? A variety of officials can perform wedding ceremonies—mayors, justices of the peace, clerks of Superior Court, judges, county clerks. Check the office in your town that issues marriage licenses to find who is qualified in your area. Ask family and friends if they

know any of these officials—it will be a friendlier occasion if the official is personally recommended or is someone you know.

Where should our civil ceremony be held? Many civil ceremonies are performed in judge's chambers, a courthouse, office or home of the official. Or it could be held at a club, home, hotel ballroom, or even at a more creative site—such as a museum, historic mansion, or park.

What should I wear? If you choose the traditional civil ceremony performed in an office or official building, with few witnesses, a dress or suit is appropriate. For a large wedding at a more formal location, wear a traditional wedding dress.

Section 3:

WORKING WITH RECEPTION PROS

PLANNING A RECEPTION

A wedding is the party of your lifetime—the one moment when you want everything to be perfect. If you're like most brides, however, you've probably never had to plan a party larger than dinner for eight or snacks and drinks for 25.

Reception planning is fun—sampling different wedding cakes, choosing gorgeous floral combinations, and just plain being in charge of how the wedding of your dreams takes shape.

Many brides and grooms, however, may be so swept up in the romance of the wedding that they do not want to stop and specify the details of flowers, catering, photography, and music in a contract. The results can be disappointing and sometimes disastrous—a different band shows up, the flowers don't resemble any that you ordered, the photographer leaves before the cake is cut.

Some general tips for reception planning:

• **Start early.** The most popular wedding service providers in your area may be booked a year or two in advance. If you begin working with service people early, you have plenty of time to get all the details right—and find a new service person if something isn't working out.

• **Be assertive, but not unbending.** Some brides forget that they are the employer and let the service providers do what they want simply because they are the wedding experts. Remember that it is your wedding and that you are the expert on what you want. Yet it's wise to listen to the ideas of experienced wedding service providers, who may have some creative ways to solve problems and make your wedding fantasies come alive.

• **Have a budget in mind.** Know approximately how much you can spend on each particular area. Before meeting with a service provider, it's a good idea to call three or four in your area to get rough estimates.

• **Specify all details in writing.** You must sign a contract or a letter of agreement with each vendor or provider, and make sure the wedding professional signs as well—or the agreement will not be enforceable. (See next section.) The contract or agreement should specify dates, times, prices, and descriptions of all services provided.

CONTRACTS

You are meeting with a wedding service provider, say a florist, and she has described floral arrangements that are just what you wanted. The florist was recommended by friends, she seems reliable, so why bring up a contract? Will she be suspicious, offended?

Perhaps, but as wedding day approaches, you will wish you had the details about your flowers in writing. You met with the florist months ago—will she have noted that you want lilies of the valley in the table centerpieces? Will she remember the correct date and time of your wedding?

Think of a contract as something that will give you, and the florist, peace of mind as the wedding approaches, and help ensure that you get the services you anticipate. Chances are, your florist and flowers will come through, but if there *is* a mistake, you can use that contract to help set things right, or at least renegotiate the bill if services deviate from what is specified in writing.

Many wedding service persons have standard contracts already prepared for you to sign; others will write out the details with you. If a service person doesn't have a contract, write down the details of what he or she will provide during your meeting. Include the date and time, and the costs. You and the service person should each sign the agreement.

You should have contracts or letters of agreement from the following:
- stationery shop (for invitations)
- caterer and rental hall
- florist
- musicians
- photographer and videographer
- wedding dress shop and men's formalwear shop
- limousine company
- baker
- bridal consultant
- rental company (for chairs, tables, linens, serving pieces, etc.)
- any other people providing a service for your wedding.

Here, other tips for your wedding service contracts:

- **Write out all details.** For example, with floral arrangements, describe the shape, size, color, number of flowers, types of flowers. Don't rely on verbal assurances—a bandleader, for instance, who *says* he will play 1940's swing music but really only knows popular tunes; a lead singer who promises she will be there.

- **Take time to understand every part of the contract.** Don't be pressured into signing immediately. If there is something you don't like or understand, ask questions. You should have time to take the contract home and have someone else look it over.

- **Make sure the merchant signs the contract.** It won't be a valid contract unless he or she signs it. Some unscrupulous businesses get the bride and groom to sign, but shrewdly avoid signing it themselves.

- **Put down as little money as possible.** The less the deposit, the more leverage you have if the firm fails to perform.

- **Beware of large cancellation fees.** Last-minute cancellation fees are understandable, but you should not have to pay large amounts if you cancel months in advance—when a caterer can rebook a room, for example, and recover any loss of income.

WEDDING CONSUMER TRAPS— AND HOW TO AVOID THEM

Unfortunately, the worst does happen occasionally: The dress you ordered never comes in, the flowers arrive wilted, the wedding photographs are too dark. Here are some common wedding frauds and disappointments—and how you can avoid them:

Wedding attire

Betty shopped for her wedding gown as soon as she got engaged—eight months before her wedding. She spent days trying on gowns and finally found the dream dress—one she had envisioned herself wearing since she was a girl. She told the Shady Lady Bridal Salon she needed it two weeks before the wedding and paid a deposit amounting to half the total price.

Two weeks before the wedding, Betty called Shady Lady to set up a time for her fitting and was told the dress hadn't come in yet. The salon claimed there was a problem on the manufacturer's end—the right fabric hadn't arrived. Her wedding date drew nearer and still no dress. In desperation, Betty went to another bridal salon, bought a dress off the rack, and had it altered. She never got back the deposit from Shady Lady, and worse, she was deprived of wearing her dream dress.

Other wedding attire rip-offs include gowns that arrive in soiled or poor condition, the wrong size, the wrong color, missing bridesmaids' capes, poorly fitted men's formalwear.

How to Avoid Bridal Attire Disappointments:
• Pay as small a deposit as possible.
• Include a cancellation provision (the store's contract may not have one), specifying that the deposit will be refunded if the clothing does not arrive on the desired date, in good condition.

• Choose a delivery date that is several weeks before you actually need the wedding dress and bridesmaids' dresses. (Men's clothing may only be available a few days before the wedding, since it is most often rented.)
• If the attire you order is not provided on time, and as ordered, consider taking the business to a small claims court to recover any money already paid.

Music

Brenda and Steve loved the band they heard at their friends' wedding—the Hood Wink Orchestra—and immediately signed them up for their own wedding. Wedding day arrived, and so did a different band!

Brenda and Steve didn't realize that many bands can operate under one name. Mr. Hood Wink, the bandleader, puts together orchestras "under the leadership of Hood Wink," according to what's needed that day. There may have been five different "Hood Wink Orchestras" playing the day of Brenda and Steve's wedding.

Other music rip-offs: The wrong number of musicians show up; a disc jockey with tapes shows up instead of live performers; the band does not know the majority of songs you had requested earlier.

How to Avoid Music Disappointments:
• Be sure your contract lists the date and site of the reception, time the band should arrive, number of hours the band will play, cost (including overtime rates), style of music to be played, and the appropriate attire for musicians.
• If there are certain musicians whom you want to appear personally at your wedding (the

bandleader, lead vocalist), specify their names in your contract and write that you want them at the event, "in person."

• Otherwise, specify the number of musicians and their instruments (for example, one saxophone player, two trumpet players).

Catering halls

Laurie and Paul booked the main ballroom of La Hoax catering facility a year in advance, paid a $500 deposit, and signed a contract. Six months later, Laurie received a call from the banquet manager saying that there had been a terrible mistake—the grand ballroom had been previously booked by another couple. They would have to move Laurie and Paul's reception to another, less formal room.

When Laurie protested, the banquet manager pointed to the contract, which stated that if the premises had been previously booked, the caterer had the right to move the couple to another room or return the deposit. Laurie and Paul had not read this small print, which cost them their dream reception.

Laurie found another reception site, although it was not as beautiful as La Hoax. Later she learned that other couples had encountered the same problem at La Hoax. The double booking was no mistake. The management promised the ballroom, and a few months before the wedding, would tell the couple there was a mistake and that they must take a smaller room. In most cases, it would be too late to find another site, so couples had to give in and accept the less desirable room.

Another catering facility rip-off involves cancellation fees. John and Emily contracted for a room in a catering hall and put down a $600 deposit toward a $2,000 reception.

Six months before the wedding, they decided they couldn't afford an extravagant reception, so they told the management they had to

cancel. He said that if they were able to rebook the room, their $600 would be refunded. He said that since they were canceling so far in advance, he would certainly be able to fill the room with another party.

The wedding date came, and so did a bill for the additional $400. The caterer was not able to fill the room, and under the terms of this contract, Emily and John were liable for 50 percent of the cost of the entire reception: $1,000.

Laws regulating contract cancellation fees vary from state to state. In some, you may only be liable for 20 percent of the original contract price—find out from your state's attorney general's office.

Other catering rip-offs: Two weddings are booked in the same room on the same day, and the later bride and her guests have to wait for the first reception to end and the room to be cleaned. If you don't read the contract carefully, you may be surprised by "hidden extras," such as gratuities, overtime fees, chair setting-up fees, extra fees for waiters or bartenders.

How to Avoid Catering Disappointments:

• Read the contract carefully, paying special attention to the cancellation clauses. While you may think you would never cancel your wedding, you may well change your reception plans—you might find another site, have to choose another date. Last-minute cancellation fees are fair, since the caterer may have already purchased food, hired waiters; but you should only have to pay a small amount—if anything—if you cancel months before, when the caterer can rebook the room and recover any loss of income. In general, the closer to the wedding date you cancel, the more you will be asked to pay. Keep down payments relatively small.

• Try to make sure that yours is the only reception that is scheduled that day in the room you choose.

• Ask about gratuities, overtime fees, coat

check fees, and any other "extra" expenses. Specify exact costs in writing; state that there are no additional fees.

• Specify a date to give the caterer a final guest count. While many caterers will ask that you pay for a minimum number of guests, try (as much as possible) to pay for the actual number who attend, rather than for a rough estimate made several months in advance.

Engagement rings

The jeweler who sold Mike a beautiful engagement ring for his fiancée, Martha, said he was giving Mike a special deal—the price of the ring was reduced from $2,000 to $1,500. A few months later, Martha took the ring to another jeweler to change the setting, and the jeweler said it was worth only $200. Several appraisers gave the same sorry estimate.

Other jewelry rip-offs: In a more complicated version of the above scenario, the jeweler suggests taking the ring to an appraiser he recommends. Reassured by the appraiser of its value, the couple buys the ring, only to find out that the appraiser is in on the fraud and has falsely inflated the stone's value.

How to Avoid Ring Disappointments:

• Know the jeweler. Call the Better Business Bureau to see if there have been any complaints filed against the company. Look for a logo on the store window, plaque on the wall, or emblem on stationery identifying the jeweler as a member of the American Gem Society. Shop at several places to get an idea of typical prices.

• Make the final sale contingent on an appraisal from an *independent* appraiser. (Tell the appraiser you want a "genuine" appraisal—as opposed to one for insurance purposes, which may be inflated.)

• Be wary of advertisements and claims of discounts, sales, price reductions. Claims of price reductions may be a way to get you to buy an inferior stone quickly.

• Don't buy a diamond unless you can look at it under natural light, near a window. Avoid jewelry stores that have blue-tinted lights overhead. All diamonds—especially less valuable yellow ones—look good under blue light.

Photography

Jane and Michael took the recommendation of friends, Beth and Don, who had used the Overexposure Studio for their wedding. A pleasant young woman had artistically captured the drama and emotion of Beth and Don's wedding. Yet at Jane and Michael's wedding, a pushy man showed up who dominated the entire wedding. He was rude to guests, delayed the wedding by insisting on endless group shots, and constantly shoved his camera in Jane's and Michael's faces, even during intimate moments like the first dance. Worst of all, the photographs were blurry and off-color.

Other photography rip-offs: The photographs don't turn out at all, or costs of additional prints may be much higher than expected. In another scenario, the photographer leaves the reception before the cake cutting, saying the contract specified four hours of coverage, beginning with the ceremony.

How to Avoid Photography Disappointments:

• Some photography studios employ several different photographers. Specify the photographer you want in writing.

• Put a clause in your contract stating that you owe no money, and that all deposits will be refunded, if the photographs don't turn out.

• Investigate "packages." While for the most part they are convenient time savers, they can also be more expensive in certain situations. One such instance: if you want a large number of prints for relatives.

• Have friends take snapshots. You can't rely on friends to capture all the important details of a wedding like a professional can, but snapshots will provide a crucial backup if the photographer's work fails.

• Meet with your photographer and go over the schedule for the wedding. Plan exactly when you will take group shots; find out how long they will take and choose a time that will not delay the reception for too long. It's a good idea to meet once at the wedding site beforehand, to discuss where the photographer will stand to get important shots.

Flowers

Robyn was very specific about the kinds of flowers she wanted in her bridal bouquet: spray roses, dreamland tulips, and camellias, all in pale pink to match the maids' dresses. But when the flowers arrived, she was dismayed to see that the roses were wilted, the tulips were orange, and carnations had been substituted for the camellias. The arrangement was much smaller than Robyn had expected. And worst of all, the flowers fell apart halfway through the reception—before the bouquet could be tossed. The florist refused to accept the blame, saying that the flowers Robyn wanted were out of season, so substitutions had to be made, and that the heat and handling during the day had affected the bouquet's condition.

How to Avoid Floral Disappointments:

• Make sure your contract specifies what the florist will do if unusual, out-of-season flowers are unavailable. Choose several substitutes and write them into the contract.

• Make the contract as detailed as possible with regard to the number, shape, size, and color of arrangements and bouquets. Indicate that you will adjust the balance of payment due if flowers are not fresh, arrangements secure.

Honeymoon

Max and Judy looked forward for months to their honeymoon at a mountain inn. When they got to the inn, however, they were told that the inn was overbooked; there was simply no room for them. The inn sent them to a decent—but less charming—guest house down the road.

Cindy and Richard wrote away to Caribbean resorts and received a number of brochures. They chose the Fraudulent Bay Cottages. What could be more romantic than having your own cottage at the beach? Plus, Fraudulent Bay was much less expensive than the bigger hotels.

When they got there, they were disappointed to see that the cottage was one tiny room and bathroom. There was a bed, but little else—no television, no radio, no rug on the floor. Just a tiny, dark, hot room. Although the room *was* cheap, the beach was an expensive taxi ride away.

How to Avoid Honeymoon Disappointments:

Overbooking does occur in hotels and on airplanes, even with written confirmation. In most cases, a hotel will find a room for you at an equivalent hotel, will transport you there, and may even pay for your stay there. If you find yourself in this situation, calmly and firmly ask to speak to the hotel manager, explain that you are on your honeymoon, and show him or her written confirmation of your reservation. Airlines have differing policies regarding overbooking, but you can avoid being bumped off a flight if you arrive at the boarding gate an hour early and check in with airline personnel—even if you already have a boarding pass. If the plane is overbooked, airlines usually offer passengers flight vouchers or cash to give up their seats, and will arrange for seats to your destination on the next available flight. If you're in no hurry, you could volunteer to give up your seats, and actually help pay for your trip! Sometimes overbooking problems at hotels and on airlines can be avoided if you call to reconfirm reservations 24 hours in advance.

• Deal with a reputable travel agent. Cindy and Richard thought they would save money by making their own travel plans. They didn't realize that travel agents rarely charge clients; instead, agents are paid commissions by the airlines and other suppliers. Try to choose a travel agent who is familiar with your destination. He or she would know which places would best suit your needs. Travel agents can put together all your tickets and paperwork. Plus, they hear of discounts and packages the general public may never be aware of, and they can tell you what paperwork you'll need (for example, passports, visas).

TIPS FROM THE BETTER BUSINESS BUREAU FOR AVOIDING WEDDING RIP-OFFS

• **Make arrangements as far in advance as possible.** You have the best chance of getting what you want by booking wedding professionals early. Popular bands and catering facilities can be reserved a year or more ahead. Some vendors charge extra if you order things on a "rush" basis. Plus, if something goes wrong, you will have more time to solve the problem.

• **Deal with reputable people.** Shop around to get a feel for fair prices in your area. Get recommendations from friends about services they have used. Call the Better Business Bureau in your area; it keeps files on various businesses and can tell you if other brides have had problems with a particular company. Beware of bargains: you want items and services of high quality.

• **Get all provisions in writing.** Include descriptions of everything you are paying for—the types of flowers, exact menu, number of personnel, etc.

• **Pay attention to cancellation policies.** Can you get a refund of a deposit if you cancel or change your wedding date? (There may be provisions that say you can get a refund up to a certain time, or no refunds unless a site can be rebooked.) Write that you will not pay, and expect a refund of any deposits already paid, if the company doesn't deliver as specified (e.g., reception food runs out, the flowers are not fresh).

Prepared with the help of Alvin Kerstein, president, Better Business Bureau of Western Connecticut.

PLANNING TIPS FOR NEW WAYS TO WED

Many brides today will be planning pre- and post-wedding parties in addition to their wedding receptions. These parties may be part of a Long Weekend Wedding, a reception far from their home as part of a Progressive Wedding, or activities at a resort before and after a Honeymoon Wedding. (See "New Ways to Wed" in Section 1.) Many weddings also have a theme or particular style: a Christmas holiday wedding; a wedding on a boat or at a country inn; a wedding with an ethnic theme; a medieval, Victorian, or Southwestern wedding. Here are planning tips for these special celebrations:

• **Enlist the help of others.** Planning a wedding and reception alone is nearly a full-time job—if your wedding is out of the ordinary, get help! *Wedding consultants* and *party planners* are professionals who can put together receptions in faraway locations, coordinate and plan many activities at a weekend or resort wedding, and make arrangements for guests' travel and accommodations. A *hotel manager* or *hotel guest relations coordinator* can help you plan events if you and all your guests are staying at one hotel (for a Weekend or Honeymoon Wedding). He or she can set up a variety of parties; plan sightseeing trips; oversee numerous activities such as scuba diving lessons, deep sea fishing, tennis matches, movies, aerobics classes. A hotel manager can also help put together your wedding reception, especially if you are getting married in a foreign country. A *tour operator* or *travel agent* will help you plan a wedding and celebration in an exotic locale. He or she can arrange for transportation and lodging for you and your guests, and get information about wedding requirements in foreign countries. A tour operator may even help with details such as finding a photographer. *Friends, neighbors,* and *members of the wedding party* can help in many ways. They can host a Long Weekend Wedding party (Friday night buffet, Saturday afternoon pool gathering, Sunday morning brunch) or a reception that is part of a Progressive Wedding; host overnight guests in their homes; help with guests' transportation. A friend could act as a guest liaison, a weekend

host or hostess to welcome guests and see that they have transportation, adequate rooms.

• **Let guests know all plans.** Be sure that guests know early on that they are not just coming to a wedding ceremony and reception and going home. Include all information in a weekend itinerary enclosed with the invitation. Once guests accept, send them specific details about travel schedules, lodging, party locations and hosts, clothes they will need, and any additional requirements, like passports, if the events are in a foreign country.

• **Make adequate preparations for an outdoor wedding.** Don't ignore the possibility of rain. Rent a tent or arrange for an alternate indoor space large enough to accommodate all guests. Set up the tent three days early to keep the ground inside dry. Thoroughly spray the area for insects the week before the wedding; have a follow-up spray the day before. Install lighting if the party will go into the evening. (You may need a generator to boost power supplies.) Make sure bathroom facilities are sufficient for the number of guests.

• **Choose favors to match your wedding theme.** For a Progressive Wedding, you could take photographs at each party and put them into a scrapbook to give to parents and party hosts. When guests arrive for a Long Weekend Wedding, consider giving them T-shirts or hats with the wedding date and the names of the bride and groom. Women at a Honeymoon Wedding on a tropical island might receive shell necklaces or leis. Guests at a Southwestern wedding could take home small cactus plants; potpourri-filled lace handkerchiefs could grace the tables at a Victorian wedding. Create ceremony programs to reflect your themes—a calligrapher's lettering can make the program look medieval, for example. Use your imagination!

WEDDING CONSULTANTS/PARTY PLANNERS

What Can They Do?

Perhaps a better question is: What *can't* they do? Some wedding consultants will take on every aspect of wedding planning, from choosing the site and getting out the invitations to supervis-ing the actual wedding on site. Other consul-tants and planners may handle one aspect of your wedding—such as decorating the inside of a reception tent or finding your dream gown and bridesmaids' dresses.

Wedding consultants might also book all

WEDDING CONSULTANT/ PARTY PLANNER WORKSHEET

Estimate #1   *Services/ideas/notes*   *Cost*

Name _____

Telephone _____

Recommended by _____

Estimate #2

Name _____

Telephone _____

Recommended by _____

Estimate #3

Name _____

Telephone _____

Recommended by _____

Final selection—name, address, telephone

_____

_____

Contract signed   Deposit paid   Balance due

_____

wedding professionals—caterers, photographer, musicians; arrange for invitations; compile guest lists; plan pre-wedding parties and Long Weekend Wedding events; make hotel and travel reservations for out-of-town guests; help the couple write their own vows and plan their ceremony. They might make sure that all service people and participants stay on schedule to make the wedding day run smoothly.

Party planners, however, specialize in pre-wedding party and reception planning rather than in ceremony and etiquette. A party planner is especially useful in creating receptions with unique themes or decorations—such as a wedding in the country, *Gone With the Wind* style, or a site with an Art Deco design.

Any bride can use the services of wedding consultants and party planners. Below, some situations in which they are particularly useful:
• Long Weekend, Honeymoon, and Progressive Weddings
• weddings being held far from where the bride is living
• an at-home or outdoor wedding that requires special services
• very large weddings
• a wedding for the bride who is too busy with career or other concerns

Find the Best

Locate a good wedding consultant by asking other wedding professionals (bridal salon personnel, caterers, florists) or brides whose weddings you have enjoyed. Or, for consultants in your area, write to: Association of Bridal Consultants, 200 Chestnutland Road, New Milford, Conn. 06776–2521; include your wedding date, phone number, and a stamped, self-addressed legal-size envelope.

Estimate the Cost

Some wedding consultants charge a flat fee for their services. Others specify a percentage (usually 15 to 20 percent) of the total wedding cost. Still others may charge by the hour. They can, however, save you money in the long run because they receive special rates on supplies and services—and these savings should be passed on to you. Furthermore, they know which suppliers are best and can command high-quality service because they represent repeat business.

Some wedding consultants offer free services to the bride. They are able to do this because they make money on commissions they receive from wedding service suppliers. Be aware, however, that this will limit your choice of suppliers.

You may also find wedding consultants in the bridal gown department, wedding gift registry, or china and silver department of stores. Since these experts are paid by the store, their services will also be free.

CATERERS/RECEPTION SITE MANAGERS

What Can They Do?

A caterer puts together perhaps the most important elements of your reception: food, drink, and sometimes the site and its decorations.

When planning a wedding, "caterer" is the first thing many people think about.

Actually, the term caterer can mean many things—from a person who prepares specialty foods to an entire company that provides a wedding site, waiters, tables, food, even bands or photographers. Find out exactly what various firms charge and what they provide.

You may work with one banquet manager who will take care of the entire site, food, and drink. If so, find out as much as you can about the facilities: Is the site large enough for all your guests? Will you be sharing facilities with other brides? (See "50 Reception Questions.")

On the other hand, the wedding you plan may involve many specialists. For example, at a wedding in a historic mansion, you first contact the person responsible for renting the space. Then you hire a caterer, bartenders, waiters, and a rental company to supply everything from the dishes and tables to a dance floor.

Find the perfect site. There are numerous possibilities for wedding reception sites. Consider banquet halls, clubs, restaurants, hotels in your area. Community centers or church/synagogue meeting halls may be inexpensive options. And there are a host of imaginative settings: country inns, boats, historic buildings, lofts, beaches, farms.

When interviewing prospective caterers or site managers, ask about the weddings they have done. Look at photographs of past events and ask for names of past clients you can call for references. It may also be a good idea to check with your local Better Business Bureau to find out if any complaints have been filed against a firm you are considering.

Determine what services cost. Be sure to get an accurate account of what's included. Sales tax, gratuities, overtime fees, may come as surprise add-ons and shatter your budget. One famous New York hotel, for example, charges an extra 19 percent of the total wedding bill to cover gratuities. Find out how costs are figured—per person for food, per bottle or per drink for liquor, per hour for waiters, and the like.

Here are some terms you may find on a catering contract, and what they mean:

Deposit is an amount you pay to reserve the site or the caterer's services. It usually ranges from about 10 to 25 percent of the total wedding costs.

Balance due is the amount remaining to be paid after the deposit. Never pay in full before the services are rendered.

Cancellation fees are fees you must pay if you cancel your reception. The closer to the wedding date you cancel, the higher the fees. At reputable firms you may owe nothing if you cancel several months before the wedding and the caterer can rebook the facility. If you cancel later and the room cannot be rebooked, you will probably have to pay an amount that covers the caterer's loss of income. And if you cancel a few days before the wedding, costs will be higher to cover food the caterer has already purchased, the waiters already hired.

Overtime costs are expenses incurred if your reception runs past the time stated in your contract. The costs should depend on how much the caterer must spend to keep the party going—wages for waiters and bartenders, additional food and drink.

Gratuities are tips given to employees. Normally gratuities are based on the total cost of food and liquor—for example, 15 to 20 percent of food and liquor costs.

Liquor costs can vary dramatically. Some firms charge per person/per hour (for example, $4 per person per hour). Some charge by the drink; others charge by the bottle; still others charge a flat fee (say, $1,000 for a four-hour open bar). How they charge may, in some areas, depend on state liquor laws. Factors such as name brands or vintage wines may influence costs. Ask your caterer about all the options, taking into consideration how much *your* guests are likely to drink.

50 RECEPTION QUESTIONS

A caterer and reception site manager can help make your wedding run smoothly. But how can you decide which professional will suit your needs best? Here, a checklist of must-ask questions to narrow your choices to the one right for you:

At Your First Meeting

Questions to ask when visiting a potential reception site:

☐ What is the rental fee? What exactly does it include?

☐ What is the maximum attendance the room or area can handle—for a seated dinner, buffet, or hors d'oeuvre reception?

☐ Is the reception site to be shared with another wedding group? How are the facilities divided? How is privacy ensured?

☐ For how many hours does the rental fee reserve the space? Are there charges for overtime? When do they begin?

☐ Are there any restrictions on when the site is available? Any price discounts for certain time periods, days of the week?

☐ Do you have a piano, other musical in-

RECEPTION HALL/HOTEL/CLUB WORKSHEET

Estimate #1

Name _____

Telephone _____

Contact _____

What's provided and cost

Food (description) _____

_____

_____

_____ $ _____

Beverages (description) _____

_____ $ _____

Cake _____ $ _____

Waiters/Bartenders _____ $ _____

Flowers/Decorations _____ $ _____

Band _____ $ _____

Photographer _____ $ _____

Limousines _____ $ _____

Coat check _____ $ _____

Parking _____ $ _____

Changing rooms _____ $ _____

Other _____

_____ $ _____

TOTAL $ _____

struments on the premises? Is there any charge for use?

☐ Are there any regulations concerning the type of music; number of musicians; duration of the music?

☐ Are there regulations on decorations, flowers, photography?

☐ Do you have air-conditioning (for warm weather weddings)? Adequate heating (for winter and early spring nuptials)?

☐ Do you have an in-house caterer or preferred list of caterers? Can I bring in the caterer of my choice?

☐ Do you have any liability insurance in the event a guest is injured?

☐ Do you have enclosed, adequate kitchen facilities? (Caterers may add surcharges for appliances—a stove, refrigerator.)

☐ Can the site be used for the ceremony?

☐ Is there a dance floor? Is dancing allowed? Where?

Questions to ask when meeting a caterer:

☐ What is the estimated cost per person for a seated dinner? Buffet? Cocktail reception? Open bar? What does the cost include?

☐ What is the staff-to-guest ratio? (For seated meals, the ratio is usually one waiter per eight to ten guests.)

☐ Have you worked at my prospective re-

Estimate #2

Name _____

Telephone _____

Contact _____

What's provided and cost

Food (description) _____

_____

_____

_____ $ _____

Beverages (description) _____

_____ $ _____

Cake _____ $ _____

Waiters/Bartenders _____ $ _____

Flowers/Decorations _____ $ _____

Band _____ $ _____

Photographer _____ $ _____

Limousines _____ $ _____

Coat check _____ $ _____

Parking _____ $ _____

Changing rooms _____ $ _____

Other _____

_____ $ _____

TOTAL $ _____

Estimate #3

Name _____

Telephone _____

Contact _____

What's provided and cost

Food (description) _____
_____
_____
_____ $ _____

Beverages (description) _____
_____ $ _____

Cake _____ $ _____

Waiters/Bartenders _____ $ _____

Flowers/Decorations _____ $ _____

Band _____ $ _____

Photographer _____ $ _____

Limousines _____ $ _____

Coat check _____ $ _____

Parking _____ $ _____

Changing rooms _____ $ _____

Other _____
_____ $ _____

                                          TOTAL $ _____

Final selection—name, address, telephone

_____

_____

Contract signed   Deposit paid   Balance due

_____

Date final guest count needed _____

Notes _____

_____

ception sites? Can you recommend other sites for a wedding?

☐ Do you have a set menu? Can the menu be modified?

☐ Can the kitchen staff adhere to special dietary restrictions for some guests who may be diabetic, kosher, vegetarian?

☐ Do you have liability coverage—including liquor liability (in case a guest drinks to excess, drives, and later sues)?

☐ Can you supply me with a list of references? (Contact two.)

☐ How much advance time is needed to confirm a reservation?

☐ Can I arrange to view the catering of another wedding reception to check food display, service style, flow, organization? Can we arrange to taste foods on the menu you suggest?

☐ Do you set the tables? Provide linens? Order floral arrangements? Coordinate the music? (Some caterers do, others *don't*!)

☐ What additional charges might be incurred other than the food, beverages, and rental of requested extras?

☐ What is the policy for payment, tipping? (Some caterers request cash, others accept checks or credit cards. Some include gratuities in the base or overall price, others do not.)

When You're Ready For Contracts

Questions to ask when reserving a reception site:

☐ Are there any additional charges for required services (i.e., security guards; rest room, coat check, or parking attendants; doormen; maintenance or lawn workers; window cleaners)? What are the charges? Is there a minimum number of hours that must be booked?

☐ Can you confirm the reservation in a letter that will outline all the details, including the room assignment?

☐ Should I have to cancel the reception, is the deposit refundable?

☐ Is adequate parking available for my guests? Will they be charged? Can these charges be waived?

☐ Are there rooms available where I, the groom, our attendants, can change into wedding attire, going-away clothes?

☐ Do you have a microphone? Is there a rental fee?

☐ How many dancers will the dance floor hold? Can we review staging, lighting, audio (and video) needs?

☐ Is there a comfortable area for guests to await our arrival from the ceremony site? Will hors d'oeuvres, drinks be served?

☐ Where is the best place to set up the receiving line?

☐ What is the name of the banquet manager? Will he or she be on hand that day? If not, who will be in charge?

☐ Is a security deposit for furniture, decor, artwork required? How much is it? When can I expect a refund?

Questions to ask when booking a caterer:

☐ How much advance time will you need to set up?

☐ Can you send me a confirmation letter including the wedding date and time, names of service help, tipping policy, decorating time, color schemes, menu, cost per person?

☐ Can I see available linens? What is the additional rental cost?

☐ How much food is enough? (Ten to twelve hors d'oeuvres per person is adequate. With buffets, offer a choice of two entrees.)

☐ Will the hors d'oeuvres be butlered or on a buffet?

☐ How much are your overtime and cancellation costs?

☐ Can you give me a ceiling on anticipated menu price increases? (Caterers quote final prices 90 days prior to the wedding due to rising food costs—an increase might be ten percent.)

☐ When will the wedding cake be delivered (if your caterer will provide you with one)? Is the cake cut by the banquet staff?

☐ Can we go over placement of the head table—on a raised platform or floor level; dais or round table?

☐ How many drinks does each bottle of liquor, champagne, provide? Is there an opening fee per bottle of champagne?

☐ Will you feed the photographers, the musicians?

☐ What is the guarantee requirement for number of guests?

☐ When must I provide a final guest count?

WORKSHEET FOR AT-HOME/ OUTDOOR/OR OTHER SITE

	Description	Rental Costs

Site: estimate #1
Contact

$ _____

Site: estimate #2
Contact

$ _____

Caterer: estimate #1   *Services Provided*

$ _____

Caterer: estimate #2   *Services Provided*

$ _____

Waiters, bartenders, clean-up help
Names/Sources

$ _____

Rental needs: estimate #1   Tent $ _____
Dance floor $ _____
Additional tents for food preparation
    or other needs $ _____
Tableware $ _____
Tables $ _____
Chairs $ _____
Linens $ _____
Power generator $ _____
Other $_____
                                    $_____

                                    TOTAL $ _____

Rental needs: estimate #2

Tent $ _____

Dance floor $ _____

Additional tents for food preparation
    or other needs $ _____

Tableware $ _____

Tables $ _____

Chairs $ _____

Linens $ _____

Power generator $ _____

Other $ _____

$ _____   TOTAL $ _____

FINAL CHOICES

Site—name, address, telephone

_____

Cost	Contract signed	Deposit paid	Balance due

_____

Caterer—name, address, telephone

_____

Cost	Contract signed	Deposit paid	Balance due

_____

Rental company—name, address, telephone

_____

Cost	Contract signed	Deposit paid	Balance due

_____

RECEPTION FOOD

Wedding receptions have never been more creative, and often this is most evident in the selection and serving of food. Will your guests sip vintage champagne as they sample caviar and smoked salmon? Will they sit down to a spicy Creole meal of shrimp, rice, corn bread, beans? Or, will they choose from an elaborate buffet table that features foods to fit every taste—Chinese egg rolls, roast beef, colorful pastas, marinated vegetables, tropical fruit salad? The

MENU WORKSHEET

Style _____ Seated _____ Buffet _____ Punch and cake _____ Hors d'oeuvres/cocktails

Hors d'oeuvres _____

_____

Salads _____

_____

Main course _____

_____

Other dishes _____

_____

Desserts _____

_____

Wedding cake _____

_____

Other ideas (food stations, sundae bar, etc.) _____

_____

type of food you serve and how you serve it depend on the following:

• **Time of day.** Serve a breakfast or brunch after a morning wedding; and a seated lunch after a noontime ceremony; cake and beverage after an early afternoon ceremony; hors d'oeuvres after a mid-afternoon ceremony; a seated or buffet dinner after a late afternoon or evening ceremony.

• **Local styles and trends.** In some areas of the country, a seated meat-and-potatoes meal is the fashion, in others, elegant hors d'oeuvres with champagne are popular.

• **Season.** Serve heartier meals in winter; lighter fare in summer. Consider, too, seasonal availability of fruits and vegetables. For example, you might serve fresh asparagus vinaigrette as a first course in late spring or summer, a hearty soup or ratatouille during colder months.

• **Budget and tastes.** More and more brides want unique choices in food—not a standard chicken and peas meal. A buffet or hors d'oeuvres reception is usually less expensive than a seated meal, and you can serve a variety of foods, including a dessert buffet. (Check prices carefully, however—an elaborate selection of elegant buffet foods may be more expensive than a simple seated meal.)

Ask your caterer about new ideas in menus and food service. Among the most popular is the food station concept. Chefs stand at a number of "stations" around the room and cook various types of food to guests' order—waffles with a selection of toppings, Japanese sushi or tempura, pastas and sauces, fresh seafood on the half-shell, caviar, ice cream sundaes.

Brides are also combining different types of service. For example, the main course may be served by waiters, but guests serve themselves at a dessert buffet.

Consider your wedding menu carefully. Personalize the meal with foods that have special meanings to you and your guests. For example, you could serve a selection of Dutch cheeses as a way of recognizing your Dutch relatives; apple pie because you and your groom love walking through a nearby apple orchard.

Ask to taste foods made by caterers, restaurants, or hotels you are considering, and check photographs of past events they have done to see that food is attractively presented and served.

RECEPTION BEVERAGES

Caterers or banquet facilities often provide beverages as part of their packages. But look carefully at the pricing policies—they vary widely. They may charge per drink, per bottle, per person, per hour, or some combination (e.g., $4 per person per hour). Decide if you want name brand alcoholic beverages or vintage wines. Ask if you may provide the liquor (which you can buy at a discount outlet), while they serve it. Discuss any additional liquor costs such as a "corkage fee" every time a waiter opens a bottle of champagne or wine.

With all these options, how can you know you are getting a fair price for your reception beverages? Talk to several caterers in your area to compare pricing policies. Discuss *all* the options with your caterer or banquet manager. For example, if you want an open bar, exactly what liquors are included? Can some be eliminated to save money? Can the hours in which it is open be limited? Consider the tastes of your guests. If you know that many of them like beer, for example, buying a keg may be the best value. Finally, keep in mind that the way reception liquor is served and priced may be determined by state law in some areas.

Alcoholic Beverages—How Much Will You Need?

Consider tastes of your guests and time of year (lighter, fruitier drinks for summer; more traditional drinks such as Scotch for winter).

On average, allow one drink per person per hour (slightly more for evening or summer). Remember that it's better to order too much than to run out.

1 bottle of wine = 6 to 8 partially filled glasses
1 quart of hard liquor = 20 one-and-a-half-ounce drinks
1 26-ounce bottle champagne = 8 servings, which comes out to a case of 12 bottles for 100 guests to have one drink each
½ keg of beer = 260 eight-ounce glasses

Non-alcoholic Beverages

With the growing interest in health and fitness, along with concerns about the dangers of drunk driving, many people are drinking fewer alcoholic beverages or abstaining altogether. Your guests will appreciate a wide selection of non-alcoholic drinks, such as:

• punches beautifully presented with flower-embedded ice and fresh fruit

• sparkling apple juice for toasts

• a water bar—a selection of bottled waters, carbonated and still

• a variety of soft drinks, juices, coffees and teas (decaffeinated, too).

BAR CHECKLIST

Number of guests _____   Cocktail hours _____ to _____

Champagne toast _____ Time _____ Wine with dinner _____ Punch bowls _____

LIQUOR

Item	Quantity	Brand	Cost
Champagne	_____	_____	$ _____
Bourbon	_____	_____	$ _____
Whiskey	_____	_____	$ _____
Gin	_____	_____	$ _____
Rum	_____	_____	$ _____
Scotch	_____	_____	$ _____
Tequila	_____	_____	$ _____
Vermouth	_____	_____	$ _____
Vodka	_____	_____	$ _____
Red wine	_____	_____	$ _____
Rosé wine	_____	_____	$ _____
White wine	_____	_____	$ _____
Punch	_____	_____	$ _____
Beer	_____	_____	$ _____
Aperitifs	_____	_____	$ _____
Brandy	_____	_____	$ _____
Assorted Liqueurs	_____	_____	$ _____
		Total liquor cost	$ _____

MIXERS/NONALCOHOLIC DRINKS

Quantity and brands (if applicable)

Collins mix _____ $ _____
Cola/Diet cola _____ $ _____
Ginger ale _____ $ _____
Soda _____ $ _____
Tonic _____ $ _____
Orange juice _____ $ _____
Tomato juice _____ $ _____
Pineapple juice _____ $ _____
Nonalcoholic punch _____ $ _____
Sparkling grape or apple juice _____ $ _____
Bottled water: still, carbonated, imported _____ $ _____
Lemon-line soda/Diet lemon-lime _____ $ _____
Iced tea _____ $ _____
Hot tea/Herbal teas _____ $ _____
Other sodas (orange, root beer) _____ $ _____
Plain water _____ $ _____
Coffee/Iced coffee _____ $ _____
Other _____ $ _____

Total $ _____

DRINK INGREDIENTS

Item	Quantity	Brand (if applicable)	Cost
Angostura bitters	_____	_____	$ _____
Cocktail olives	_____	_____	$ _____
Cocktail onions	_____	_____	$ _____
Ice	_____	_____	$ _____
Lemons and lemon peel	_____	_____	$ _____
Limes	_____	_____	$ _____
Superfine sugar	_____	_____	$ _____
Tabasco sauce	_____	_____	$ _____
Other	_____	_____	$ _____
_____	_____	_____	$ _____
_____	_____	_____	$ _____

Total drink ingredients cost $ _____

BAR EQUIPMENT

Item	Number	Item	Number
Bottle openers	_____	Water pitchers	_____
Can openers	_____	Drink recipe book	_____
Cocktail shakers	_____	Cocktail napkins	_____
Corkscrews	_____	Stir sticks	_____
Ice buckets	_____	8-oz. glasses	_____
Ice tubs	_____	4-oz. glasses	_____
Knives	_____	Champagne glasses	_____
Spoons	_____	Wine glasses	_____
Strainers	_____	Serving trays	_____
1 ½-oz. jigger	_____	Shaker, blender, or hard mixer	_____
		Other	_____
		Equipment costs, if any	$ _____
		TOTAL BAR COST	$ _____

STATIONERS

Meeting with a Stationer

Choose a stationer and place your invitation order at least three months before your wedding. The stationer will need several weeks to order the invitations (about four weeks for engraving); you'll need at least a week to address them (more if you plan to use a calligrapher). They must be mailed six to eight weeks before the wedding in order to allow adequate time for planning and responses.

Count on one invitation for every married couple, and for couples who live together. Your clergymember and spouse, as well as your attendants, should also receive invitations. You need not invite dates of single guests, but if you do, send the escort a separate invitation (avoid writing "and Guest" on the envelope), at his or her address. Order a number of extra invitations as keepsakes for you, your mother, and your fiancé's mother.

There are three types of printing processes that are available:

• Engraving is the most expensive, but also the most traditional and formal. The paper is pressed onto a specially treated steel or copper plate so that the letters are slightly raised from the page.

• Thermography is a printing process that fuses ink and powder to resemble engraving. Due to recent advances in this technique, thermography can be hard to distinguish from engraving, although the quality varies from printer to printer. Thermography is always less costly than engraving—usually about half the price because you don't have to pay for plates.

• Offset printing is the most affordable, with many colors and styles available, but the look is less formal.

Many different paper styles are also available. The most formal invitations are engraved on the top page of a double sheet of white or ivory paper.

New ideas for wedding invitations include:

• pastel, moiré, pearlized, or exquisite, hand-made papers

• colored borders, flowers, decorations, or ribbons

• photographs of the bride and groom enclosed or printed on the front

• confetti enclosed

• invitations to match a theme wedding—for example, a piece of parchment with Old English type for a Renaissance Fair wedding.

Calligraphy has become increasingly popular for wedding invitations. Literally, calligraphy means "fine penmanship," but it has come to mean an elegant italic script. Calligraphers often take several weeks to address wedding invitations. Today, many stationery stores have computerized calligraphy machines that create perfect script in a short time and can be used for invitations as well as addresses.

What You Will Need

In addition to invitations, you may order the following:

Announcements are generally sent to people who are not invited to the wedding: faraway friends, business associates, acquaintances. Paper, printing, and format are similar to invitations. They should be addressed and ready to mail immediately after the wedding.

Thank-you stationery is needed once the invitations go out. The classic thank-you note is written in blue or black ink on folded gray,

pearl, ecru, or white paper, often called "informals." You may choose to have your stationery monogrammed (with your maiden name initials for use before the wedding; your married name, if different, for notes sent after the wedding). Just as there are creative, colorful wedding invitations, there are many options in stationery you can use for thank-you notes.

Reception response cards save guests from writing acceptance or regret notes. Guests fill in their names, check whether they're coming, and return them in the provided stamped and addressed envelopes. Traditionally they are *not* used with formal invitations—a personal reply is preferred.

Ceremony cards are used when the ceremony is held at a public place—such as a museum or historic site—and there is a chance that someone not invited might wander in unwittingly. Guests must present the card at the door for admittance.

Pew cards indicate special seating positions. They are most often used for very large, formal weddings.

Rain cards inform guests invited to an outdoor wedding of the location of an alternate site, in case of inclement weather.

Travel cards tell guests about wedding day transportation arrangements—such as a bus to take them between hotel, ceremony, and reception. A card may also indicate parking locations and if fees or gratuities have been paid.

Maps to the ceremony and reception are becoming frequent accompaniments to invitations. They aid out-of-towners in finding locations, ensure guests arrive on time. Have them drawn and printed in the same style as invitations. Be prepared with extras at the ceremony site.

Long Weekend Wedding cards alert guests to the fact that there are additional festivities planned. This insert gives guests a schedule of events, suggestions for lodging, transportation, an idea about appropriate dress.

Name cards let people know what name you will use after the wedding. They are particularly useful when a woman retains her own name, or when a couple adopt a hyphenated form of both their names.

At-home cards announce your new address, the date you will be ready to receive mail—and visitors—there.

Ceremony programs add a personal touch to your wedding. Whether they are printed and beautifully bound, or simply photocopied, they always include names of participants; information about the order and content of the ceremony; lists of musical selections, readings. Thoughts on marriage and biographies of participants may also be included.

Napkins and matchbooks, pens and pencils, may be ordered from many stationers with the bride's and groom's names and wedding date.

Mailing How-To's

• Order envelopes early so you can begin addressing while waiting for printing or engraving to be completed.

• Write out all names, street/avenue/road, states, etc., on the envelope. (Nothing should be abbreviated except Mr., Mrs., and Ms.) If several members of a family are to be invited, avoid using the phrase "and Family." Address the outer envelope to the heads of the household. List children invited on the inner envelope. For example:

Outer envelope:
Mr. and Mrs. Edward James Farrell
24 King Street, Apartment 24
Anywhere, Ohio 12345

Unsealed inner envelope:
Mr. and Mrs. Farrell
Monica and Malcolm

• A folded formal invitation is slipped into the inner envelope with the folded side down. The less formal invitation is not folded, but placed in the envelope so that the side with lettering will face the recipient when the inner envelope is opened.

• Extra enclosures such as reception cards, at-home cards, maps, may be placed next to the engraving or printing.

• Tissues placed by the stationer to prevent smudging while the ink dries on engraving may be discarded or left in, as you prefer.

• The unsealed inner envelope is placed in the outer envelope so that the guest's name comes immediately to view. Write just Mr., Mrs., Ms., or Miss, and the last name; children's first names are written underneath.

• Include a return address. The U.S. Post Office requests that all return addresses appear on the upper left corner.

Classic Type

Invitation typefaces vary according to your taste. Your stationer will have traditional samples, such as the ones below, from which you might choose.

Florentine Script

Venetian Script

Shaded Antique Roman

Park Avenue

Stuyvesant Script

Riviera Script

SAMPLE INVITATION WORDINGS

Standard Invitation

Mr. and Mrs. Andrew Lyle Smith
request the honour of your presence
at the marriage of their daughter
Mara Jean
to John Reginald Jones
Saturday, the sixth of June
at four o'clock
First Congregational Church
Newtown, Massachusetts

Reception Card

Reception
immediately following the ceremony
Shady Knoll Country Club
Seventy-nine Horseshoe Lane
Newtown, Massachusetts

Combined Ceremony/ Reception Invitation

Mr. and Mrs. Andrew Lyle Smith
request the honour of your presence
at the marriage of their daughter
Mara Jean
to
John Reginald Jones
Saturday, the sixth of June
at four o'clock
First Congregational Church
Newtown, Massachusetts
and afterwards at
Shady Knoll Country Club

R.s.v.p.
63 Rogers Street
Newtown, Massachusetts 12345

One Remarried Parent Hosts

Mr. and Mrs. Donald Jones
request the honour of your presence
at the marriage of her daughter
Susan Ann Miller
to
John David Smith
Saturday, the eighth of March
at three o'clock
All Saints' Church
New York, New York

His Parents Host

Mr. and Mrs. William Smith
request the honour of your presence
at the marriage of
Susan Ann Miller
to their son
John David Smith
Saturday, the eighth of March
at three o'clock
All Saints' Church
New York, New York

Invitation to Reception Only

Mr. and Mrs. Charles Miller
request the pleasure of your company
at the wedding reception of their daughter
Susan Ann
and
John David Smith
Saturday, the eighth of March
at half after four o'clock
The Edwardian Towne House
113 East Sixty-seventh Street
New York, New York

Your Parents Share Planning

Mr. and Mrs. Charles Miller
request the honour of your presence
at the marriage of their daughter
Susan Ann Miller
to
John David Smith
son of Mr. and Mrs. Leo Smith
Saturday, the eighth of March
at three o'clock
All Saints' Church
New York, New York

Two Remarried Parents Host

Mrs. Donald Jones
and
Mr. Charles Miller
request the honour of your presence
at the marriage of their daughter
Susan Ann Miller
to
John David Smith
Saturday, the eighth of March
at three o'clock
All Saints' Church
New York, New York

You're the Host

The honour of your presence
is requested at the marriage of
Susan Ann Miller
to
John David Smith
Saturday, the eighth of March
at three o'clock
All Saints' Church
New York, New York

You Host Your Second Wedding

The honour of your presence
is requested at the marriage of
Susan Miller Smith
to
Lawrence Edward White
Saturday, the eighth of March
at three o'clock
All Saints' Church
New York, New York

Parents Host Your Second Wedding

Mr. and Mrs. Charles Miller
request the honour of your presence
at the marriage of their daughter
Susan Miller Smith
to
Lawrence Edward White
Saturday, the eighth of March
at three o'clock
All Saints' Church
New York, New York

Children Invite Guests to Marriage of Their Parents

Jason and Nicole Smith
and
Samantha, Adam, and Jennifer Jones
request the honour of your presence
at the marriage of their parents
Candace Wilson Smith
and
William Robert Jones
Saturday, the sixth of July
at four o'clock
First Presbyterian Church
Newell, Idaho

Your Parents Issue Traditional Wedding Announcements

Mr. and Mrs. Charles Miller
have the honour of announcing
the marriage of their daughter
Susan Ann
to
John David Smith
Saturday, the eighth of March
One thousand, nine hundred and ninety-one
New York, New York

You Reaffirm Your Wedding Vows

The honour of your presence
is requested at the reaffirmation
of the wedding vows of
Mr. and Mrs. John David Smith
Saturday, the eighth of March
at three o'clock
All Saints' Church
New York, New York

Sample Informal Wordings

Bill and Marge Smith
and Tom and Barbara Rowe
invite you
to share in the joy
of the marriage
uniting our children
Nicole and Jason
Four p.m.
Unitarian Church
New Hope, California

or

Tom and Beth Grant
ask those dearest to us
to join us in worship and celebration
of the marriage of our daughter
Marcia Jill
to
Bill Smith
Saturday, July 5th
9:30 a.m.
First Presbyterian Church
Newell, Idaho

Response Card

M_____

_____*accepts*
_____*regrets*
Saturday, the sixth of June
Shady Knoll Country Club

INVITATION WORKSHEET

My invitation will read:

_____

request the honour of your presence

at the marriage of their daughter

_____

to

_____

_____

_____

_____

_____

_____

and afterwards at

_____

Please respond

_____

_____

STATIONERY WORKSHEET

Estimate #1   _Number_   _Cost_

Name _____   Invitations _____

Telephone _____   Announcements _____

                              Thank-you notes _____

Response cards _____

At-home cards _____

Napkins/Matchbooks _____

Programs _____

Maps _____

Rain/Travel cards _____

Long Weekend Wedding cards _____

Other _____

TOTAL $ _____

Estimate #2   Invitations _____

Name _____   Announcements _____

Telephone _____   Thank-you notes _____

Response cards _____

At-home cards _____

Napkins/Matchbooks _____

Programs _____

Maps _____

Rain/Travel cards _____

Long Weekend Wedding cards _____

Other _____

TOTAL $ _____

Final choice—name, address, telephone

_____

Contract signed   Deposit paid   Balance due

_____

INVITATION PROOFREADING CHECKLIST

Proofreading date _____   Envelopes ready _____   Invitations ready_____

When the printer or stationer asks you to review your invitation wording and order, read it carefully, compare it to the one you wrote out on the Invitation Worksheet, and answer the following questions:

_____ Is the invitation worded the way *you* want it?

_____ Do the lines fall in the proper places (*to* on one line, the entire date on another)?

_____ Is everyone's name spelled correctly—your parents', yours, your groom's, his parents', if they are listed?

_____ Is there a *u* in the word *honour*?

_____ Do the day of the week and the date correspond? (Check a calendar.) Is the time written in words, not numbers? Is it correct?

_____ Are the names of the ceremony and reception sites spelled right? Are any addresses complete and correct?

_____ Are the commas in the right places? Apostrophes? Are there periods after all abbreviations?

_____ Is the paper the color you chose? The lettering style? What about any borders or designs?

Corrections if any _____

_____

_____

Pickup or delivery date_____   Cost per hundred $ _____

Number of invitations to order _____   Total invitation cost $ _____

RECEPTION MUSIC

Music sets the tone of your reception. The lilting melodies of classical waltzes contribute to a romantic, formal atmosphere; lively, popular rock music gets everyone dancing. Consider the following when choosing your music:

• **Size of reception site.** A soft trio would be lost in a big hall; a loud band would overpower a reception in a small room.

• **Tastes of guests.** It's hard to please everyone, so consider bands that can play a variety of tunes. Most guests prefer softer music while eating—save the rock for dancing later on.

• **Extra services provided by the band.** Would you like a master of ceremonies who can announce reception events like the cake cutting? Some bands provide children's entertainment; others use professional staging and lighting effects.

The right music will add immeasurably to everyone's enjoyment of the reception—so you'll want to be sure to make a good choice when hiring musicians. Here are tips on selecting a band:

□ Get word-of-mouth references from friends and relatives or contact your local musicians union.

□ Find out how many musicians are in the band, what instruments they play. Request an audition tape if you haven't heard them before. Or arrange to hear them play if they are performing in public.

□ Inquire about breaks—how many will the musicians take and for how long? Do they expect refreshments?

□ Ask if they can perform the music you and your guests like. Can they play the ethnic selections you want? If not, are they willing to learn them?

□ Ask if the bandleader will be present for your reception—often an orchestra has several groups performing under its name. You might want to specify that his or her name appear in your contract, along with the name of the group's lead vocalist.

□ Discuss how active you want the bandleader to be in making announcements—your first dance, toasts, the cake cutting, bouquet and garter tosses.

□ Request that musicians dress in a style and formality suited to your wedding.

□ Request that a representative for the group visit your reception site ahead of time to ensure that there's adequate room for equipment, enough electrical outlets.

□ Be prepared to pay a deposit beforehand; the remainder of the fee is usually paid at the end of the reception.

□ Specify names, hours, the band will perform, date, site, cost—including overtime rates—in writing.

RECORDED MUSIC

Recorded music, a popular option, is available on pre-recorded, reel-to-reel tapes. Or a disk jockey may be present to choose songs based on the guests' reactions and your pre-requested selections. A disk jockey may also act as a master of ceremonies. Below are some of the advantages to recorded music:

• Disk jockeys and their equipment are now of excellent quality.

• The set-up requires less space than a band.

• Songs sound exactly as recorded, and a wide variety is available.

• The music is continuous.

• The cost can be half that of a live band.

How to find a good disk jockey or someone to make a tape? Ask friends or the reception site manager for recommendations. If you choose a company unknown to your friends, ask for references, former clients.

If you want a disk jockey, find out in advance how he or she works. Some pride themselves on sizing up the crowd or sensing the pace of the party and don't like to take requests. Others only specialize in certain types of music. If you and the groom have specific musical preferences, make sure the disk jockey you hire is willing to play whatever you want.

Ask to see a demo tape of your disk jockey

performing at a wedding. Then sign a contract with the disk jockey or tape technician, listing hours to be worked, agreed fee and overtime policy, site, appropriate attire, name of disk jockey, time of first dance, style of music and particular songs. If he or she is unfamiliar with your reception site, meet there prior to the wedding to choose a place to set up, and make sure there are enough electrical outlets and other necessities.

RECEPTION MUSIC SUGGESTIONS

First Dance Songs

"As Time Goes By," by Hupfeld

"I'll Always Love You," sung by Taylor Dane

"Always," sung by Atlantic Star

"You Are the Sunshine of My Life," sung by Stevie Wonder

"(I've Had) The Time of My Life," sung by Bill Medley, Jennifer Warnes

"Endless Love," sung by Diana Ross, Lionel Richie

"Just You and I," sung by Melissa Manchester

"Saving All My Love for You," sung by Whitney Houston

"Always," by Berlin

"It Had to Be You," by Jones

"Theme from *Ice Castles* (Through the Eyes of Love)," sung by Melissa Manchester

Father/Bride Dance Songs

"Daddy's Little Girl," by Burke and Gerlach

"Over the Rainbow," by Arien and Harburg

"Moon River," by Mancini and Mercer

"Sunrise, Sunset" (*Fiddler on the Roof*), by Back and Harnick

"Thank Heaven for Little Girls" (*Gigi*), by Lerner and Loewe

"Through the Years," sung by Kenny Rogers

"Misty," sung by Johnny Mathis

"The Greatest Love of All," sung by Whitney Houston

"The Wind Beneath My Wings," sung by Bette Midler or Lou Rawls

"Turn Around," sung by Harry Belafonte

"Daddy's Hands," sung by Holly Dunn

"The Time of Your Life," sung by Paul Anka

"My Heart Belongs to Daddy," by Porter

Other Reception Crowd-Pleasing Dance Songs

"La Bamba," sung by Ritchie Valens or Los Lobos

"Pink Cadillac," sung by Bruce Springsteen or Natalie Cole

"Shout," sung by Otis Day & the Knights

"Do You Love Me?" sung by The Contours

"I Heard It Through the Grapevine," sung by Marvin Gaye

"Jump (for My Love)," sung by The Pointer Sisters

"Old Time Rock and Roll," sung by Bob Seger

"Respect," sung by Aretha Franklin

"New York, New York," sung by Frank Sinatra or Liza Minnelli

"Celebration," sung by Kool & The Gang

"Mony Mony," sung by Tommy James and The Shondells

"Twist and Shout," sung by The Isley Brothers

RECEPTION MUSIC WORKSHEET

                                          Type of Music/Notes   *Cost*

Estimate #1

Name _____

Telephone _____

Number of musicians _____

Recommended by _____

Estimate #2

Name _____

Telephone _____

Number of musicians _____

Recommended by _____

Estimate #3

Name _____

Telephone _____

Number of musicians _____

Recommended by _____

Final selection—name, address, telephone

_____

_____

Contract signed   Deposit paid   Balance due

_____

RECEPTION MUSIC CHECKLIST

Reception Activity	Time	General Kind of Music or Specific Selections
Receiving Line	_____	_____
	_____	_____
	_____	_____
Arrival of Bride and Groom	_____	_____
	_____	_____
First Dance	_____	_____
Seating at Bride's Table	_____	_____
Cake cutting	_____	_____
Dancing or Background	_____	_____
	_____	_____
	_____	_____
Special Requests	_____	_____
	_____	_____
	_____	_____

RECEPTION ENTERTAINMENT

In addition to music, you may want to have entertainment at your wedding reception. This grand tradition dates back to ancient times, when acrobats and pageants heralded the marriages of royalty.

Some ideas for reception entertainment:
• comedian (be sure to review his or her material ahead of time)
• light or laser show
• mime
• fireworks
• skywriting above the reception site
• slide show or video about the couple—including baby pictures, a story about how you met, information about the families
• costumed musicians—perhaps a Dixieland group, Renaissance-style minstrels, bagpipers.

Finding and Hiring Entertainers

• Get recommendations from friends, if possible. Otherwise check the yellow pages under

Dance with: Father _____ _____

Mother _____ _____

Tossing of Bouquet _____ _____

Throwing of Garter _____ _____

Departure of Bride and Groom _____ _____

Last Dance _____ _____

Other _____ _____

_____ _____

_____ _____

Orchestra or bandleader _____

Number of musicians _____

Instruments _____

Hours of music _____ to _____ Continuous music? Yes _____ No _____

Regularly hourly rate _____ Overtime rate _____

Total reception music cost $ _____

"Entertainers" or "Entertainment Bureaus." Also note news stories and advertisements in local newspapers, magazines. Check with the Better Business Bureau to see if any complaints have ever been filed against the company or individual.

• Talk to the booking agent (or performer) about your preferences, party mood and location, size of audience, length of performance.

• If possible, preview recommended artists at another party.

• Draw up a contract specifying the individual performer(s), arrival time, length of act, scheduled breaks, performance details such as songs or routines, attire. Be sure both parties sign.

• Find out what equipment is needed (sound system, electrical outlets, spotlight), and make arrangements with reception site manager to rent, if necessary.

FLORISTS

Flowers have been part of weddings since ancient Roman times, when brides carried bunches of herbs under their veils (perhaps to ward off evil spirits). Later, brides held orange blossoms as symbols of purity. Today, flowers are found in every part of the wedding: the bride and her attendants carry bouquets, the groom and his men wear boutonnieres, grandmothers and other special guests are honored with corsages or hand-held bouquets. Flowers and garlands embellish the church ceremony site, and floral arrangements decorate the reception tables and other celebration areas.

Begin to look for a good florist at least three months before the wedding. Photographs of past weddings, recommendations of friends, acceptance of your ideas, flexibility, and knowledge are key elements. Compare costs, too.

Once you have chosen your florist, it's time to plan each arrangement. Give your florist as much information as possible: bring swatches of fabric from the wedding dress and bridesmaids' dresses, photographs of the dresses, details about mothers' and groom's attire. The florist should probably visit the ceremony or reception site if he or she is unfamiliar with it to plan how best to decorate it.

Get all the floral descriptions in writing, figure out costs, and sign a contract together. Here, floral ideas and tips:

Bride's Bouquet

• Choose a bouquet that goes with your dress and body proportions. Some brides with an ornate dress may prefer simpler flowers; petite brides may choose smaller bouquets.

• The shapes, styles, and colors of bridal bouquets are practically unlimited. Choose from small nosegays, baskets, single blooms, or silk flowers. One popular trend: Carry an arm-

Crescent-shaped cascade of flowers

ful of long-stemmed flowers on one arm—presentation-style. Or consider a tussy-mussy, a finger-held bouquet of small flowers and fragrant herbs.

• White is the traditional color for bridal bouquets (and there are many types of white flowers to mix together—for a textured look). Many brides are also choosing vibrant blues, deep pinks, and purples, or white with accents of yellow or pink flowers.

• Flowers have romantic meanings (a rose signifies love; lily of the valley, happiness), so you may want to create a bouquet with a message. Some bouquets include a sprig of ivy, which symbolizes fidelity. Or choose flowers that have special meanings to you and your groom—wild daisies to remind you of the summer walk when he proposed.

• Wearable flowers are new bridal acessories. Florists can create fresh flower boas, necklaces, and bracelets, or tuck them in pockets, headpieces, hats.

• A flower-covered prayer book or Bible is a beautiful touch for a large religious wedding.

• Silk flowers can look very lifelike—and are less perishable than fresh flowers. You might include some silk flowers among the fresh blooms. (Perhaps have a silk replica of your fresh bouquet made, to save over the years.)

• Your florist and library will have details on the methods of flower preservation. Some florists suggest that you have a special bouquet made to throw, so that you can preserve yours as a keepsake. One easy way to preserve flowers is to microwave them. (Check a microwave cookbook for directions.) Artists in your area may also dry, mat, and frame wedding bouquets according to the colors and style requested. (Ask your florist and your friends for references; inquire at any bridal shows held in the area, or at your wedding gift registry.)

• Flowers and other ornaments in your hair look beautiful for the reception, when the veil comes off. Also order "going-away flowers" for your travel outfit.

Hand-tied bouquet of long-stemmed flowers trimmed with ribbon

Round flower ball

Bridesmaids' Flowers

• The honor attendant's bouquet is often different in color and size from the bridesmaids' flowers. Attendants' bouquets are usually similar in shape to the bride's bouquet, but smaller and in harmony with the wedding colors.

• If any bridesmaids have allergies to pollen, your florist may suggest silk flowers or varieties of fresh blooms that are low in pollen.

Flower Girls

• Traditionally flower girls carry baskets of loose petals to strew in the aisle before the bride. However, brides have been known to slip on the petals, so many flower girls today carry silk petals, miniature bouquets, or small baskets of flowers.

• Small flowers are most appropriate for small flower girls—lily of the valley, sweetheart rosebuds, violets, the new miniatures of many well-known varieties.

Groom and His Attendants

• The groom and ushers traditionally wear boutonnieres in their left lapels. Besides a traditional white carnation, consider a rose, lily of the valley, stephanotis, for the best man and groom. Just as bridal bouquets are becoming more colorful, so are the flowers that the groom and his men are wearing. Other choices: oncidium orchids, cornflowers, delphinium—especially in colors that match the wedding color schemes.

• Often the groom wears a flower found in the bride's bouquet. You could literally pluck this blossom from your bouquet at the altar. (Ask your florist to wire the flower for easy removal.) After handing your bouquet to your honor attendant, you could then pin the flower to his lapel.

• Your groom might also choose a flower

with meaning, such as forget-me-not, which symbolizes true love.

• Fathers should receive boutonnieres too, so they can be identified among the guests.

Corsages For Mothers and Significant Others

• Traditionally mothers and grandmothers receive flowers in colors that complement their dresses. (Find out these colors in advance so the florist has time to order flowers.) The standard corsage is pinned to the dress just below the shoulder. Many women, however, prefer the more modern look of flowers around their wrists or attached to gloves, purses, or waistbands, so delicate material isn't damaged.

• A small bouquet or single blossom can substitute for a corsage.

• You may also want to give some sort of floral decoration to other wedding participants: ceremony reader or soloist, guest book or gift attendant, wedding consultant, Long Weekend Wedding coordinator. If you aren't able to include your groom's sisters in your bridal party, be sure to honor them with a corsage too.

Ceremony Flowers

• Order floral decorations for your ceremony that match the size of the church, synagogue, or room, the formality of your ceremony, and budget. Position vases of flowers (the simplest decoration) on either side of the altar, or huge sprays and garlands of flowers near the altar and entrances, as well as flowers and garlands on every pew (the most elaborate).

• Flowers and foliage decorations should direct attention to the front of the church and to the bridal couple. Overly elaborate arrangements can be distracting, while small ones get lost. Potted plants that can be used later are an economical compromise.

• The church or synagogue may be already decorated for another occasion, or you may be able to share floral costs with another bride who is using the same site at a different time that day. (Your clergymember can help you get in touch.)

• New trends in ceremony decor: Hang flowers on the church door to announce a wedding is taking place. Use a lot of foliage such as ferns, ivy, ficus trees, palm trees. Set up an arbor of flowers at the altar to frame the bride. (The traditional huppah at a Jewish ceremony may be an arbor of flowers.)

Nosegay trimmed with ribbons to mark aisle seat of church pew

Reception Flowers

• Floral arrangements are appropriate on buffet tables, cake table, near the band, on mantels or staircases, near the entrance or area where the receiving line is positioned.

• Keep centerpieces low to encourage conversation. They need not be identical, but should complement or match the overall color scheme.

• Cluster small bud vases in the middle of each reception table. When the wedding is over, each guest takes home a bud vase as a favor.

• Consider combining non-floral decorations—such as twinkling lights, mirrors, balloons, candles.

• Warm a large room with ficus trees, palms, other greenery, rented for the day.

• Consider edible centerpieces—colorful fruit baskets sprinkled with flowers, spun sugar sculptures, miniature tiered wedding cakes.

THE LANGUAGE OF FLOWERS

AMARYLLIS—*Splendid beauty*
APPLE BLOSSOMS—*Temptation*
BACHELOR'S BUTTON—*Celibacy*
BLUEBELL—*Constancy*
DAFFODIL—*Regard*
FORGET-ME-NOT—*True love*
GARDENIA—*Joy*
HONEYSUCKLE—*Genuine affection*
IVY—*Fidelity*
JASMINE—*Amiability*
LILY OF THE VALLEY—*Happiness*

MYRTLE—*Love*
ORANGE BLOSSOM—*Purity, loveliness*
RED CHRYSANTHEMUM—*I love you*
RED TULIP—*Love declared*
ROSE—*Love*
VIOLET—*Modesty*
WHITE CAMELLIA—*Perfect loveliness*
WHITE DAISY—*Innocence*
WHITE LILAC—*First emotions of love*
WHITE LILY—*Purity and innocence*

FLOWER CHECKLIST

DECORATIONS FOR THE CEREMONY SITE (church, hotel, etc.)

Where	Kinds of flowers	Color	Number of arrangements	Cost
Altar or canopy	_____	_____	_____	$ _____
	_____	_____	_____	$ _____
	_____	_____	_____	$ _____
Pews	_____	_____	_____	$ _____
Aisles	_____	_____	_____	$ _____
Windows	_____	_____	_____	$ _____
Doors	_____	_____	_____	$ _____
Other	_____	_____	_____	$ _____
_____	_____	_____	_____	$ _____
_____	_____	_____	_____	
			TOTAL	$ _____

Other decorations provided

What	Where	How many	Flowers, if any	Cost
Candles	_____	_____	_____	$ _____
Candleholders	_____	_____	_____	$ _____
Aisle runner	_____	_____	_____	$ _____
Other	_____	_____	_____	$ _____
_____	_____	_____	_____	$ _____
_____	_____	_____	_____	$ _____
			TOTAL	$ _____

Delivery

Ceremony site _____

Address _____   Phone _____

Person to see _____

Date _____   Time _____

FLOWERS FOR THE WEDDING PARTY

Bride

Style of bouquet _____

Kinds and colors of flowers _____

_____

_____

Ribbon color _____

Cost $ _____

Maid or matron of honor

Style _____

Kinds and colors of flowers _____

_____

Ribbon color _____

Cost $ _____

Bridesmaids _____ How many _____

Style _____

Kinds and colors of flowers _____

_____

Ribbon color _____

Cost of all $ _____

Flower girl

Style _____

Kinds and colors of flowers _____

Ribbon color _____

Cost $ _____

Mother of the bride

Style of corsage _____

Kinds and colors of flowers _____

_____

Ribbon color _____

Cost $ _____

Delivery of flowers for the bridal party

Place (home of bride, church, etc.) _____

Address _____ Phone _____

Person to see _____

Date _____ Time _____

Cost $ _____

Groomsmen, fathers, ring bearer _____ How many _____

Kind and color of boutonnieres _____

Cost $ _____

Delivery of flowers for the groom's party

Place (church, hotel, etc.) _____

Address _____ Phone _____

Person to see _____

Date _____ Time _____

Mother of the groom

Style of corsage _____

Kinds and colors of flowers _____

_____

Ribbon color _____

Cost $ _____

Delivery

Place (home of groom's parents, church, etc.) _____

Address _____ Phone _____

Person to see _____

Date _____ Time _____

Other person (bride's grandmother, groom's grandfather, aunts, etc.) _____

Style _____

Kinds and colors _____

Cost $ _____

Delivery address _____ Phone _____

Date _____ Time _____

Other _____

Style _____

Kinds and colors _____

Cost $ _____

Delivery address _____

Date _____   Time _____

TOTAL COST OF FLOWERS FOR THE WEDDING PARTY $ _____

DECORATIONS FOR THE RECEPTION

Where	Kinds of flowers	Color	Number of arrangements	Cost
Receiving line area	_____	_____	_____	$ _____
Buffet table	_____	_____	_____	$ _____
	_____	_____	_____	$ _____
	_____	_____	_____	$ _____
Bridal table	_____	_____	_____	$ _____
Parents' table	_____	_____	_____	$ _____
Guest tables	_____	_____	_____	$ _____
	_____	_____	_____	$ _____
Cake table	_____	_____	_____	$ _____
Cake knife, top of cake, etc.	_____	_____	_____	$ _____
Punch table	_____	_____	_____	$ _____
Bandstand	_____	_____	_____	$ _____
Other _____	_____	_____	_____	$ _____
_____	_____	_____	_____	$ _____
_____	_____	_____	_____	$ _____
			TOTAL	$ _____

Delivery

Reception site _____

Address _____   Phone _____

Person to see _____

Date _____   Time _____

Party flowers (for the bridesmaids' luncheon, rehearsal dinner, etc.)

	Where	Kinds of flowers	Color	Number of arrangements	Cost
Buffet table	_____	_____	_____	_____	$ _____
Bridal table	_____	_____	_____	_____	$ _____
Guest tables	_____	_____	_____	_____	$ _____
Other _____	_____	_____	_____	_____	$ _____
_____	_____	_____	_____	_____	$ _____
				TOTAL	$ _____

Delivery

Party site (bride's home, restaurant, etc.) _____

Address _____   Phone _____

Person to see _____

Date _____   Time _____

Flowers for special guests _____

Style, kinds, colors _____

Cost $ _____

Delivery address _____

Date _____   Time _____

TOTAL COST OF PARTY FLOWERS $ _____

FLORIST WORKSHEET

Estimate #1

		Ideas	Costs
Name _____		Bridal bouquet _____	
Telephone _____		_____	$ _____
		Bridesmaids' Flowers _____	
		_____	$ _____

Mothers'/Other participants _____

_____ $ _____

Groom's/Men _____

_____ $ _____

Ceremony _____

_____ $ _____

Reception _____

TOTAL $ _____

Estimate #2

Ideas   *Costs*

Name _____   Bridal bouquet _____

Telephone _____

_____ $ _____

Bridesmaids' Flowers _____

_____ $ _____

Mothers'/Other participants _____

_____ $ _____

Groom's/Men _____

_____ $ _____

Ceremony _____

_____ $ _____

_____

Reception _____ $ _____

TOTAL $ _____

Final selection—name, address, telephone

_____

_____

Contract signed   Deposit paid   Balance due

_____

PHOTOGRAPHERS

Your marriage ceremony will be over in a few minutes, and the reception will be over in a few hours, but the photographs and videotape of your wedding hopefully will last a lifetime. It is essential that the people who photograph and videotape your wedding be professionals whom you trust.

There are two types, or styles, of wedding photographs:

Formal portraits: These posed shots are usually taken before the wedding, and are often sent with wedding announcements for publication in newspapers. Portraits of you alone, you and your groom together in street clothes, are often taken for newspaper engagement announcements.

Wedding photographs: These photographs are taken at the actual ceremony and reception, and include candids, formal groupings (of your entire family, all the attendants), and documentation of the important reception events (the first dance, friends toasting you). The same photographer can take your formal portraits and your wedding photographs, or you may choose two different professionals. Some photographers can take portraits at the wedding site, either with a studio-type backdrop they provide or against an outdoor setting. Remember that posing for formal portraits during the reception will take time away from your guests.

New Trends in wedding photography to consider:

• The photojournalistic approach, in which the photographer takes shots as if he or she were covering a news story. The photographer stays in the background, rather than lining people up and asking them to smile. There are no posed shots, but a collection of true-to-life vignettes.

• Black-and-white photographs are finding their way back into wedding albums—a classic look that may age better than color.

• Photo displays of the bride and groom from birth to marriage are mounted at the wedding, especially near the receiving line.

• Polaroid snapshots are given to guests as a favor.

• Soft-focus portraits evoke a romantic feeling. The photographer darkens or clouds the corners slightly to draw attention to the expression of the bride.

• Double exposures or special filters are used to create images such as candles, water, stars, as a background for a sensitive portrait.

As with any wedding service, the best way to find a good wedding photographer is through the recommendations of friends and recent brides. Ask caterers, florists, and other wedding personnel for names, too. Find out if the photographer is a member of the Professional Photographers of America (which has a "Code of Ethics for Wedding Photography").

Questions to Ask Photographers

• Can you see sample wedding albums? Do they include styles that you like—such as diffused lighting, outdoor settings, multiple exposures? Do the pictures capture emotions?

• If you are working with a large studio, who will be the actual photographer covering your wedding? Take recommendations of specific photographers and interview before you make your selection.

• Does the photographer seem willing to listen to your concerns? Avoid those who seem to have a set way of doing things.

• Does he or she have experience at your wedding site? Are there any restrictions in the church or synagogue—such as no flash allowed?

• Do you want the photographer to wear attire similar to that of the wedding guests? Or will you allow creative license?

• When will wedding day posed pictures be taken, and how long will it take? If you don't wish to follow the tradition of the groom not seeing the bride before the wedding, take group shots before the ceremony. Taking them between the ceremony and reception, or during the reception, are other options (as long as you still have a receiving line first and guests aren't kept waiting too long).

• What will photography cost? Will you pay by the hour? If so, does this include transportation time, travel expenses? Or is there a standard wedding package? Can photographs be ordered individually, and for how much? Is an album included? Are your original proofs part of the package? What styles of wedding albums are available?

• When will the previews or proofs be ready? How long may proofs be kept before the prints are ordered?

• How long does the photographer keep negatives? (You may not be able to afford many prints right away, but want the option of ordering more in coming years.)

PHOTOGRAPHY WORKSHEET

Estimate #1   *Comments about style*

Name _____   _____

Telephone _____   _____

Recommended by _____   *Costs (per print? per hour?)*

                                        _____

Estimate #2   *Comments about style*

Name _____   _____

Telephone _____   _____

Recommended by _____   *Costs (per print? per hour?)*

                                        _____

Final choice—name, address, and telephone

_____

_____

Contract signed   Deposit paid   Balance due

_____

Formal Portrait Tips

• If you want your formal portrait to appear in the newspaper, time your photography session carefully. Some newspapers need photographs a few weeks before the wedding.

• For engagement photographs, ask your photographer about backgrounds. As a general rule, wear medium to dark tones with a dark background, light colors for a light background. (Avoid loud prints and plaids.)

• Makeup should be subtle. Remember that lights intensify colors.

• To make sure your wedding dress is wrinkle-free, bring it to the studio in a garment bag and change there. Some photographers may take your photograph at the final fitting at your bridal salon.

• Anywhere from a few days to a few weeks after your portrait session, the photographer will send you previews or proofs. At that time,

you'll decide on the various sizes and quantities of prints you want to order. Don't forget to order enough for friends and relatives.

Wedding Candid Tips

• Visit the ceremony site with your photographer. Figure out where everyone can stand to get the shots you want.

• Sign a contract with details such as date, locations, start and finish times, cost, overtime fees, name of photographer who will attend, elements of the package you are buying.

• Give the photographer a list of shots you will want him or her to be sure to take on the wedding day.

• Assign someone in the wedding party (honor attendant, a sister) to point out all of the guests whose photographs should be taken during the reception.

WEDDING PHOTOGRAPHS

Your maids scrambling for your bouquet, your father dabbing a tear from his eye . . . On the list below, check off which special moments you'd like to see in *your* wedding album. Then clip out the list and take it to your photographer—just to be sure he or she captures *all* those happy wedding memories on film.

BEFORE THE CEREMONY

_____ Bride in dress
_____ Bride with mother
_____ Bride with father
_____ Bride with both parents, stepparents
_____ Bride with honor attendant
_____ Bride with maids
_____ Bride touching up makeup, hair
_____ Bride at gift table
_____ Everyone getting flowers

_____ Bride leaving house
_____ Bride, father getting in car
_____ Groom alone
_____ Groom with best man
_____ Groomsmen getting boutonnieres
_____ Other moments dressing
_____ _____
_____ _____
_____ _____

AT THE CEREMONY

_____ Guests outside church, other site

_____ Bride, father, getting out of car

_____ Bride, father, going into church

_____ Ushers escorting guests

_____ Groom's parents being seated (or in procession)

_____ Bride's mother being seated (or in procession)

_____ Soloist and organist

_____ Groom and groomsmen at altar (or in procession)

_____ Bridesmaids coming down aisle

_____ Maid or matron of honor

_____ Flower girl and ring bearer

_____ Bride and father

_____ Giving-away ceremony

_____ Groom meeting bride

_____ Altar or canopy during ceremony

_____ Bride and groom exchanging vows

_____ Ring ceremony

_____ The kiss

_____ Bride and groom coming up aisle

_____ Bride and groom on church steps

_____ Bride alone in the chapel

_____ Bride and groom among guests, wedding party

_____ Bride and groom getting in car

_____ Bride and groom in back seat of car

_____ Other ceremony moments

_____ _____

_____ _____

_____ _____

POSED SHOTS BEFORE THE RECEPTION

_____ Bridesmaids looking at bride's ring

_____ Bride's and groom's hands

_____ Bride and groom together

_____ Bride with parents

_____ Groom with parents

_____ Bride and groom with honor attendants

_____ Bride and groom with children

_____ Bride with her attendants

_____ Groom with his attendants

_____ Bride, groom, all the wedding party

_____ Bride, groom, all the parents

_____ Other post-ceremony moments

_____ _____

AT THE RECEPTION

_____ Bride and groom arriving

_____ Bride and groom getting out of car

_____ Bride and groom going into reception

_____ The receiving line (posed)

_____ Receiving line (spontaneous unposed)

_____ Bride and groom in receiving line

_____ Bride's mother in receiving line

_____ Groom's mother in receiving line

_____ Buffet table

_____ Friends serving punch

_____ Bride, groom, at bride's table

_____ Parents' table

_____ Bride, groom, dancing

_____ Bride, her father, dancing

_____ Groom, his mother, dancing

_____ The musicians

_____ Bride, groom, talking to guests

_____ Passing the guest book

_____ The cake table

_____ Bride, groom, cutting the cake

_____ Bride, groom, feeding each other cake
_____ Bride, groom, toasting
_____ Throwing and catching bouquet
_____ Groom taking off bride's garter
_____ Throwing, catching, the garter
_____ Wedding party decorating car
_____ Bride changing into going-away clothes
_____ Groom changing
_____ Bride and groom saying good-bye to parents

_____ Bride and groom ready to leave
_____ Guests throwing rice
_____ Bride and groom getting in car
_____ Guests waving good-bye
_____ Rear of car departing
_____ Other reception fun

_____ _____
_____ _____
_____ _____
_____ _____
_____ _____

VIDEOGRAPHERS

As more people own video cassette recorders (VCRs), more brides and grooms want to preserve the action of their weddings on video. A video brings your wedding day to life years later, and it is fun and romantic to play the tape for everyone, especially for those who couldn't attend.

There are three main types of wedding videos to consider:

The *nostalgic video* starts with vintage photographs of you and your groom. From there, it might show the two of you in a favorite scenic spot. Scenes from the ceremony, reception—even honeymoon—complete the tape; often they are interspersed with shots of family members sharing special memories of you. Costs for this type of video can run high.

A *documentary-style video* uses only scenes of the wedding day. It may include shots of you and your groom getting ready beforehand, scenes of guests arriving, panoramas of your ceremony and reception sites. Your groom can wear a cordless microphone to record your vows at the altar. During the reception, the videographer might conduct interviews, capture guests' insights on marriage, childhood anecdotes about you two.

A *straight-shot format*, where only one camera is used, is the least expensive option since it eliminates the need for editing. Still, the videographer can add small touches—such as including your names and wedding date in the beginning of the tape, and/or a musical introduction.

Finding a Videographer

• Since the field is new, there are many inexperienced videographers. Be sure yours has experience. Ask to view sample tapes of weddings, and get references.

• Ask local photography studios for sources. (They may provide videotaping services themselves.) Check, too, with other newlyweds and wedding professionals such as caterers or bridal consultants. You could also write to the Professional Photographers of America, 1090 Executive Way, Des Plaines, IL. 60018.

Questions For a Videographer

• How many camera assistants will he or she need that day?

• What equipment will he or she use? Will special lighting, electrical outlets, be needed?

• Will he or she be as unobtrusive as possible, or more like a wedding participant—interviewing guests, getting close to the bride and groom to capture important moments like the first dance?

• What will the video cost? Are there ways to cut down on the total price, such as eliminating music and credits?

When You've Decided On a Videographer

• Set up a meeting at the wedding site for him or her *with* the still photographer—to coordinate their activities, figure out placement of cameras, discuss how lighting can be kept to a minimum, etc.

• Sign a contract with details such as date, locations, start and finish times, number of cameras, amount of editing, name of camera persons, appropriate dress for videographer and all assistants, costs.

VIDEOGRAPHY WORKSHEET

Estimate #1

Name _____

Telephone _____

Recommended by _____

Comments about style

_____

_____

Cost _____

Estimate #2

Name _____

Telephone _____

Recommended by _____

Comments about style

_____

_____

Cost _____

Final choice—name, address, and telephone

_____

_____

Contract signed   Deposit paid   Balance due

_____

TRANSPORTATION

Amidst all the other wedding details, don't forget to figure out something very important: How will you, your bridal party, and guests get to the wedding? Limousine service is the most elegant, and is available in most areas. (Make arrangements at least three months before the wedding.) You will probably also need friends to help transport out-of-town or elderly guests.

Limousines

Depending on your budget, you may hire one limousine or many. Traditionally one limousine picks up you and your father and takes you to the wedding site, while your mother and bridesmaids ride in one or several other cars or limousines. The groom's parents or grandparents may also be picked up by car. After the ceremony, you and your new husband travel to the reception site in the same car you and your father arrived in. You might even take it to the airport or a hotel after the reception.

Most limousine services charge by the hour, starting at the time the car leaves the garage until it returns. Thus, it's better to hire a company that's located near your wedding site. Other things to look for when hiring a limousine:

• Ask if there is a minimum rental time. Are gratuities for the driver included in the price? Is a deposit required? Will it be refunded if we cancel? When is the balance due? (If it's due on the wedding day, ask what the form of payment is—and assign a member of the wedding party to deliver it.) If the groom's family will be paying for the limousines, have the bill sent directly to their home.

• Visit the limousine office and see that their insurance and city licenses are in order. Ask to see the vehicle you will be renting. Does it have seat belts, other features you would like—such as a bar or stereo?

• If the cars are "out," it may mean that the company doesn't own its own vehicles. Instead, the company may be renting cars from other firms, which increases the chances that the car you want may be unavailable on wedding day. Specify the car you want in a contract.

Other Drivers

If you don't hire professional drivers for your wedding party, assign friends with clean, comfortable cars to drive them. Friends can also help drive out-of-town guests or anyone else who is unable to drive. Be sure to thank drivers by paying for a tank of gas and a car wash—and a small gift, too. Use the Driver's Checklist to help them know who to pick up, when, and where.

Getting Away in Style

Many brides and grooms choose a unique vehicle to transport them to the reception, or from the reception to the honeymoon site or other destination. Among the options: helicopter, horse-drawn carriage, horseback, fire engine, hot-air balloon, boat or gondola, antique or luxury car, private plane, bicycle, horse-drawn sleigh at a winter resort.

Decorating the Getaway Car

Traditionally, male attendants sneak out of the reception to festoon the getaway car with "Just Married" decorations. The custom of tying tin cans to the back of getaway cars, and honking horns, is probably symbolic of the belief that the noise would ward off evil spirits. Here are some other ideas:

• Safety first. Don't obstruct the driver's view in front or back. Avoid glue, cellophane tape, or rubber cement, which many damage the car's finish. And make sure attendants have the right car beforehand.

• Names of bride and groom and "Just Married" should be painted in white shoe polish that washes off with water. (Before painting on the names, dab a small amount of polish on an un-obtrusive part of the car, to be sure it washes off easily.)

• Use balloons, signs, crepe paper. Some party stores sell ready-made getaway kits.

• A florist can decorate the car with garlands of flowers, using floral tapes and clips that won't harm the paint.

WEDDING DAY TRANSPORTATION WORKSHEET

TO THE CEREMONY SITE

Name	Time and place of pickup	Who will drive
Bride		
Father		
Mother		
Maid/Matron of Honor		
Bridesmaids		
Groom		
Best Man		
Ushers		
Groom's Parents		
Grandparents		
Other Guests		

TO THE RECEPTION SITE

Name	Time of pickup	Destination	Who will drive

Bride and Groom _____

Bridal Attendants _____

Groom's Attendants _____

Bride's Parents _____

Groom's Parents _____

Grandparents _____

Other Guests _____

_____

FROM RECEPTION SITE TO HOTEL, HOME, ETC.

Name	Time of pickup	Destination	Who will drive

Bride and Groom _____

Bridal Attendants _____

Groom's Attendants _____

Bride's Parents _____

Groom's Parents _____

Grandparents _____

Other Guests _____

_____

_____

_____

_____

_____

_____

_____

LIMOUSINE WORKSHEET

Estimate #1

Name _____   Price _____

Telephone _____   Comments _____

Recommended by _____   _____

Estimate #2

Name _____   Price _____

Telephone _____   Comments _____

Recommended by _____   _____

Final Choice—Name, address, telephone

_____

_____

Contract signed   Deposit paid   Balance due

_____

DRIVER'S CHECKLIST

(Give a copy to each driver.)

Driver's name _____

Address _____ Phone _____

Passengers

1. Name _____

   Address _____ Phone _____

2. Name _____

   Address _____ Phone _____

3. Name _____

   Address _____ Phone _____

4. Name _____

   Address _____ Phone _____

5. Name _____

   Address _____ Phone _____

Address of gathering place _____

Arrival time _____

Ceremony site _____

Ceremony address _____

Arrival time _____

Directions _____

_____

_____

Reception site _____

Reception address _____

Arrival time _____

Directions _____

_____

_____

_____

_____

_____

Luggage stored in trunk (time, number of bags) _____

CAKES

Cake is the one element no wedding reception, no matter how small, can do without. Your caterer may provide a wedding cake as part of the overall menu package, or you may purchase it separately from a baker, especially if you want a unique design. There are many choices in flavors and decorations available:

• Traditional wedding cakes are made of white or yellow sponge cake or fruit cake, frosted in white.

• New flavors: chocolate, carrot, banana, lemon, spice, cheesecake, or a combination of several of these.

• Fillings: mousse, praline, or a variety of fruit fillings—including lemon—are popular.

• Frostings: Bakers can use buttercream or

BAKER'S WORKSHEET

Estimate #1

Name _____

Telephone _____

Recommended by _____

Description and comments

_____

_____

Price $ _____

Estimate #2

Name _____

Telephone _____

Recommended by _____

Description and comments

_____

_____

Price $ _____

Final Choice—Name, address, telephone

_____

_____

Contract signed   Deposit paid   Balance due

_____

WEDDING CAKE CHECKLIST

Number to serve _____

Size of cake _____

Shape _____

Cake flavor _____

Filling flavor _____

Icing flavor and color _____

Decoration description _____

_____

Cake topper description _____

_____

Cake knife included?   Yes _____ No _____

Cutting instructions _____

_____

_____

_____

Cost $ _____

Groom's cake?   Yes _____ No _____

Description _____

How many packages _____

Cost $ _____

Delivery _____

Reception site _____

Address _____ Phone _____

Person to see _____

Date _____ Time _____

Total cake cost $ _____

gum paste to create fantastic floral or basket-weave effects. The cake might be embellished with elaborate sugar flowers, fruit, gold filigree.

• Shapes: Wedding cakes come in many different shapes to reflect the couple's interests—a ski slope, your city's skyline, double rings, hearts, castles, Bibles. Tiers of petit fours are the American version of the traditional French *croque-en-bouche* (a tower of caramel-covered cream puffs).

• Cake toppers: Decorations atop the cake include the traditional bride and groom figurines; figurines dressed in the spirit of the couple's interests and hobbies (tennis outfits, scuba gear); porcelain keepsake statuettes personalized to resemble the couple in coloring, bridal outfits; other figures such as cherubs, birds, Cupids, wedding bells; fresh flowers.

• Groom's cake: This grand tradition is experiencing a revival. Groom's cakes may be brandied fruit or chocolate layers, in creative shapes such as a top hat or champagne bottle. They may also be whimsical representations of grooms' favorite hobbies or sports. In some areas of the country, the groom's cake may be cut and served at the rehearsal dinner, but traditionally guests are given a small box with a slice to take home from the wedding reception. Legend has it that a woman who puts a piece under her pillow will dream of the man she will marry.

Wedding Cake Shopping Tips

• Start shopping for a wedding cake about three months before the wedding.

• Look through magazines for ideas, and bring these pictures with you when you shop for a cake decorator.

• Ask to see photographs of other wedding cakes the baker has created, and taste some samples.

• Get the baker's recommendations on what types of cake, frostings, and cake shapes will hold up during your reception, especially if it will be a lengthy one, or during hot weather.

• Discuss cake set-up; arrange for the baker to work with the banquet manager to see that the cake is displayed properly. Ask that the baker work with the florist as well, to coordinate any floral decorations on the cake.

• What is the price? Will there be extra fees for delivery, set-up? Who will cut the cake after the bride and groom have shared their first slice? (Register for a cake knife to be used for your cake-cutting ceremony; it will become a keepsake you will enjoy using on each anniversary, and on all special occasions.)

• Get details in writing—size, shape, flavor, color of cake; delivery information; payment schedule.

TIPS ON TIPPING

Certain wedding professionals customarily receive tips. Here are suggestions on whom to tip, when, and how much. Remember, these are guidelines—you may tip more or less depending on local custom or feelings about the quality of service you received.

Whom to tip	How much	When, and by whom
Caterer, club manager, hotel banquet manager, bridal consultant	1–15% for extra-special services only; fee usually covers everything. If gratuity is not covered in fee, tip 15–20%.	Reception hosts pay bill on receipt. Add any special tip to payment.
Waiters, waitresses, bartenders, table captains	15–20% of bill given to captain or maître d'hôtel to distribute to rest of staff.	If included, reception hosts pay tips with bill. If not, right after reception.
Powder room attendants, coat room attendants, in hotels or clubs.	50¢ per guest, or arrange a flat fee with the hotel or club management.	If a flat fee, reception hosts pay it with bill. If not, right after reception.
Florist, photographer, baker, musicians you hire, limousine driver	15% for driver; others tipped only for extra-special service, 1–15%.	Ceremony hosts tip driver at reception site. Add other tips to bill payments.
Civil ceremony officials (judge, justice of the peace, city clerk)	Usually a flat fee ($10 and up). Some judges cannot accept money. Ask.	Groom gives fee to best man, who pays after the ceremony.
Clergymembers (minister, rabbi, priest)	Usually a donation ($20 and up), depending on ceremony size. Ask.	Groom gives donation to best man, who pays after the ceremony.
Ceremony assistants (altar boys, sextons, cantors, organists)	Sometimes covered by church fee, or ask clergy what's customary ($5–$25).	Ceremony hosts pay church fee when billed; separate fees, tips, after service.

Section 4:

WEDDING ATTIRE GUIDE

SHOPPING FOR A BRIDAL GOWN

Shopping for your wedding dress is one of the most exciting aspects of wedding planning. Nothing makes you feel more like a bride-to-be than the transformation you see in the dressing room mirror. There are several things you should know, however, before visiting your local bridal salon. Buying a wedding dress isn't like buying a shirt or a new pair of pants!

• Shop early. You will need to order your wedding gown at least six months before your wedding, even earlier if you need to dress ahead of time for a bridal portrait.

• Know your style. Look at pictures in bridal magazines; tear out photos of favorite gowns, and note the names of the manufacturers. Consider the formality of your wedding and what looks good with your figure type. (See following charts.)

• Work up a budget. Wedding dresses range in price from hundreds of dollars to thousands. Most styles are available in different price ranges—the difference is in the quality of materials and finishing details. Don't forget to budget for accessories! A headpiece, strapless bra, special petticoat, shoes, hosiery, and jewelry can all add up to hundreds of dollars.

• Make an appointment. Many bridal shops or bridal departments of large department stores require advance notice. Allow about an hour and a half for your appointment.

• Bring a friend or your mother. It's a good idea to have someone you trust accompany you, but don't confuse the issue with more than two people.

• Take along accessories. For try-ons and fittings, bring shoes of the style and heel height you will wear, and a strapless bra if you want a bare-shouldered look. The salon will provide a selection of petticoats and slips. An heirloom veil, a special necklace, gloves, and anything else you plan to wear on wedding day should come with you, as well.

• Choose the dress. Bridal shops stock sample gowns, usually in size eight or ten. Your saleswoman can pin or hold the sample gowns so you can envision them in your size. Once you have chosen the dress you want, the salon orders it in the size closest to yours. You then go in for a first fitting, during which the dress is altered in many ways to suit you perfectly. Personal wishes—the addition or subtraction of sequins and pearls, a change in neckline, longer or shorter sleeves—are also accommodated at this time, for a fee.

WEDDING FASHIONS

Wedding fashions differ for very formal, formal, semi-formal, and informal celebrations. The time of day and location are also a factor. How to choose? While styles do change from year to year, the following guidelines will help you, your groom, your mothers, and the wedding party dress appropriately and attractively.

	VERY FORMAL	FORMAL EVENING	FORMAL DAYTIME	SEMI-FORMAL	INFORMAL
Bride	Floor-length gown of satin, lace, or peau de soie, with a cathedral or chapel train. Long, full-length veil and headpiece with lace, beading, silk flowers, perhaps fur. Long sleeves or gloves to cover arms. Shoes to match. Full bouquet or flower-trimmed prayer book.	Traditional, floor-length dress with chapel or sweep train. Veil or mantilla flowing to hem. Same accessories as very formal, but a simpler bouquet.	Traditional, floor-length dress with a shorter chapel or sweep train. Shoulder- or fingertip-length veil, or hat. Matching gloves, shoes. Less elaborate bouquet, accessories, than at formal evening wedding.	Trainless, floor-length or short dress in chiffon, jersey, or lace. Chapel or ballet veil with long dress; elbow- or shorter-length veil, hat, or flowers in hair, with short dress. Shoes to match. Small bouquet or flower-trimmed prayer book.	An elegant street-length suit or dress (in any color except black). Accessories should include a nosegay, wristlet, or corsage to wear.
Mothers	Floor-length evening or dinner dresses (not all black or white) in shades that blend with—rather than match—maids' dresses. Small hats or veils, shoes, gloves. Matching flowers.	Long dinner dresses. (Both the mothers should dress in similar styles). Small hats or veils optional (unless expected in a house of worship). Gloves optional. Matching flowers.	Street-length dresses. Small hats or veils optional (unless expected in a house of worship). Gloves optional. Matching flowers.	Elegant street-length dresses similar to the bridesmaids' style—most likely elegant, street-length dresses. Matching accessories.	Elegant street-length dresses similar to the bridesmaids' style—most likely elegant, street-length dresses. Matching accessories.

	VERY FORMAL	FORMAL EVENING	FORMAL DAYTIME	SEMI-FORMAL	INFORMAL
Groom, men	*Before 6 p.m.* Black or gray cutaway coat, gray and black striped trousers, gray waistcoat, formal white shirt with wing collar. Striped ascot, gray gloves, black shoes, socks. *After 6 p.m.* White tie. Black tailcoat, satin-trimmed trousers, white piqué waistcoat, stiff-front shirt with wing collar, French cuffs. Studs, white piqué bow tie, white gloves, patent leather pumps, black socks. Top hats optional.	Black tie: Black or charcoal gray dinner jacket with matching trousers, white pleated-front shirt with turned-down or wing-tip collar and French cuffs, a black vest or cummerbund. Black shoes, socks, and bow tie. Patterned accessories optional.	*Traditional*: Black or gray stroller, striped trousers, gray waistcoat. White shirt with turned-down collar, striped tie. Black shoes and socks. Gray gloves optional. *Contemporary*: Formal suit in white or light colors for summer; darker shades for fall. Dress shirt, bow tie, vest or cummerbund.	*Traditional*: Solid dark suits with plain white shirts, four-in-hand ties. Black shoes with long socks. *Contemporary*: Dinner jacket or formal suit, dress shirt. Bow tie, vest or cummerbund. For a summer wedding, white linen jackets with black or gray trousers.	Traditionally styled jackets and neckwear—perhaps with patterned accessories—in the same mood as the bride's attire.
Bridesmaids	Floor-length dresses similar to bridal gown style, material. Floral wreaths, ribbon headbands, lace hats, or flowers in hair. Long sleeves or gloves to cover arms. Matching shoes, bouquets, jewelry.	Floor-length dresses in a style similar to the bride's dress, for a unified look. Complementary headpieces, shoes, bouquets, jewelry. Gloves are optional.	Floor-length dresses (street-length, for a small ceremony or one early in the day). Matching headpieces and shoes. Gloves are optional. Bouquets or parasols with summery styles.	Simple long or street-length dresses to match bridal style, or identical flowered or solid skirts with different-hued blouses. Gloves, hats, flowers for hair, optional. Matching shoes and jewelry. Small bouquets, wristlets, or flowers at collars, waists.	Dresses or suits similar to the bride's—perhaps in a style that can be worn again. Wristlets or corsages.

• Leave a deposit. You will usually be asked to leave a deposit totaling half the price of the gown. Find out about the store's cancellation policy. The price of one fitting is usually included, but additional fittings or alterations may cost more.

• Arrange for fittings. Your dress should be delivered to the store within six to eight weeks. Schedule your first fitting, bring along wedding accessories, and review with salon personnel any changes you'd like to have made. Additional fittings may be necessary. After your final fitting, find out when you can pick up your dress, or arrange to have it delivered (in time for your formal portrait). You may want to store it at the salon until just before the wedding if storage space is limited at your home.

FINDING THE PERFECT DRESS

Here's how to find the dress that looks best with *your* figure type.

If you're short and petite (five feet four inches and under), look for petite-sized dresses. Shop for dresses with neat seams or lace appliqués that run up and down lengthwise. Consider empire, princess, or A-lines with small collars and cuffs, trim at the neckline and shoulders to draw the eye upward. Try to avoid belts; if you want one, it should be narrow.

If you're tall (five feet nine inches plus), look for dresses with trim that wraps all around, wide midriffs and sashes, large collars, big cuffs, raglan or butterfly sleeves, flared or tiered skirts, low necks.

If you have a full figure (you could lose 20 pounds or so), consider a princess silhouette featuring vertical panels with no waist seam, or the straight, sleek lines of a chemise. Avoid a figure-hugging sheath or trumpet skirt. Taffeta or or-

GOWNS FOR EVERY BODY SIZE Left to right: Petite, tall, slender, full-figured.

ganza will be more alluring than overly shiny fabrics like satin. To minimize hips, a basque or dropped-V waist works well. Leg-of-mutton sleeves, which are full and then taper downward, flatter full arms. Intricate embroidery or lace near the neckline plays up facial features; vertical beading on the center (rather than sides) of the gown elongates the body. Forgo abundant ruffles, flounces, or layers of lace that may thicken proportions.

If you're slender (you think you need to gain a few pounds), you can choose fabrics that have texture, sheen, nap, or horizontal ribbing, such as satins, velvets, or brocades. Choose a dress with a gathered or dirndl skirt, long puff sleeves, a bloused-bodice top, a cropped jacket, a sash in a color different from the rest of the dress, a wide sculpted collar.

If you have a thick midriff and waist, aim for the slimming effect of a lifted waistline and A-line skirt. Avoid tight waists, cummerbunds, and shaped midriffs in contrasting colors.

If you have a slender midriff and waist, give yourself a little shape with a dress featuring a well-defined midriff, gathered or pleated skirt, natural or sashed waistline. The sash could be in a pale color such as a delicate pink.

Broad shoulders? Look for dresses with smooth, set-in sleeves, low Vs or high covered necks. Stay away from puffed or leg-of-mutton sleeves, bare necklines, broad collars, haltered tops, shoulder pads.

Narrow shoulders? Drape them with cape collars or capelets. Accent them with sleeves that gather at the top, necklines that are bare or widely curved, and shoulder pads built into the dress.

Big bosom? Stick to V-, U-shaped, or high necklines with a keyhole yoke. Avoid cinched waists, empire styles that come up high under the bust, clingy jerseys.

Wide hips? Choose an A-line or gently flared half circle of a skirt. Balance yourself top and bottom by choosing a broad collar or portrait neckline, and puff sleeve.

BRIDAL SHOP TALK

Decisions, decisions—satin or organza? Chapel train or ballet-length? A fresh floral wreath or lacy Juliet cap? Once you speak the wedding-fashion language, shopping for a unique look will be simple, exciting. Take this glossary on bridal salon visits.

Silhouettes

Ballgown—off-the-shoulder yoke nipping into a natural waist with full skirt.

Basque—natural waist with V-front . . . a full skirt.

Empire—small, scooped bodice with high waist, a slim yet full skirt.

Princess—slim-fitting style, with vertical seams flowing from shoulders down to hem of flared skirt.

Sheath—narrow, body-hugging style without a waist.

Lengths and Trains

Street Length—hem just covering knees.

Intermission Length—hem falling slightly below or midway between the knee and ankle in front, floor-length behind.

Ballet Length—hem swirling to ankles.

Floor Length—hem fully skimming the floor.

Sweep Train—shortest train, barely sweeping the floor.

Court Train—a train extending one foot longer than the sweep train.

Chapel Train—most popular of all bridal trains—trailing about one-and-one-third yards from waist.

Cathedral Train—tumbling two-and-one-half-yards from waist.

Extended Cathedral Train—unfolding nearly three yards from waist.

Fabrics

Brocade—heavy fabric with interwoven, raised design.

Chiffon—delicately sheer . . . a simple weaving—often of silk or rayon—with a soft or stiff finishing.

Eyelet—open-weave embroidery used for decorations.

Moiré—silk taffeta that, when illuminated, glistens like water.

Organza—sheer, crisply textured fabric, almost . . . transparent.

Silk-faced Satin—brimming with body, with a lustrous sheen.

Slipper Satin—light, soft . . . a more closely woven fabric.

Taffeta—smooth, glossy . . . a finely textured fabric with body.

Tulle—tiny-meshed net of silk, cotton, or synthetics.

Polyester may also be used alone or blended with natural fibers.

Laces

Alençon—originated in Alençon, France; a pretty, delicate, yet durable design, outlined with cord on net ground.

Chantilly—from Chantilly, France; graceful floral sprays on fine lace background, outlined with silk threads.

Schiffli—a machine-made, delicate floral embroidery.

Venise—heavy, raised floral design, first made in Venice.

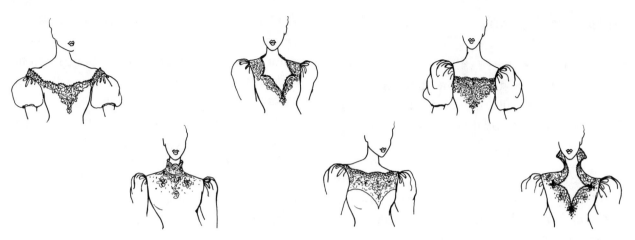

NECKS Top, left to right: Off-the-shoulder, sweetheart, square. Bottom, left to right: High, bateau, Queen Anne.

Necklines

High—collar just brushing the chin.

Boat or Bateau—gently following curve of the collarbone . . . high in front and back, opening wide at sides, ending in shoulder seams.

Off-the-shoulder—gracefully hovering above bustline.

Queen-Anne—rising high at the nape (back) of neck, then sculpting low to outline a bare yoke.

Square—shaped like a half of a square.

Sweetheart—shaped like the top half of a heart.

Sleeves

Bishop—fuller in the lower forearm, then gathered at wrist into a wide cuff.

Dolman—extending from an armhole so large it creates a cape-like effect, often fitted at wrist.

Leg-of-mutton (or Gigot)—full, loose, rounded from shoulder to slightly below elbow, then nipped in at wrist.

Melon—extravagantly rounded from shoulder to elbow.

Puff—gathered into gentle puff near shoulders.

SLEEVES Top, left to right: Fitted, leg-of-mutton, puff. Bottom, left to right: Melon, dolman.

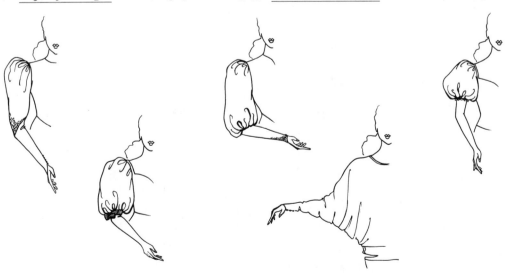

Headpiece Glossary

Shopping for a headpiece will go more smoothly if you know what to call the different styles available, how to identify the look you want. Here, a glossary of bridal headpiece terms:

Banana Clip—curved hair ornament with spring-action grip to hold a large section of hair; may be embellished with jewels, tulle, silk flowers, beading, etc.

Bow—loops of ribbon or fabric worn at crown of head or nape of neck; may include ribbon or tulle streamers.

Fabric-covered Ponytail Band—circle of elastic encased in gathered decorative fabric, such as satin or brocade; may be adorned with beads, sequins, etc.

Floral Wreath—circlet of fresh, silk, or delicate porcelain flowers that rests atop the head or mid-forehead; may be adorned with ribbon streamers, tulle.

Garden Hat—wide-brimmed, face-framing hat of straw, lace, satin, or other stiff, lightweight material; brim, frequently boned to hold shape, may be decorated with ribbon, silk flowers, etc.

Half-Hat—small hat covering no more than half the crown of the head.

Headband—wide ornamental strip of stretch satin, elastic, plastic, or other flexible material worn across the top of head from ear to ear; may be adorned with flowers, feathers, bows, beads, etc.

Juliet Cap—small, round cap that fits snugly on top of head; often covered with lace or satin and decorated with pearls or semiprecious stones.

Mantilla—lace head scarf of Spanish origin, worn loose around the face and often secured with a comb.

Pillbox—small, flat-topped, straight-sided round or oval hat worn on top of the head.

Pouf—small gathered puff of tulle attached to back of headpiece.

HEADPIECES-1 Top, left to right: Juliet cap, fabric ponytail band, pouf with fingertip veil.
Bottom, left to right: Mantilla, snood.

Profile Comb—thin piece of shell, wood, metal, or plastic with rows of teeth, worn asymmetrically on one side of head or centered in back; often embellished with clusters of fresh or silk flowers, lace, pearl sprays.

Snood—knitted or crocheted net that encases hair at back of head or nape of neck; may be attached to a hat, bow, clip adorned with flowers.

Tiara—crown, with or without veiling, worn atop the head; may be decorated with pearls, gemstones, rhinestones, crystals, or lace.

Turban—long scarf of fine linen, silk, or other fabric draped or preconstructed in soft folds around the head; often decorated with jewels.

Blusher—loose veil worn forward over face or back over the headpiece; often attached to longer, three-tiered veil.

Cathedral Length—cascading three and one third yards from headpiece, usually worn with cathedral train.

Chapel-Length—falling two and one third yards from headpiece; usually worn with chapel train.

Fingertip—most popular length, gracefully touching the fingertips.

Fly-away—multilayers that brush the shoulders, usually worn with an informal, ankle-length dress *or* a style with too-pretty-to-hide details in back.

Veils

Ballet or Waltz Length—falling to the ankles.

Bird Cage—falling just below chin, gently shirred at the sides, and usually attached to hats.

Most veils are made of a nylon material called illusion. Embellishments often include poufs, which are small gathers of veiling on the crown of a headpiece. Floral wreaths often have flowing silk or satin ribbons called streamers, tied into sentimental "love knots."

HEADPIECES-2 Top, left to right: Picture hat, profile comb, garden hat. Bottom, left to right: Floral wreath, pillbox hat.

BRIDAL HEADPIECE

The headpiece is the crowning touch of the total bridal look. Here are tips for buying one that flatters your face and wedding dress:

Choose a headpiece to go with your gown. Try them on together. If your gown is rich in detail, opt for an elaborate or richly detailed headpiece; with an understated dress, a simple headpiece is best. Your headpiece should be the same color as your gown and made of the same fabric or lace with, perhaps, matching beads, sequins, crystals.

The veil length should be in keeping with the length of the gown: cathedral- or chapel-length veil with a train; ballet-length with a hem that skims floor or ankles; chin-length blusher with a knee-length dress. The back of your gown is often just as beautiful as the front, and will be seen by guests as you stand at the altar. Even if it will be partially covered by a long veil during the ceremony, it will be admired at the reception, when your headpiece and veil come off. Or select a headpiece with less voluminous tulle, such as as garden hat or wreath.

Fit the headpiece to your figure and face. The wide brim and low crown of a garden hat can flatter a long face. A round face is elegant framed with a pillbox or high tiara. To deemphasize a short, full figure, stay away from billowy veils; instead try a wreath, perhaps with the new delicate porcelain flowers, and shorter veiling.

Consider your hairstyle. If you like smooth, pulled-back hair, choose a small, exquisitely ornamented headpiece. Accent a chignon with a profile comb, or pillbox. You can tame volume, thick curls, with a snood of netting decorated with metallic threads, sparkling jewels. For short hair try a Juliet cap or floral wreath. A lace mantilla or tiara will complement any hair length.

Make sure it's comfortable. Can you turn your head, bend over, without fearing the headpiece will come loose? Secure the headpiece with white hairpins or small combs; before wedding day, practice walking, dancing, without losing the headpiece.

Reception headpiece hints. Want to wear your headpiece at the reception, but concerned about ease of movement? Ask your salon to attach the tulle to the headpiece with snaps or Velcro® so it can be removed after the ceremony. Or switch to a smaller hair ornament for the reception—a profile comb, satin bow, silk or fresh flowers, strand of pearls. Be sure your hairstyle will work well with both your ceremony veil *and* reception ornament.

SHOES

A bride 10 or 20 years ago probably thought little about her wedding day shoes: Only plain white pumps were available. Today, however, wedding shoes are a work of art! In a variety of shapes and adorned with beading, bows, pearl edging, rhinestones, sequins, satin rosettes, ruffles, or lace, they complete your look of head-to-toe elegance. Look for beautiful fabrics: moiré with leaf or rose patterns, faille with gold threads or embroidery, damask, brocade. Even dyeing techniques have improved these days, making color matching easier for you and your attendants. Here are some shoe-shopping tips:

• Start looking for shoes as soon as you've selected a gown; this leaves time for comparisons and custom work.

• Coordinate shoes with the style of your gown. A sweeping train goes well with pumps; with a contemporary knee-length dress, consider slingbacks.

• Don't neglect comfort. You will be standing several hours. Don't let aching feet or blisters ruin your wedding.

• Consider heel height. A medium heel offers elegance and support. Ballet-style slippers are lovely if you don't want to add height. Mar-rying outdoors? High or spiked heels might sink into grass.

• Shop for shoes in the afternoon, when your feet are likely to be largest. (They normally swell during the day.)

• Wear shoes around home to break them in a bit before the wedding. Scuff the bottoms to prevent slipping.

• Takes shoes to each dress fitting to determine proper hem length.

LINGERIE AND ACCESSORIES

Wedding lingerie serves a dual purpose: It shapes and smooths your wedding gown, and adds its own beauty and romance to the way you feel. For wedding night, you'll want something extravagantly elegant—even if you only wear it for two minutes.

Here's what you need, and buying tips:

Slip or petticoat. Slips and petticoats that go under your wedding dress can usually be purchased at the same place you buy your gown. The right petticoat can improve the shape and movement of your wedding dress. Hoops hold the shape of the fullest skirt. A stiff petticoat of tulle, organdy, taffeta, or nylon tricot works well with a slightly less full skirt. A slim sheath needs a body-clinging liner with a side slit. If you choose a petticoat that shows, look for one decorated with lace or ribbons.

Bras. The proper bra can define and emphasize your bust, or minimize it, if need be. A variety of styles are available today, designed to go with a wide selection of wedding dresses. Note: Be sure no telltale straps will show. An off-shoulder gown needs a strapless bra. With a sheer-back dress, try a low-back bra or, as most bridal consultants recommend, have a bra built into the dress. Try on several different bra styles with your gown, and be sure your choice is comfortable—you'll be wearing it for hours.

Panties. Buy panties in the same fabric and color as your bra—perhaps stretch lace or stretch satin in white, ivory, nude. Favorite styles: string bikinis, control-top briefs, tap pants (with a longer leg).

Hosiery. All whites and ivories are not created equal. Take a close look at the color of your gown. Does it have a soft pink or peach hue? Then sheer pale pink or peach hose might look wonderful. A dress with gray tones? Try a silvery stocking. Look for interesting textures and patterns—side ribbon or braid designs, satin and tulle rosettes, rhinestones or bows at the ankle. Some brides feel most comfortable in pantyhose; others choose a sexy garter belt or a lace-top, thigh-high stocking. Shopping tip: Buy a spare pair of hosiery in case you get a run on wedding day.

Gloves. Glove length depends on your gown. Short gloves go with a long-sleeved gown; a short sleeve or strapless dress gives you more options in glove length. Glove length is measured by buttons: A 1-button glove stops at the wrist, the 16-button style covers the entire arm.

Choose gloves according to season and the fabric and ornamentation of your dress. Warm weather calls for cotton or crochet; cool-season options include stretch satin, taffeta, kid leather, nylon with lycra. Gloves can echo a design element of your gown—ruffles, pearls, beading, ribbons, rhinestones, lace cuffs. For a special look, try gloves with gold threading, pastel embroidery, blush pink satin rosettes or bows.

Bags. A wedding day bag should be small and coordinate with your gown. Look for interesting shapes: round, top-hat shaped, rectangular, canteen, semi-circle. Or try a soft drawstring bag. Fabric options include silk, satin, faille, brocade, ottoman, velvet, metallic mesh—in shades of white or ivory to match your dress. You can add bright accents: beads, braid, bows, pearls, sequins, satin rosettes, rhinestones, tassels. Or pin a favorite brooch on a plain bag.

Jewelry. Pearls are a classic wedding day look and can be worn in many ways. A gown with a sweetheart or portrait neckline looks stunning with a pearl choker. Accent a V-back gown with a long strand of pearls clipped at the neck, trailing down back. A simple bodice can be dressed up with a long strand of pearls, perhaps with a rhinestone or diamond pendant at the end. You can also wear a pearl bracelet or braid pearls through your hair.

Choose earrings that flatter your headpiece and hairstyle. An ornate veil looks best with simple button earrings; eye-catching drop earrings complement a simple headpiece or hat,

upswept hair.

Wear heirloom jewelry in new ways, too: Pin a grandmother's brooch to your handbag; wear an aunt's pierced earrings clipped to your gloves; fasten a locket to your headpiece; or wear a necklace in your hair like a tiara.

Seasonal accessories. Celebrate spring with a flower ball: A round base is wrapped with lace, covered with tiny blossoms, and attached to a long satin ribbon. A summer bride can carry a parasol or crocheted fan. In cool weather, consider a shawl embroidered in the hues of attendants' dresses. Wearing a fur-trimmed winter gown? You may wish to carry a fur muff.

Bibles and books. Some brides choose to carry a family Bible or prayer book, which can be covered with embroidered brocade or petit point, decorated with ribbons and flowers. Between the pages, tuck a rose or bookmark hand-lettered with a favorite passage. You might also carry a Victorian posy book of pressed flowers or a leather-bound volume of treasured poems.

Garters. Appliquéd or embroidered hearts, flowers, dice (for luck), holiday motifs (pumpkins, flags, Christmas trees), add interest to a lace or satin garter. Or personalize it with "something old, new, borrowed, blue." Sew on a piece of lace from your mother's wedding gown, a new blue ribbon, a jewel borrowed from a friend.

ATTENDANTS' DRESSES

Attendants' dresses should complement the bride's in style and degree of formality. The style of dresses is up to you, but most brides get some input from their attendants. You may want to pick out three or four dresses you like and let them make the final selection. Keep their budgets, tastes, and figures in mind—and try to choose dresses that can be worn again.

Most often, the bridesmaids wear identical dresses, while the honor attendant wears a dress differing slightly in color or style. There is no hard-and-fast rule, as long as they all coordinate. For example, if you have bridesmaids with very different figure types, they might wear dresses in the same fabric, but different styles.

Attendants' dresses can be ordered from the

bridal salon. Or you can choose the fabric and style, and each attendant can be responsible for producing her own dress. Customarily bridesmaids pay for their own wedding attire, but it's perfectly acceptable for the bride to make a gift of some or all of their outfits if there are money problems that would prevent participation of dear friends or close relatives.

When dresses are ordered through a bridal salon, attendants can go for fittings at their convenience. If each lives in a different town, however, the best choice is a style from a national manufacturer that is available in their hometown bridal shop. Measurement forms (which list dimensions such as bust, waist, hips, etc.) are usually available from the bridal shop. Bridesmaids might fill in the forms and send them back, so one bridal salon can get the dresses in their sizes. If bridesmaids can arrive a few days before the wedding, there will be time to make any alterations. Otherwise, have the store mail them out, and each attendant can use her own seamstress for alterations.

Specify the style and color of attendants' accessories—shoes, hosiery, gloves, simple jewelry—and help bridesmaids locate them. If any special undergarments are needed, such as a strapless bra or slip with a slit, be sure bridesmaids know about this. Will attendants wear petticoats? If so, you may want to select these yourself, to be sure each petticoat will have matching trim, be equally full.

Junior bridesmaids may wear dresses identical to those of regular bridesmaids, or they may wear more youthful styles—for example, a gown with ruffles or a higher neckline, shoes with lower heels.

Flower girls wear long or short dresses that complement the wedding style. White dresses are charming, sashed to match the bridesmaids' dresses. Flowers or ribbons are appropriate in the hair.

Mothers of the bride and groom wear dresses that reflect the formality of the wedding (long gowns for a formal evening wedding, tea-length for afternoon). Traditionally the bride's mother selects her dress first and describes it to the groom's mother, who finds one in a harmonizing style and color. The mothers' dresses should also complement the color of the bridesmaids' gowns.

BRIDAL ATTIRE CHECKLIST

WEDDING GOWN PURCHASED AT:

Contact person _____ Telephone _____

Description of dress: _____

_____

_____

Date ordered _____ Cost _____

Delivery date _____ Deposit paid _____

Balance due _____

Fitting dates _____

Date dress will be ready _____

HEADPIECE/VEIL PURCHASED AT:

Contact person _____ Telephone _____

Description _____

_____

Date ordered _____ Cost _____

Date headpiece will be ready _____ Deposit paid _____

Balance due _____

SHOES PURCHASED AT:

Contact person _____ Telephone _____

Description _____

Date ordered _____ Cost _____

Additional costs for dyeing, etc. _____

Date shoes will be ready _____ Deposit paid _____

Balance due _____

OTHER ACCESSORIES

	Date purchased	Other facts (any alterations, additional costs)
Petticoat/slip		
Bra		
Panties		
Hosiery		
Gloves		
Earrings		
Necklace		
Bracelet		
Garter		
Other		

BRIDESMAIDS

Description of dress, size, where purchased, payment information, etc.

Maid/matron of honor _____

_____

Bridesmaid 1 (name) _____

_____

Bridesmaid 2 _____

_____

Bridesmaid 3 _____

_____

Bridesmaid 4 _____

_____

Bridesmaid 5 _____

_____

Fitting dates for bridesmaids: _____

Date dresses will be ready _____

Contact person _____ Telephone _____

Headpieces purchased at: _____

Headpiece description _____

Contact person _____ Telephone _____

Cost _____ Deposit paid _____ Balance due _____

Date headpieces will be ready _____

Shoes purchased at: _____

Shoe description _____

Contact person _____ Telephone _____

Cost _____ Additional cost for dyeing? _____

Date shoes will be ready _____

Accessories (bras, slips, jewelry, etc.) _____

_____

_____

FLOWER GIRL

Dress purchased at: _____

Description: _____

Additional information (if fittings/extra costs are necessary) _____

_____

Hair decoration: _____

Shoes: _____

Flower basket or bouquet description: _____

Other accessories: _____

MEN'S FORMALWEAR

What should the groom wear? His attire depends on the hour and degree of formality of the ceremony. (See Wedding Fashions chart at the beginning of this section.) Read this section and together discuss his fashion preferences. Today's groom has many choices.

The tuxedo—as the hip-length dinner jacket with formal trousers is commonly called—is most appropriate for a formal wedding that takes place after 6 P.M., but this versatile style has been adapted for daytime ceremonies as well. White tie is still the *only* attire for a very formal evening wedding. Grooms who wish to honor tradition wear a debonair stroller or cutaway for a formal daytime ceremony. For a less formal wedding, the groom may choose a dark suit or cream-colored dinner jacket.

Today's formalwear allows for more variety and personal style. How can your groom be sure he's making the right choice? He should start by seeking the guidance of a professional at a formalwear shop. He might ask about single-breasted versus double-breasted jackets; shawl, peaked, and notch collars; bow ties, ascots, and four-in-hand neckwear; whether to wear a vest or cummerbund; and how to coordinate his accessories with bridesmaids' attire. He should also consider cuff links, studs, pocket squares, suspenders. For an up-to-date, personalized look, your groom may select accessories in one of the newest fabrics—brocade, tapestry, paisley, plaid.

Nowadays, fathers of the bride and groom usually wear formal attire that matches the groom and his attendants. The bride's father traditionally escorts the bride down the aisle, which makes him a member of the wedding party. The groom's father may also walk down the aisle, and will certainly be seated in a position of honor.

Ring bearers might wear cotton or wool Eton suits with short pants and knee socks. For very formal weddings, pantaloons in silk or velvet might be topped with a silk blouse. An older boy usually wears a scaled-down version of the men's formalwear.

In most cases, grooms and attendants rent their formalwear. If your groom will be attending black-tie parties in the future, however, this might be a good time to buy a tuxedo. Some tips on tuxedo rental:

Selection. A men's formalwear store is usually the best place to rent wedding attire. These shops have large selections and can do quick alterations. Looking for a particular suit, perhaps one spotted in a bridal magazine? If the store doesn't have it in stock, it can probably be ordered. Note: Accessories such as vest or cummerbund, suspenders, shirt, studs, cuff links, ties, even shoes, may or may not be included in one package price.

Groom and attendants should be measured for formalwear about three months before the wedding. Out-of-towners can visit their own local formalwear shop, then send their measurements to the groom. Ushers who live far away should arrive a day or two before the wedding, to allow time for alterations.

Size. Shirts should hug the neck. Pants should reach shoes, with a slight "break." Waistbands are usually adjustable. Jackets should fit snugly around shoulders (no arm bulges), with some room at the waist. Jacket sleeves should end at the wrist bone, and show from one-quarter to one-half inch of shirt cuff.

Picking up the suit. In general, suits can be picked up two or three days in advance. Make sure there are no stains, fabric snags, cigarette burns. Jackets should have the same number of buttons on each sleeve. Everything should be tried on. If the store owns an industrial hemmer, the pant leg length can be adjusted in about

GROOM'S WEDDING CLOTHES CHECKLIST

☐ VERY FORMAL   ☐ EVENING   ☐ STROLLER
☐ FORMAL   ☐ WHITE TIE AND TAILS   ☐ DARK SUIT
☐ SEMI-FORMAL   ☐ BLACK TIE   ☐ CONTEMPORARY
☐ INFORMAL   ☐ DINNER JACKET
☐ DAYTIME   ☐ CUTAWAY

Men's formalwear store _____ fitting date _____ time _____

Date ready _____

GROOM	Size	Cost		Size	Cost
Trousers _____		$ _____	Neckwear _____		$ _____
Shirt _____		$ _____	Collar _____		$ _____
Coat _____		$ _____	Other (suspenders, cuff links, studs, pocket squares) _____		$ _____
Vest/cummerbund _____		$ _____			$ _____

Total cost of groom's clothes $ _____

BEST MAN	Size	Cost		Size	Cost
Trousers _____		$ _____	Neckwear _____		$ _____
Shirt _____		$ _____	Collar _____		$ _____
Coat _____		$ _____	Other (suspenders, cuff links, studs, pocket squares _____		$ _____
Vest/cummerbund _____		$ _____			$ _____

Total cost of best man's clothes $ _____

USHERS	Trousers size	Shirt size	Coat size	Vest size	Other accessories
Name _____					$ _____
Name _____					$ _____
Name _____					$ _____
Name _____					$ _____

Total cost of *each* usher's clothes $ _____

10 minutes. A tailor can do small alterations, such as turning up sleeves, sewing on buttons.

Returning the suit. It is customary for the best man to return the groom's suit the first working day after the wedding. Ushers should return their own suits promptly to avoid late charges. Food and beverage stains can usually be dry cleaned, but clothing that is more seriously damaged may have to be paid for.

GROOM'S GLOSSARY

These are the definitions and details you need to know to outfit your groom:

Tuxedo—worn for formal weddings after 6 P.M. The black or gray jacket may be single- or double-breasted, with shawl, peak, or notch lapels in satin or grosgrain. It is worn with matching formal trousers. A white or ivory *dinner jacket*, with formal black trousers, is another alternative during warmer months.

White Tie—most formal menswear style, consisting of a black coat with tails, matching trousers, a tie and vest in white piqué, and a winged-collar shirt with stiff, white piqué front.

Cutaway (or morning coat)—the formal daytime equivalent of a tailcoat, in black or gray with striped trousers, winged-collar shirt, ascot.

Stroller (or walking coat)—cut slightly longer than a suit jacket, in black or gray, and worn before 6 P.M. with striped trousers, a laydown-collar shirt, and four-in-hand tie. (The *only* other option for a daytime wedding is a dark formal business suit.)

Laydown collar—a turned-down collar (like a business shirt) but in a formal fabric.

Winged collar—the most formal dress shirt with a stand-up band collar and folded-down tips. Pleating styles and subtle patterns may vary according to the season's fashion.

Vests—worn to cover the trouser waistband in matching or contrasting fabric.

Cummerbunds—also worn to cover the trouser waistband (instead of vest) with the pleats facing up, and a coordinating bow tie.

Suspenders—also called braces, they may be worn along with cummerbunds.

Bow ties—made of formal fabric and worn with tuxedos, dinner jackets.

Four-in-hand ties—a knotted tie similar to a business tie but in a more formal fabric.

Ascots—double-knot ties with ends folded over, worn with stickpins, winged collars.

Studs and Cuff Links—worn in place of buttons on formal shirts. They come in gold- or silver-tone, precious metals, or a mix of various designs.

Boutonnieres—flowers (which coordinate with the bride's bouquet) worn on the left lapel.

Pocket Squares—a small, visible pocket handkerchief of linen, silk, or other dressy fabric.

Section 5:

PARTIES

SHOWER GUIDE

Bridal showers are pre-wedding parties at which small gifts—usually for the couple's new home—are given. At the traditional all-female shower, friends and relatives give the bride kitchen items or lingerie. Today, however, as more grooms take an active interest in their homes, "co-ed" (male/female) showers are on the rise. These parties shower the bride- and groom-to-be with presents they can use on their honeymoon, for their bar and kitchen, to re-model their home, for their hobbies.

Traditionally, good friends of the bride and groom host the shower. Another couple, a male friend, or group of friends could also play hosts. Except for certain areas of the country where it is the accepted custom, close relatives such as a mother or siblings should not host showers because it looks too much like the family is asking for more gifts.

As a bride, your role in shower planning is minimal, except to provide names and addresses of guests and the location of your bridal registry, if hosts ask for them. If bridesmaids, friends, or relatives are hosting or attending several showers in your honor, bridesmaids should tactfully tell these repeat guests that, in order to conserve their budgets, they need only give the bride and groom one gift. At the shower, graciously thank guests for each gift and later send a written thank-you note. Also thank your shower hosts with flowers or small gifts.

Here, more shower planning tips:

• **Whom to invite.** In general, only people who are invited to the wedding are invited to a wedding shower. One exception would be a shower held at an office or club for colleagues and acquaintances who probably would not attend the wedding. At a traditional female shower, female relatives (mothers, sisters, grandmothers) are invited from both the bride's *and* groom's sides.

• **When to hold a shower.** Showers may be given from two months up to two weeks before the ceremony. In fact, your shower might even be held a few *days* in advance of the big event—if that's the only time long-distance family members and friends will be able to gather before the wedding.

Keep work schedules of those involved in mind, making sure that principal guests are able to attend at the time you've chosen. What about surprise showers? They can be fun, but may backfire when a busy bride suddenly has other plans at party time. Invitations are mailed or

SHOWER CHART

Theme: _____

Hostess: _____

Date: _____ Time: _____

Place: _____

Guests	Gift	Date thank-you notes sent
1 _____	_____	_____
2 _____	_____	_____
3 _____	_____	_____
4 _____	_____	_____
5 _____	_____	_____
6 _____	_____	_____
7 _____	_____	_____
8 _____	_____	_____
9 _____	_____	_____
10 _____	_____	_____
11 _____	_____	_____
12 _____	_____	_____

guests called at least three weeks in advance of the shower date. If there's absolutely no time before the wedding, a shower can even be given after the couple returns from their honeymoon.

• **What happens at the party.** Invited guests arrive about half an hour before the bride to set up a gift box display. Someone is assigned to write down who gives each gift as it is opened, another to collect ribbons and make the bouquet that is traditionally used at the rehearsal in place of a real bouquet.

Depending on the time of day, refreshments or even a meal is served after the gifts are opened. Popular options: a Saturday afternoon barbecue, Sunday brunch, or an evening cocktail, dinner, or dessert party during the week.

SHOWER THEMES

Many shower hosts choose themes for gift giving and decor. Consider:

• **His-and-hers.** Male and female friends attend and give presents the couple can use together: wine, blankets, garden equipment, compact discs (CDs), videotapes.

• **Bar.** The couple receive items they can use to set up a bar: glassware, liquor and wine, coasters, trays, and other utensils.

• **Garden.** For the couple who will be moving to a home with a yard, rakes, hoses, hand tools, outdoor furniture, and garden books are perfect small gifts.

• **Luxury.** This type of shower works well for an all-female gathering. Gift ideas include certificates for treatments at a beauty spa, satin lingerie, bubble bath, specialty foods.

• **Honeymoon.** Travel items for the hon-

SHOWER CHART

Theme: _____

Hostess: _____

Date: _____ Time: _____

Place: _____

Guests	Gift	Date thank-you notes sent
1 _____	_____	_____
2 _____	_____	_____
3 _____	_____	_____
4 _____	_____	_____
5 _____	_____	_____
6 _____	_____	_____
7 _____	_____	_____
8 _____	_____	_____
9 _____	_____	_____
10 _____	_____	_____

eymoon and after: portable alarm clock, guidebooks, tote bags, camera, small leather goods, are all ideal presents.

• **Kitchen, bathroom, or bedroom.** A shower can be designed to help stock a particular room of the house. Kitchen showers include spices, utensils, small appliances, bowls, canisters; a bathroom shower might call for wastebaskets, towels, rugs; for a bedroom shower, expect sheets, clock, closet accessories, blankets, or a comforter.

• **'Round-the-clock.** The host assigns a time of day to each guest, who brings a gift the couple could use at that time. For example, at 7:00 A.M., a subscription to the morning paper, a coffeemaker; 4:00 P.M., a teapot; 7:00 P.M., a corkscrew; 8:00 P.M., an espresso maker. A 'Round-the-clock shower opens the door to gifts in every room.

• **Office.** Co-workers join forces (and finances) to give the bride one wonderful present: a group gift for her new home, or more per-

SHOWER CHART

Theme: _____

Hostess: _____

Date: _____ Time: _____

Place: _____

Guests	Gift	Date thank-you notes sent
1		
2		
3		
4		
5		
6		
7		
8		
9		
10		

SHOWER CHART

Theme: _____

Hostess: _____

Date: _____ Time: _____

Place: _____

Guests	Gift	Date thank-you notes sent
1 _____	_____	_____
2 _____	_____	_____
3 _____	_____	_____
4 _____	_____	_____
5 _____	_____	_____
6 _____	_____	_____
7 _____	_____	_____
8 _____	_____	_____
9 _____	_____	_____
10 _____	_____	_____
11 _____	_____	_____
12 _____	_____	_____
13 _____	_____	_____

sonal office items such as an attaché case, or fine stationery embossed with her new name.

• **Service.** Rather than bringing gifts, guests offer a service, such as cooking a gourmet dinner, after the couple return home from their wedding trip.

• **Handycouple.** Friends bring bride- and groom-to-be tools, pledge to spend a day help-ing with future home fix-up projects (painting a room, cleaning the yard).

Other shower ideas include: Library—books and magazine subscriptions; Entertainment—discs, games, videocassettes; Indoor Garden—plants, pots, watering cans; Sports—gear for the couple's favorite sport.

SHOWER GAMES

Games are fun to play at parties, especially with a younger crowd. And since nearly any party game can be given a bridal theme, the possibilities are endless. Guests could "pin the boutonniere on the groom," for example, instead of pinning the tail on the donkey. Take a popular board game like Trivial Pursuit or A Question of Scruples, and make the questions wedding or marriage-related. Scramble marriage-related words such as *siks* for kiss or *ubtquoe* for bouquet and have guests unscramble them. Finally, perhaps the most popular shower game is "bridal bloopers." Someone writes down the bride's words as she opens her shower gifts: "This is incredible!" or "How did you know what I wanted?"—and then reads them back as "What Suzanne will say on her wedding night."

BRIDESMAIDS' PARTIES

Bridesmaids' parties are customarily given by the bride to thank her bridesmaids and to have one last "all-woman" gathering before the wedding. The party could be hosted by the bridesmaids as well, or combined with the groom's party for his attendants.

If bridesmaids are coming from out of town, the most convenient time for a gathering may be wedding morning or afternoon. Traditionally a luncheon is hosted by the bride the day of the wedding for the bridesmaids, the bride's and groom's mothers, and other female guests at a club or restaurant.

However, many brides choose to have the luncheon a few days or a few weeks before, when things are more relaxed. Just about any style of party is acceptable: an afternoon tea party, dessert and champagne, an elegant meal at a restaurant, a cozy luncheon at home. It's a time for a bride to reminisce with close friends. Some may choose to have a "bachelorette" party marking her final outing as a single woman, complete with a trip to an all-male revue, bar, or dance club.

At the party, the bride gives her attendants their thank-you gifts and goes over the wedding day schedule. A traditional bridesmaids' party activity is to bake a ring or thimble inside a pink cake. The woman who finds the ring or thimble in her piece will be the next to marry. Another safer version of this tradition (which eliminates the possibility of breaking a tooth) has become a part of the cake-cutting ceremony in the coastal South. At the reception, before bride and groom cut the wedding cake, single female guests pull at the ends of ribbons sticking out of the bottom of the cake. Tied to the end of each ribbon are small silver ornaments—a fleur-de-lis represents wealth; an anchor means hope, a heart, love. The woman who gets the small silver ring is next to marry.

BRIDESMAIDS' PARTY CHECKLIST

Location: _____

Date and time: _____

Date invitations sent: _____

Guests: _____

_____

_____

_____

Menu and beverages: _____

_____

_____

Additional activities/notes: _____

_____

BACHELORS' PARTY

At the traditional bachelors' party, the groom gets together with his male friends. The festivities can be organized by the best man or any of the groom's friends, or the groom himself can play host.

The old, stereotypical bachelors' party conjures up visions of a scantily dressed woman jumping out of a cake, followed by lots of heavy drinking. Today, however, it can be any type of gathering the groom enjoys: a sporting event, beach party, concert, fishing trip, or picnic. Or the party could be a luncheon or dinner at a restaurant, hotel suite, club, or private home.

The groom proposes a toast to his bride after the meal or at some point during the party. After the toast, it's an old tradition for the men to smash their champagne glasses so that they may never be used for a less worthy purpose. If you intend for this custom to be carried out, warn the club or restaurant ahead of time and arrange to pay for the broken glassware.

A bachelors' party is held within a few weeks of the wedding, but never the night before—participants may need time to recover. The groom should probably give his attendants their thank-you gifts at the rehearsal dinner, when they are less likely to be lost or damaged.

If drinking alcoholic beverages will be part of the bachelors' party, arrangements must be made for taxis, limousines, or sober friends to drive the participants home.

OTHER PRE-WEDDING PARTIES

Wedding Work Parties. Friends gather to help you with wedding tasks, such as addressing invitations, lettering place cards, or figuring out the reception seating. Everybody shares snacks or a meal, and while friends enjoy time with each other, important wedding work also is accomplished.

Tasting Parties. Friends help you choose the hors d'oeuvres, cake, wine, punch, or champagne you will serve at your reception. Have bakers and caterers make samples, buy several brands of champagne, or try out different punch recipes. Provide blindfolds and rating cards and put everyone to "work."

CHECKLIST FOR ADDITIONAL PRE-WEDDING PARTIES

Type of party: _____

Date and time: _____

Location: _____

Contact person and telephone number: _____

Guests: _____

_____

_____

_____

_____

_____

Menu and beverages: _____

_____

_____

_____

Activities and notes: _____

_____

CHECKLIST FOR ADDITIONAL PRE-WEDDING PARTIES

Type of party: _____

Date and time: _____

Location: _____

Contact person and telephone number: _____

Guests: _____

_____

_____

_____

_____

Menu and beverages: _____

_____

_____

Activities and notes: _____

_____

REHEARSAL DINNER

A dinner or some sort of party usually follows the wedding rehearsal, which is generally held the day or evening before the wedding. Even when a small wedding does not require a rehearsal, an intimate dinner on the eve of the ceremony is a friendly way to welcome close family and friends and let them get to know one another before the wedding.

Hosts. The groom's parents customarily host the rehearsal dinner. Friends or relatives of the bride, however, or the couple themselves,

can also decide to host this "night before the wedding" festivity.

Guests. Everyone who attends the wedding rehearsal should be invited to the rehearsal dinner: attendants and spouses; clergy and spouse; parents and grandparents; parents of children in the wedding. Out-of-town guests who arrive the night before the wedding are often included, as well as other close friends and relatives. Hosts on a budget might limit the party to wedding participants only.

Planning. A rehearsal dinner can range from an elaborate formal banquet to a poolside picnic, potluck supper, brunch, or dessert buffet and coffee. A seated dinner, however, is still the most popular choice.

The hosts of the party might include traditional family drinks or foods. If the groom's family lives far away, the bride and her family can help organize the event. For example, the bride's mother might give the groom's mother a list of restaurants available on a particular date, so she can make the necessary arrangements by telephone.

In most cases, the rehearsal dinner is more understated than the wedding, with fewer guests and simpler food, drink, and decor.

Although invitations may be telephoned, written ones are preferable, since there may be a variety of wedding-related parties during that period and guests can easily be confused.

Activities. The rehearsal and dinner following are often the first times the family and friends of the groom meet the family and friends of the bride. You will want to get things off to a warm start by introducing people to one another. Use place cards and a seating plan so people get to meet each other. A slide show, video, or book with pictures of the bride and groom from babyhood onward would also break the ice. Don't leave other family members and friends out of the presentation!

If there haven't been bridesmaids' and bachelors' parties, you two can give all of your attendants their gifts at the rehearsal dinner and go over any last-minute instructions for the wedding at this time.

Toasts are historic. First, there is the customary salute to the couple by the best man. The groom then follows with a toast to the bride and his new in-laws; then the bride toasts him and his family. Attendants might want to toast also. From there, other guests propose toasts that include anecdotes about the bride and groom. (Brief ones are enjoyed more than lengthy ones.) Though there is more time for speeches at a rehearsal dinner than at the wedding itself, it's not a license to talk too long.

Don't let the champagne toasting get out of hand, especially if the wedding is the next morning. The groom or a friend could wind things up by thanking the hosts and reminding everyone that the most important event still lies ahead.

The rehearsal dinner may also double as an occasion to celebrate a reaffirmation of parents' or grandparents' wedding vows, an anniversary, an important birthday, or some other family milestone.

YOUR WEDDING GIFTS

YOUR WEDDING GIFTS

Wedding invitations are the official signal to family and friends that the festivities are about to begin. Traditionally only those guests who accept your invitation send wedding gifts, but many other people who have known either the bride and groom, but for some reason cannot attend the wedding, send them also. Guests may send gifts any time before the wedding and up to a year afterward.

You must write down who sent what gift as soon as you receive it, or you'll lose track. Use the following guest list chart, devise your own, or keep your records on a home computer—because a thank-you note is mandatory for every gift you receive, and you must know whom to thank.

Wedding Gift Registries

If you've ever shopped for a wedding gift, you know how difficult it is to choose the right thing. The gift should be something the couple will use, something that goes with their color schemes and decor—yet guests often have little information about their tastes and needs. Now that you're getting married, you can help your guests by listing your preferences at the wedding gift registry in your favorite store. The wedding gift registry helps you receive what you both want and need. And as items are chosen, the consultant will take them off your list, resulting in fewer duplicates and returns.

Virtually all major department stores have wedding gift registries, as do specialty china, glass, and silver gift shops. Unexpected places, such as gourmet shops, museum gift shops, hardware stores, travel agencies, even liquor stores, have them also. If a store doesn't have a wedding gift registry, you could ask the manager to create one especially for you.

A wedding gift registry works like this: Together you meet with a gift consultant and, after looking at all the options, list the items you want and the quantities you will need. (Many stores have checklists and computers to make this easier.) When guests come to the store, they are handed a copy of your registry list from which to choose a gift. Another possibility: A guest can telephone a store and the consultant can either mail the registry list or read off specific items. The guest can order a gift and pay by credit card or store charge without traveling at all. Whether it's used by phone or in person, the wedding gift registry can be a convenience for everyone.

It is especially thoughtful to choose a gift

from the registry and add a personal touch. For example, a guest might select a crystal dish and fill it with the couple's favorite chocolates; a toaster with a newspaper subscription.

Other helpful hints for using the wedding gift registry:

• Register for gifts in a wide range of prices—wooden spoons, measuring cups, soap dishes—as well as crystal, china, and silver. The tableware section in this book will help you determine what you need and how much.

• Spread the word to your friends and bridesmaids about your registry locations. Never write the information on wedding invitations. A shower hostess, however, may include your registry information on a shower invitation.

• Be diplomatic. When guests ask what you'd like for a wedding gift, tell them where you're registered, not specifics. You may mention a gift that's too expensive, or one they personally don't like.

• Diversify by registering in several different stores. If you're getting married in the town where you grew up, for example, but live miles away, register in both locations.

Gifts of Money

Gifts of money are customary in some neighborhoods. They are also popular with brides who have lived on their own, or been married before, and have collected many household basics. Or the couple may want to buy a home or car, or plan to move, and don't want to add to their possessions immediately.

If you prefer monetary gifts, let your mother and close friends discreetly spread the word. Never write your gift preference on your wedding invitations.

Choose a trustworthy friend to hold on to checks and cash you receive at the wedding. You can endorse the checks and he or she can deposit your gifts while you are on your honeymoon.

Damaged Gifts

If a gift arrives damaged, determine from the wrappings who sent it. If it's from a store, call the customer service department, or any other number that may be listed in the papers that accompany the gift, and report the problem. The store will probably replace the gift at no charge; there is no need to tell the giver about the damage.

If the gift was wrapped and sent by an individual, call that person and explain what happened. The package will probably be insured against breakage, so he or she will be able to get reimbursed.

Gift Exchanges

Even if you use the wedding gift registry, gifts you can't use will still arrive. Think carefully before exchanging them. Each is from someone close to you who will look for it when visiting your home, so it's more thoughtful to avoid hurt feelings and keep the gift. (It is not necessary to use it every day, but rather on the occasions when that person visits.) On the other hand, if the giver is unlikely to find out about the exchange, it may be practical to take it back and get something you really need. Don't ask the person where the gift was purchased and don't mention the exchange in your thank-you note.

Gift Displays

In some areas of the country, it is sometimes customary for a wedding gift display table to be on view during the reception. Gifts can be grouped by category (appliances on one side, silver on another), or mixed. Set out one place setting of your dinnerware, flatware, and glassware. In cases where people have given you checks, you can write the giver's name and "check," but don't list the amount. Decorate the gift display with flowers, ribbons, or greenery.

Give some thought to security. You may want to assign or hire a guard for the gifts, especially during the wedding and when the house is empty. Also, check with your insurance company about a temporary floater policy that will cover your gifts until they are moved into your new home (which is thus covered by your regular homeowner's insurance).

Not everyone will have the space to set up a gift display, however, and if you are returning to your hometown to get married from a distant location, you may prefer to have all gifts sent to your residence in another city. (List a mailing address on your wedding gift registry list; friends can also spread the word.)

Gifts at the Reception

Encourage guests to send gifts directly to your home, rather than bringing them to the reception. But since some people will bring gifts to the reception anyway, set aside an area where they will be safe. This could be an attended coat check area at a hotel, restaurant, or club; or a table in a locked closet. Assign a friend to collect the gifts, make sure they are safely stored, and later transport them to your home after the wedding.

Don't open gifts at the wedding. Cards can easily get lost, and guests who didn't bring gifts will feel uncomfortable.

TABLEWARE GUIDE

A large portion of your preferences for wedding gifts will be things for your table. Your choice of china, crystal, silver, and linens will dress your table up or down, quickly change the look, feel, and season of your table.

Dinnerware, commonly referred to as "china," includes place settings as well as serving pieces.

Flatware, commonly referred to as "silverware," includes place settings and serving utensils. Flatware may be sterling silver, silverplate, or stainless steel, and may be accented with gold.

Glassware combines both "crystal" and barware and includes glasses for wine, water, champagne, cocktails, brandy, juice, beer, and soft drinks.

Holloware refers to serving pieces and vessels (such as bowls, platters) that have height and depth (as opposed to flatware). These could be made of many materials, from sterling silver, silverplate, or pewter to glass, porcelain, wood, or other materials. Included are items like salt and pepper shakers, sugar and creamer, serving bowl, vegetable dish, butter dish, gravy/sauce

boat, pitcher, candleholders, vase, tea or coffee service, cake plate, punch set.

Linens. Choices for tablecloths and place mats include fabric prints or solids, textured wovens or straw, or lace.

Tableware Selection Tips

• You and your fiancé will want to decide what type of entertaining you prefer: casual country? buffets with red and white checkered cloths and rustic backgrounds? formal dinner parties with white linen and sparkling crystal? Perhaps you will alternate.

• Think creatively about tableware elements. Pair dinnerware with contrasting patterns in flatware, crystal, and accessories. A traditional rule is: Mix two patterned and one plain, one patterned and two plain; dinnerware pattern with bright flowers, ornate flatware, and smooth blown glassware. Or select a dinnerware pattern of fine white china banded with blue, simple flatware, and cut crystal glassware.

• Tableware can also be coordinated through

design motifs, such as beading or braiding, that are repeated throughout the dinnerware, flatware, and crystal. Look for a rhythm repeated in the three elements, or effective contrasts for dramatic effect. Consider textural interest, colors accented off each other, mixed materials.

• Collect extra pieces for variety and personality. Stores and galleries offer unique designs in tableware items, such as colorful service/buffet plates to go under dinner plates, craftware serving pieces, demitasse cups (plus a va-riety of cups and saucers), crescent salad dishes, compote bowls, colored glassware, an assorted table linen wardrobe. Consider found objects to decorate your table. (Make it a visual surprise!) For instance, an item from your jewelry box—or even the garden shed—adds interest.

Choose two sets of tableware items—one casual (or everyday set), one fine china (for more special occasions)—that can mix and match if necessary.

REGISTRY CHECKLIST

This checklist is the perfect helpmate for selecting your wedding gifts. First, read each column, and note the patterns, manufacturers, and number of items you'd like. Later, when you two visit the store's wedding gift registry, bring this list along—to easily record your preferences. (Your store may offer items not included below—from exercise weights to pasta makers—so write these choices under "other.") As gifts arrive—mark the items received, and keep up-to-date!

	FORMAL/QTY	CASUAL/QTY
☐ Service Plate		
☐ Buffet Plate		
☐ Serving Bowl		
☐ Platter		
☐ Gravy Boat		
☐ Teapot		
☐ Coffeepot		
☐ Sugar/Creamer		
☐ Other:		

Dinnerware

MANUFACTURER

FORMAL PATTERN _____
CASUAL PATTERN _____

	FORMAL/QTY	CASUAL/QTY
☐ Dinner Plate		
☐ Dessert/Salad Plate		
☐ Bread/Butter Plate		
☐ Tea Cup/Saucer		
☐ Coffee Cup/Saucer		
☐ Demitasse/Saucer		
☐ Mug		
☐ Soup/Cereal Bowl		
☐ Rim Soup		
☐ Cream Soup/Saucer		
☐ Fruit Bowl		
☐ Salad Bowl		
☐ Egg Cup		

Flatware

MANUFACTURER

FORMAL PATTERN _____
CASUAL PATTERN _____

	FORMAL/QTY	CASUAL/QTY
☐ Dinner Fork		
☐ Dessert/Salad Fork		
☐ Dinner Knife		
☐ Soup Spoon		
☐ Tea/Dessert Spoon		
☐ Cream Soup Spoon		
☐ Iced Tea Spoon		
☐ Demitasse Spoon		
☐ Steak Knife		
☐ Butter/Pastry Knife		
☐ Butter Spreader		
☐ Serving Spoon		
☐ Pierced Spoon		

FORMAL/QTY   CASUAL/QTY

☐ Serving Fork
☐ Cold Meat Fork
☐ Gravy Ladle
☐ Pie Server
☐ Cake Knife
☐ Sugar Spoon/Tong
☐ Lemon Fork
☐ Carving Set
☐ Salad Servers
☐ Silver Chest
☐ Other:

Glassware

MANUFACTURER

FORMAL PATTERN _____
CASUAL PATTERN _____

FORMAL/QTY   CASUAL/QTY

☐ Goblet
☐ Claret
☐ White Wine
☐ All-Purpose Wine
☐ Champagne Flute
☐ Champagne Saucer
☐ Iced Beverage
☐ Cocktail
☐ Highball
☐ Old-Fashioned
☐ Beer Mug
☐ Pilsner
☐ Brandy
☐ Sherry
☐ Liqueur
☐ Fruit Juice
☐ Finger Bowl
☐ Other:

Serving Pieces/Holloware

PATTERN   REC'D.

☐ Serving Bowl
☐ Serving Platter
☐ Covered Casserole
☐ Quiche Dish

PATTERN   REC'D.

☐ Soufflé Dish
☐ Chafing Dish
☐ Soup Tureen
☐ Well & Tree Platter
☐ Gravy/Sauce Boat
☐ Bread Tray
☐ Serving Tray
☐ Tea Service
☐ Coffee Service
☐ Cream/Sugar
☐ Cake Plate
☐ Dessert Dishes (set)
☐ Compote
☐ Salt/Pepper
☐ Trivet
☐ Cheese Board
☐ Candlesticks
☐ Napkin Rings
☐ Salad Bowl
☐ Bonbon/Nut Dish
☐ Other:

Barware/Entertainment

PATTERN   REC'D.

☐ Ice Bucket
☐ Wine Cooler
☐ Decanter
☐ Pitcher
☐ Punch Bowl Set
☐ Corkscrew/Opener
☐ Jigger/Bar Tools
☐ Wine Rack
☐ Coasters
☐ Other:

Kitchenware

MANUFACTURER   MODEL

☐ Toaster
☐ Toaster Oven
☐ Coffee Maker
☐ Coffee Grinder
☐ Food Processor
☐ Blender

MANUFACTURER MODEL

- [ ] Stand Mixer
- [ ] Hand Mixer
- [ ] Deep Fryer
- [ ] Slow Cooker
- [ ] Electric Skillet
- [ ] Steamer
- [ ] Wok/Utensils
- [ ] Hot Tray
- [ ] Electric Knife
- [ ] Can Opener
- [ ] Juicer
- [ ] Microwave Oven
- [ ] Microwave Cookware
- [ ] Skillet sizes:
- [ ] Saucepan sizes:
- [ ] Ice Cream Maker
- [ ] Stock Pot
- [ ] Tea Kettle
- [ ] Dutch Oven
- [ ] Roasting Pan
- [ ] Bakeware
- [ ] Baking Dish sizes:
- [ ] Mixing Bowls
- [ ] Measuring Set
- [ ] Thermometer/Timer
- [ ] Utensil Set
- [ ] Cookbook:
- [ ] Other:

Cutlery

MANUFACTURER MODEL

- [ ] Cutlery Set
- [ ] Sharpening Tool
- [ ] Knife Block
- [ ] Other:

Electronics

MANUFACTURER MODEL

- [ ] Television
- [ ] Video System
- [ ] Stereo System
- [ ] Telephone
- [ ] Radio/Clock Radio

MANUFACTURER MODEL

- [ ] Camera Equipment
- [ ] Calculator
- [ ] Home Computer
- [ ] Other:

Home Equipment

MANUFACTURER MODEL

- [ ] Iron/Ironing Board
- [ ] Vacuum/Carpet Sweeper
- [ ] Tool Box
- [ ] Smoke Alarm
- [ ] Security Device
- [ ] Fire Extinguisher
- [ ] Sewing Machine
- [ ] Other:

Linens

MANUFACTURER STYLE QTY

TABLE SIZE:
- [ ] Formal Cloth/Napkins
- [ ] Casual Cloth/Napkins
- [ ] Place mats
- [ ] Napkins

BED SIZE:
- [ ] Flat Sheet/Fitted Sheet
- [ ] Automatic/Electric Blanket
- [ ] Pillow Case/Sham
- [ ] Blanket
- [ ] Throw Blanket
- [ ] Comforter/Duvet
- [ ] Bedspread
- [ ] Mattress Pad
- [ ] Pillows

BATH
- [ ] Bath Towel
- [ ] Hand Towel
- [ ] Face Cloth
- [ ] Bath Sheet
- [ ] Guest Towel

BATH ACCESSORIES
- [ ] Shower Curtain
- [ ] Bath Scale
- [ ] Showerhead Massage

	MANUFACTURER	STYLE	QTY
☐ Hair Dryer			
☐ Other:			

Decorative Accessories

	MANUFACTURER	STYLE
☐ Vase		
☐ Lamp		
☐ Clock		
☐ Mirror size:		
☐ Area Rug size:		
☐ Decorative Art/Object		
☐ Other:		

Luggage

	MANUFACTURER	MODEL
☐ Garment/Hanging Bag		
☐ Suitcases		

	MANUFACTURER	MODEL
☐ Duffel		
☐ Other:		

Stationery

	COLOR	STYLE
☐ Letterhead		
☐ Informals		
☐ Address Book		
☐ Other:		

General

☐ Furniture
☐ Closet/Storage System:
☐ Exercise/Sporting Equipment:
☐ Hobby:
☐ Storage/Cedar Chests
☐ Other:

YOUR DINNERWARE

Fine dinnerware or china sets the tone for a beautiful table setting. The two of you will discover a wide variety of dinnerware colors and textures. Here is information on the several types of dinnerware to help you choose.

China/Porcelain. Quality dinnerware that is durable, but made from highly refined clays and minerals. It is completely non-porous. (It won't absorb food stains.)

Bone china contains bone ash and is extremely translucent. If you hold it up to the light, you can see the silhouette of your hand through it.

Stoneware is made from coarser clays than porcelain, making it more informal in appearance. It is popular for casual designs and ovenware products.

Earthenware is made from a mixture of clays, is semi-porous and slightly less durable, usually vividly decorated.

Oven-to-tableware includes porcelains and other types of clay that have a manufacturer's guarantee that they will not chip, crack, or craze (develop fine cracks in the glaze) within a specified number of years.

Plastics are durable, chip-resistant, and often brightly decorated. Melamine, the best quality, is stain-resistant.

How Much Will We Need?

Dinnerware is usually sold in five-piece place settings. A place setting for a fine china pattern would include a dinner plate, dessert/salad plate, bread and butter plate, cup and saucer. (A casual dinnerware place setting would substitute a small bowl for the bread and butter plate.) You can register for as many place settings as you think you can use, based on how many people you usually serve when entertaining.

Most dinnerware services include soup bowls (great for pasta), vegetable dishes, platters, tea or coffee set, espresso cups, as well.

Tips For Buying Dinnerware

• Pick up cups. Consider how they feel to hold, as well as how they look. Both bride and groom should do this.

• Notice plate shapes. Is it a spacious *coupe* (rimless) or a deeper *shouldered* (rimmed) design?

• Hold up plates. Do they reflect light brightly, look smooth? Are they free from waves, bumps, or pinholes? Is bone china translucent when you hold it up to light?

• Check price and availability. "Open stock" means dinnerware—even one plate at a time—is available as long as the pattern is being manufactured. Some stores will notify you if your pattern goes on sale. If the pattern is being discontinued, and is available at a closeout sale, you may save money and complete a set, but you

DINNERWARE CHECKLIST

PATTERN NAME   Fine china _____ Everyday dinnerware _____

MANUFACTURER   Fine China _____ Everyday dinnerware _____

	FINE CHINA			EVERYDAY DINNERWARE		
	Quantity on hand	Quantity desired	Price	Quantity on hand	Quantity desired	Price
Dinner plates						
Salad plates						
Bread and butter plates						
Cups and saucers						
Fruit and cereal bowls						
Soup plates						
Cream soups						
Demitasse cups and saucers						
Vegetable serving dishes						
Platters						
Salad or serving bowl						
Gravy boat						
Butter dish						
Sugar bowl and creamer						
Teapot						
Coffeepot						
Tureen						
Salt and pepper shakers						

may not be able to replace any pieces that later break. (Your wedding gift registry may be able to steer you to companies in your area that sell discontinued patterns.)

Dinnerware Care

• Scrape leftovers off plates with a paper towel or soft brush, not a knife or any other hard utensil.

• Check manufacturer's recommendations about using a dishwasher. Most dinnerware is dishwasher safe—if you arrange dishes careful-ly. The high temperatures of the dry cycle may soften metallic banding on dishes, which may rub off if dishes touch one another, or the dish-washer rack. Do not use the heat-dry setting on the dishwasher when washing fine china.

• When hand washing, use a rubber mat or dish towel to cushion the bottom of the sink, and put a rubber nozzle on the faucet tip to pre-vent chips.

• Never use abrasive cleaners, steel wool pads, or scouring powder on dinnerware. If you wish to remove stains, rub gently with a borax cleaning compound.

• To store fine dinnerware, stand cups up straight or hang them from round hooks. Stack-ing can damage the handles. Plates are best stacked with felt protectors or paper plates be-tween them—to prevent the bottom of one plate from scratching the top of another.

• To avoid cracking, never put a cold dish in the oven unless it's marked "oven-to-tableware," and don't cook with dinnerware unless you know it's flame-proof. Metal-banded dinnerware should never be put in a microwave oven; the finish may be marred.

YOUR FLATWARE

Sterling silver has great beauty and intrinsic value that will be treasured for generations to come. Made from 925 parts pure silver and 75 parts of a mixed alloy for strength, each piece of this precious metal bears a hallmark or im-print, "sterling," and the maker's mark to attest to its value and quality. Sterling can be embel-lished by *chasing* (sculpting by hand), *embossing* (a die impression), or *engraving* (a light surface cutting).

Sterling is available in a bright mirror finish or a satin finish. In time and with regular use, silver develops a lustrous *patina*, or tiny scratches that give it a soft glow. Sterling will never wear out, and it will become more beautiful with time. Use your sterling silverware every day, with every meal, on a rotating basis, so all will tarnish less and develop a patina at the same rate. When you do polish it (perhaps twice a year), use a good quality silver-cleaning polish or bath, never a chemical dip, which may be too harsh and remove micro-thin layers of silver, as well as remove the dark antiquing added to offset the detail on certain traditional chased designs.

Sterling may go in the dishwasher if it is loosely stacked and dried by hand—to avoid the damaging heat of the dry cycle. However, some manufacturers recommend hand washing.

Store silver in a drawer or chest lined with protective, tarnish-preventing cloth. If you aren't using it often, store it in an airtight chest.

A typical six-piece place setting consists of dinner knife, dinner fork, soup spoon, salad fork, teaspoon, and butter spreader. Serving pieces are an excellent addition to your silver chest, as are demitasse spoons (for serving es-presso), luncheon knives, fish forks and knives. Remember, just as with china, you could select serving and accessory pieces in patterns differ-ent from your place settings (simple vs. ornate). Choose serving pieces separately—each with a unique personality and style.

SILVER CHECKLIST

PATTERN NAME Silver _____ Everyday flatware _____

MANUFACTURER Silver _____ Everyday flatware _____

	STERLING			EVERYDAY		
FLATWARE	Quantity on hand	Quantity desired	Price	Quantity on hand	Quantity desired	Price
Teaspoons						
Soup spoons						
Salad forks						
Butter spreaders						
Dinner knives						
Dinner forks						
Cream soup spoons						
Demitasse spoons						
Iced drink spoons						
Cocktail or oyster forks						
Steak knives						
Serving forks						
Serving spoons						
Salad servers						
Soup ladle						
Cream or sauce ladle						
Sugar tongs						
Sugar spoon						
Jelly server						
Butter server						
Pie or cake server						
Carving set						
Pasta server						
Teapot						
Coffeepot						
Sugar and creamer						
Tray						
Large platter						
Smaller platter						
Vegetable serving dishes						
Gravy boat and tray						
Sauce bowl and tray						

FLATWARE	Quantity on hand	Quantity desired	Price	Quantity on hand	Quantity desired	Price
Bread tray						
Butter dish						
Water pitcher						
Salt and pepper shakers						
Bowls for flowers, candy, fruit, etc.						
Compotes						
Candlesticks (high)						
Candlesticks (low)						
Coasters						
Cocktail shaker						
Ice bucket						
Trivets						

YOUR GLASSWARE

Glassware is either hand-blown or machine-made. When glass is **hand-blown**, it's created one piece at a time by a skilled glassblower. The result is a very fine, delicate, uniquely shaped piece of glass—a work of art. **Machine-made** glass is either blown or molded mechanically, many pieces at a time, into uniform shapes. **Cut glass** is decorated by hand-cutting on stone wheels, or it is pressed in by machine. Typical cut glass decorations include leaf or flower motifs, diamond designs, geometric patterns. **Etched glass** had fine-line, lacy patterns made by a wax and acid process. **Pressed glass** is formed in patterned molds to give the glass dimensional, raised designs. **Lime glass** is the type of glass used for inexpensive, casual glasses because it contains lime and soda, or other alkalis. **Lead crystal** contains lead oxide and other alkalis, and is used for making finer-quality goblets, vases; crystal pitchers, bowls, dishes, etc. **Full lead crystal** is the highest-quality glassware and must have a lead content of at least 24 percent in the United States. The lead gives it a characteristic brilliance and sparkle, but also softens the crystal so precise designs can be cut by hand into the crystal.

There are also **colored glasses** (produced by mixing various mineral salts with the other glass-producing materials), **milk glass** (which is an opaque white), and **cased glass** (which is coated with layers of colored glass to give it a two-tone effect).

What Glassware Will You Need?

There are two basic types of glassware: stemware (which are drinking glasses or other pieces that are on stems, such as wine glasses), and barware (which consists of drinking vessels without stems, such as glasses for everyday beverages or cocktails). You will probably start with a basic, "all-purpose" stemware shape, such as a nine-ounce goblet for wine, water, and juice; champagne flutes; and several barware styles, such as a short "old-fashioned" glass and a taller highball glass.

GLASSWARE CHECKLIST

PATTERN NAME Crystal _____ Everyday glassware _____

MANUFACTURER Crystal _____ Everyday glassware _____

	CRYSTAL			EVERYDAY GLASSWARE		
	Quantity on hand	Quantity desired	Price	Quantity on hand	Quantity desired	Price
Water goblets						
All-purpose wine						
Flute/champagne						
Fruit juices						
Iced beverages						
Old-fashioned						
Highballs						
Sours						
Cocktails						
Pilsners						
Cordials						
Brandy snifters						
Pitchers						
Decanters						
Dessert or salad bowl						
Individual plates and bowls						
Punch set						

Later you can add wine glasses in different shapes for individual wines—Bordeaux, Burgundy, white, sweet wines, sherries. Also add cordial glasses, brandy snifters, and accessories, such as decanters.

Buying Tips

• Make sure glasses feel comfortable and balanced when you hold them.

• Examine cuttings. They should be sharp, precise. Hand-cut patterns will be deeper, more exact, than machine-cut.

• Glasses should be clear and sparkling, smooth on the edges, and uniform in shape and thickness with handmade glassware. However, you may spot slight variations, such as bubbles or minor size differences. These are all a testament to their handcrafted character; they are not just regimented, machine-made objects.

Caring For Glassware

• Store glasses in cupboards—away from dust and steam. Line shelves with paper, plastic, or rubber covering to cushion against chipping.

• Stand glasses upright, not turned upside down. They were not designed to balance this way and will collect shelf odors in the bowls.

• Check with the manufacturer before putting fine glassware in the dishwasher. Generally, if glassware is thin, delicate, or has gold or platinum decorations, it should be washed by hand.

• To wash by hand, line the sink with a rubber mat or with a dish towel, or use a plastic dish pan. Put a rubber nozzle on the faucet to prevent accidental chipping. Use warm, soapy water. A drop of laundry bluing or ammonia will give glasses added luster. Rinse glassware in very warm water; drain upside down on a dish rack or heavy dish towel.

• Once almost dry, polish to a sparkle with a lint-free cloth. Cradle the bowl in your hand, rather than holding the glass by the stem; with too much stress, the stem may snap off.

• To prevent cracking, avoid sudden temperature changes—don't drop ice into a hot glass or put hot drinks into cold glasses. If you want to serve beverages, such as Irish coffee, special heat-tempered glasses are available.

YOUR LINENS

Linens refer to sheets, pillowcases, blankets, towels, as well as tablecloths, napkins, and place mats. You can list all these items in wedding gift registries at department and bed and bath stores.

Bedding

A generation or two ago, sheets were always white and needed ironing. Today, sheets come in a vast array of colors and patterns, and in a number of fabrics that eliminate the need for ironing. Here are some things to look for when buying sheets:

Fabric. The more threads per square inch, the softer and finer the sheet. Percale, a popular option, has more threads (and is thus more expensive) than muslin. Feel the fabric—but don't forget to consider its washability and durability.

Size. Sheets come in sizes to fit standard twin, double, queen, or king-size beds. The package should list the exact dimensions of the sheet; if you have doubts about the right size, measure your bed and compare.

Other bedding needs. After you've picked your sheets, look for coordinating pillowcases and shams (pillow covers); comforter and duvet (a covering for a comforter) or bedspread; bedskirt; curtains; table skirts. Extra flat sheets can be used for creating bedskirts, table skirts, shower curtains, or other accessories. You will also need blankets, mattress covers or pads, and pillows. Think about the pillow's size, content, degree of firmness, as well as accessory pillows.

Towels. Towels come in many different textures with different absorbencies. A velvety texture feels soft, but may not dry as well as a rougher-textured terry. You can coordinate towels, rug, and shower curtain. Also register for towels in different sizes: bath sheet, bath, hand, face cloth. And select guest towels—to be used when entertaining. Personalize your towels with monograms or a favorite motif.

Table Linens

Pick table linens to go with your dinnerware and dining room decor. You will probably need at least one fine linen or lace tablecloth for elegant dining, several casual ones for every day. You will probably also want a selection of place mats. Napkins are a necessity and should go with your tablecloths and place mats. However, your linens can make a strong fashion statement. Bold colors or interesting designs can change the mood of the table for each party, and give a routine table setting a face-lift. Consider getting eight or a dozen colorful, unique, inexpensive cotton napkins. When serving a casual buffet, oversize, 24-inch square napkins are the best choice for laps; team them with smaller napkins for hands and mouth. Also select cocktail napkins for the bar.

BASIC LINENS LIST

Per Bed

1 fitted mattress pad
6 sheets (fitted and flat)
2 winter-weight blankets
1 electric blanket with dual controls
pillows (as many as you like)
3 pillowcases for each pillow
comforter or duvet

Extras:

mattress covers
summer-weight blankets
bedspread or blanket and pillow protectors

Bath:

8 bath towels
8 hand towels
8 washcloths
2 bath mats
shower curtain

For Your Guests

4 sheets per bed (fitted and flat)
2 pillowcases for each pillow
1–2 blankets
2–4 sets of towels
6 fingertip towels

YOUR MONOGRAM

Once you've chosen the name you'll use after you marry, you may also want to select a monogram to personalize such things as your silver, towels, stationery.

There was a time when almost every wedding gift—from pillowcases to crystal stemware—bore a monogram. And today that trend is again popular. Worried that wedding guests won't know that you're not changing your name after marriage? List your monogram preference at the wedding gift registry.

The letters of the customary, three-part monogram are the bride's initials—that of her first name, maiden name, and new last name, in that order, provided the letters in the monogram design are all the same size. But if one letter is larger than the others, it's the new married name initial. You may want a combination of your first name initial, your husband's first name initial, and your married initial above or below the two. If you will keep your own name, you can have a joint monogram—your first and last initials stacked over his—with a decorative motif in between (similar to the second-from-the-top monogram).

Caution: If your initials spell a word like BAD or JAR, choose a monogram design in which the last initial is the center, and larger than the other two: bDa or jRa.

Where to put your monogram? Simple silver is a "natural" gift to personalize. (Many patterns even have a monogram shield.) Very ornate silver is sometimes marked on the back, although this can't be done with knives that are decorated all around. Some silver styles have their own alphabets especially designed to harmonize with them. Often the silver monogram most easily engraved is a single initial—that of your married last name. Plain linens display a monogram to the best advantage. Patterned linens usually don't show off a monogram well unless the pattern is limited to a narrow border—printed, woven, or embroidered. Some jacquard towels have plain areas in the design where the monogram may be placed to excellent advantage.

Your monogram design might vary to suit the item that will carry it. Styles range from traditional to contemporary, from ornate to tailored. Four popular ones are illustrated below:

1. Elaborate intertwined initials.
2. Block capitals in a triangle—centered with a star.
3. Tailored oval or diamond shapes.
4. Three letters not contained in a shape, with either the middle letter or the last one the largest.

OTHER APPLIANCES AND TOOLS

Depending on your cooking and entertaining needs, there are a number of small appliances you will probably want right away. List the following on your wedding gift registry: blender, electric can opener, toaster, automatic drip coffee maker, wok, food processor, miniature electric food chopper, stand or hand mixer, popcorn maker, iron, ice cream maker.

YOUR COOKWARE

Today's cookware market is seasoned with a wide variety of styles and materials. The two of you might choose from decorative ceramics, temperature-resistant glassware, and updated metals with shiny finishes or brightly colored enamel coatings. How to tell what's best? Here is a guide to cooking utensils:

Aluminum

Aluminum is the most popular cookware material because it quickly and evenly spreads heat throughout the sides and bottom of the pan. Aluminum pans are best purchased with non-stick surfaces which are non-porous, keep the heat within, and are easy to clean. Because it's lightweight, aluminum is a good choice for stock pots, roasting pans, and other large, difficult-to-handle items. The heavier the gauge (thickness) is, the more durable—and costly—the utensil.

Stainless Steel

If you're looking for exceptionally durable cookware, stainless steel is the answer. It doesn't dent, stain, or scratch, and won't corrode or tarnish permanently. Stainless steel by itself, however, is not a good heat conductor. Check to see if it is bonded or sandwiched with copper or aluminum.

Cast Iron

Cast-iron utensils are excellent for browning, frying, stewing, and baking because they absorb heat slowly and distribute it evenly. Since cast iron is porous and rough, it must be seasoned periodically to prevent rusting, keep food from sticking. Enameled cast iron has all the same advantages, but it doesn't require seasoning. Be careful not to overheat it, however, or the finish may chip or develop fine cracks.

Copper

Copper is the oldest cookware metal and the best conductor of heat. Copper serving utensils are also excellent for keeping food warm at the table. Copper items are always lined with silver, tin, stainless steel, or a non-stick finish because any direct contact with copper can cause foods to discolor and is not healthy. Polish the exteriors periodically with a commercial copper cleaner to maintain appearance.

Porcelain Enamel

Also called enameled steel, porcelain enamel is metal covered with a durable glass. Porcelain enamel combines the heat-conducting qualities of metal with an easy-care surface that won't interact with food, stain, scratch, or peel. Higher-quality versions often have stainless steel rims.

Glass and Pyroceramics

One dish that goes from freezer to oven to table is ideal for busy cooks. Glass and pyroceramic utensils fit the bill and are easy to maintain due to non-stick, non-porous surfaces. Be sure to look for a warranty against thermal breakage (due to extreme changes in temperature).

Microwave Cookware

If you two registered for a microwave, give special consideration to cookware materials. As a rule, metallic utensils cannot be used because they reflect microwaves *away*, preventing food from cooking. There are some microwave utensils that contain a combination of metal and plastic for better overall cooking. Glass, ceramic, and plastic utensils generally work well for microwave cooking.

Non-stick Surfaces

The main lure of non-stick pots and pans? They're a snap to clean! Non-stick surfaces also need little or no cooking oil. When cooking, always use wood or nylon utensils, as metals can mar the surface. Non-stick surfaces are also dishwasher safe, or can be cleaned with detergent and sponge. Be sure to recondition them, according to the manufacturer's directions.

Cookware Care

Before using your new cookware, read the manufacturer's instructions carefully. Wash utensils first in warm, sudsy water to remove manufacturing oils. Tools made of wood, plastic, or metal with a non-stick coating are less likely to scratch cookware finishes. Allow metal cookware to cool after use before immersing in water (extreme temperature changes can cause warping in some materials) and use mild detergent; abrasive cleansers can harm finishes.

Source: The Cookware Manufacturers Association, Lake Geneva, Wisconsin.

KNIVES

A good knife will last for decades. You'll be less likely to cut yourself with a sharp knife than a dull one, since it will do the job on the first try.

Knife blades are made from either high-carbon steel, stainless steel, or high-carbon stainless steel. High-carbon stainless steel is usually the best choice, since it is strong, does not rust, pit, or stain, and can be resharpened when it becomes dull. Handles, too, come in various materials. Choose one that won't become slippery when wet or greasy. Make sure the handle is tightly attached to the blade.

You will probably need at least four good knives. A **chef's knife** is a large, heavy knife for chopping whole foods. A **paring knife** is a miniature version of the chef's knife and is used for smaller cutting tasks. Use a long, thin **slicing knife** for cutting cooked meats and vegetables. A **serrated knife** has a scalloped edge and is used for cutting bread, tomatoes, or other foods with a tough skin and soft interior.

STOCKING YOUR KITCHEN

Here is a checklist of basic kitchen tools and accessories to complement your registry checklist. What you will need will depend on how much you cook and entertain.

_____ 2 saucepans: 1-qt., 2½ qt.	_____ Rolling pin
_____ 2 skillets: 8-in., 10-in.	_____ Pastry brush
_____ Double boiler	_____ Pastry blender
_____ Stockpot	_____ Flour sifter
_____ Kettle	_____ Muffin tin
_____ Dutch oven	_____ Spring form, removable bottom
_____ Roasting pan with rack	_____ Tube (angel food cake) pan
_____ 2-qt. round casserole	_____ Soufflé dish
_____ 2-qt. rectangular baking dish	_____ Quiche plate

___ 2 cake pans: 9-in. rounds	___ Molds, different sizes
___ Cookie sheets	___ Custard cups or ramekins
___ 2 loaf pans	___ Poached egg pan
___ Pie plate	___ Oven thermometer
___ Set of mixing bowls	___ Meat thermometer
___ Wooden spoons	___ Boning knife
___ Utensil set (ladle, masher, etc.)	___ Carving knife and fork
___ Wire whisk	___ Knife rack or holster
___ Rotary egg beater	___ Garlic press
___ Measuring cups and spoons	___ Egg slicer
___ Salad bowl and servers	___ Salad spinner
___ 3-knives: 3-in., 5-in., 8-in.	___ Apple corer
___ Bread knife with serrated edge	___ Bulb baster
___ Knife sharpener	___ Barbecue skewers
___ Wooden cutting board	___ Rubber bowl scrapers
___ Grater	___ Spice rack
___ Colander and strainer	___ Storage canisters or mason jars
___ Metal tongs	___ Turntable for cupboard shelf
___ Corkscrew	___ Serving trays
___ Can and bottle opener	___ Paper towel rack
___ Vegetable peeler	___ Apron
___ Reamer (citrus juicer)	___ Food processor
___ Salt and pepper mills	___ Microwave oven
___ Kitchen shears	___ Slow cooker
___ Funnels, large and small	___ Coffee grinder
___ Coffee maker	___ Juice extractor
___ 60-minute timer	___ Pressure cooker
___ Plastic storage containers	___ Deep fryer
___ Ice trays	___ Waffle iron
___ Vegetable and dish scrubbers	___ Ice cream maker
___ Dish towels	___ Wok
___ Pot holders	___ Hot tray
___ Dish drainer	___ Fondue pot
___ Drawer organizer for cutlery	___ Clay cooker
___ Wastebasket	___ Fish poacher
___ Vegetable steamer	___ Melon ball scoop
___ Blender	___ Ice cream scoop
___ Toaster or toaster oven	___ Biscuit and cookie cutters
___ Electric mixer with dough hook	___ Pastry bag and attachments
___ Kitchen scale	___ Trussing needle, lacing pins
___ Marble pastry slab	___ Cookbook holder

THANK-YOU NOTE GUIDE

• Send a written thank-you note for every gift you receive—even if you have already thanked the giver in person. (You should write thank-you notes to your fiancé and parents for their gifts, and for all that they have done to help plan your wedding.)

• Send thank-you notes within two weeks of receiving a gift that arrives before the wedding, within a month after the honeymoon for gifts received on wedding day or shortly afterward. Guests may send gifts up to one year after the wedding.

• If you are very busy, or have a large number of gifts, you can send printed cards to let givers know their gifts have been received. *Always* send a written thank-you later.

• Sign notes with your maiden name before the wedding; your married name (if you plan to use it) afterward. Never send stationery with your married name *before* the wedding.

• For the classic thank-you note, choose folded notepaper in white or ivory, and write in blue or black ink. For a personalized, contemporary look, use colorful, decorated paper, and perhaps enclose a wedding photograph.

• Encourage your groom to write thank-you notes, especially to his relatives and friends he knows well. Customarily the writer of the note signs it; the other is mentioned in the letter. (For example, "John and I love salads, and we can't wait to eat them out of such an elegant bowl." Sign the note, "Fondly, Mary.")

• A thank-you note to a married couple may be addressed to the wife (with her husband mentioned in the body of the letter), or addressed to them both.

• You can write one note to a large group (such as co-workers) who give a joint gift. Individual thank-you notes are a must for bridesmaids—even for a joint gift.

If you aren't really sure what the gift is, simply describe it.

Dear Miss Martin,

Thank you for the beautifully engraved silver piece. You can be sure John and I will give it a place of honor in our new apartment. I hope that someday our home will be as warm and personal as I've always remembered yours. Thank you again.

Sincerely,
Ann Brown Smith

If it's a joint gift, write a group note, then thank everyone in person.

Dear Coworkers,

Thank you, thank you for the place setting of china! Now John and I have service for twelve — just what we need to host the annual partners' dinner. How did you _ever_ guess? Seriously, we do appreciate it — and I can't wait to get back with our honeymoon snapshots for you to see.

with much affection,
Ann Smith

Five Quick Steps to the Perfect Thank-You Note

1. Address the note to the person who gave you the gift. Traditionally you write to the woman if it's a married couple: *"Dear Mrs. Nelson."* Or you can address both husband and wife. It's a joint gift from more than four people? Address the group as a whole: *"Dear Friends."*

2. In the first sentence, say thanks—and make sure to name the gift. *"Thank you so much for the plaid blanket you and Mr. Nelson sent."* (Notice how you mention the husband.) If you aren't sure what the gift is, simply describe it: . . . *"the lovely etched crystal piece."*

3. Mention something more about the gift— like how perfect it is for your home: *"Since we'll be moving to Vermont, the blanket is sure to keep Bob and me warm through the long winters ahead."* If the gift is money, tell what you'll put it toward. Slip your groom's name in, too.

4. Add another thought—maybe a comment about the wedding plans or a visit that will involve the gift giver: *"So glad you'll be at the wedding—you two always get everyone dancing!"* Then say thanks again.

5. Sign off. Use your maiden name before the wedding, your new married name after— both first *and* last if you don't know the gift giver well.

If you haven't met the gift-givers yet, mention a time when you might.

Dear Mrs. Robins,
    Thank you very much for the blender you and Mr. Robins sent. John tells me you always served the thickest milkshakes in town — and now we can too! I can't wait to meet you both at the wedding. Again, many thanks.
        Sincerely yours,
        Ann Brown

If it's a gift of money, let the giver know how you'll be using it.

Dear Uncle Ed,
    Thank you so much for the generous wedding check. It was a wonderful surprise. John and I have added it to savings earmarked for a car — and thanks to you, we're almost there. We'll be driving around to see you soon!
        Love,
        Ann

If it's a gift you don't like, say how clever it is. Returning it? Don't tell!

DEAR BOB AND JAN,
    THANKS SO MUCH FOR THE LAMP. THAT'S A GUM MACHINE TOO! ANN AND I HAVEN'T STOPPED TALKING ABOUT IT — AND IT'S SURE TO BE A CONVERSATION PIECE WHENEVER WE HAVE PEOPLE OVER. YOU TOO ARE ALWAYS SO CLEVER AND FUN. WE HOPE YOU'LL BE AMONG OUR FIRST GUESTS.
        YOUR PAL,
        JOHN

GIFTS FOR ATTENDANTS AND OTHERS

Traditionally the bride and groom each give their attendants identical gifts, but give the honor attendants (maid or matron of honor, best man) something special. You can, however, personalize all gift choices and give each attendant a different gift. Child attendants should get small gifts, too. Choose something appropriate for their ages.

Distribute the gifts for the bridesmaids at a bridesmaids' party, or with the ushers' gifts at the rehearsal dinner. Present your flower girl and ring bearer their gifts at a quiet time when they will appreciate them.

It is also thoughtful to give presents to various wedding helpers. The type of gift depends on how much the person did for you and how close you are. For example, old friends who hosted a dinner dance in your honor might receive a sterling silver picture frame; a neighbor who housed a bridesmaid for a night may get a house plant in a decorative basket. People you should thank with gifts include:

• friends and relatives who host wedding-related parties, such as showers, Weekend Wedding, or Progressive Wedding events
• ceremony soloists or musical performers—if they are friends; professionals are, of course, paid
• ceremony readers
• children who help pass out wedding programs or rice
• guest book attendant
• person in charge of wedding gifts at the reception
• friends who drive out-of-town guests to and from lodging, and on wedding day drive important participants and others from ceremony to reception
• out-of-town friends who offer to act as guest liaisons
• baby-sitters who are close friends

• friends who house or host wedding participants or guests
• anyone who helps in a special way, such as a friend who has studied flower arranging and gives expert advice on your floral arrangements; a co-worker who switches shifts with you so you can shop

Some couples also give their parents gifts and a loving note at wedding time—to thank them for their help in putting on the wedding, and as keepsakes of a memorable day.

Wedding gifts from parents are special and meaningful. Typically they would pass down heirloom items, such as a silver tea set or antique jewelry, or give a substantial present for the couple's new home, such as a silver flatware set or furniture. The groom's parents may wish to pay for the honeymoon as their present to the couple. Either set of parents may give money the couple can use for buying a home, car, or other large item.

Finally, the bride and groom often exchange gifts. You might give your groom a gold watch, silver cuff links, or luggage; he might give you jewelry. (Pearls are often the traditional gift.) Personalize these items by engraving or embossing them with your initials, and if possible, your wedding date, a few sentimental words.

Gift Ideas for Bride's Attendants

• leather or silver picture frame
• bracelet (gold, silver, or with stones such as onyx)
• silver compact
• perfume atomizer
• appointment or address book
• jewelry box
• crystal vase or ring holder
• pen and pencil set

Gift Ideas for Groom's Attendants

- key ring
- silver bar jigger or mug
- letter opener
- wallet
- money clip
- pen and pencil set
- Swiss Army knife
- tie clip

Gift Ideas for Child Attendants

- inexpensive jewelry
- bride and groom dolls
- tickets to circus or ice-skating show
- games
- cassette tapes
- coin bank

Gift Ideas for Other Wedding Helpers or Parents

- picture frame with a photo of the bride and groom
- laminated or framed wedding invitation
- silver plate or bowl
- crystal vase or paperweight
- fruit, cheese, or wine basket
- plant in decorative basket
- tickets to sporting event or concert
- notepaper
- gift certificate
- coffee mug set
- book
- scented soaps
- perfume bottle with favorite scent

Section 7:

FOR THE TWO OF YOU

BRIDAL BEAUTY COUNTDOWN

When preparing for a big event, timing is everything. A new type of exercise regime, a longer hairstyle, new makeup or a series of facial treatments, dental or doctors' appointments, have to be scheduled early enough to allow for fine-tuning, to get the maximum results.

Six Months Before:

• Try a new hairstyle for your wedding day and after. Show your headpiece to the stylist so your hair can be designed for it. Or choose a headpiece that goes with your chosen hairstyle.

• Get into a health routine—exercising, eating right—so that you're not run-down by wedding day.

• See a dermatologist about any existing skin problems.

Three Months Before:

• Get check-ups—dentist, doctor, gynecologist, ophthalmologist.

• Get a professional manicure; keep up the nail-care routine at home.

• Treat yourself to a facial; ask about skin-care routines to use at home.

• Experiment with new makeup looks. You can get free make-over demonstrations at most cosmetics counters. Or get a professional, personalized analysis by a makeup artist.

One Month Before:

• Schedule a makeup lesson if necessary. Buy new makeup (if you didn't after earlier analysis) which works best with your skin type and color.

• Make a hair appointment for a few weeks before the wedding and, if desired, on wedding day. A popular option is to have a hairstylist come to your home on wedding day to style your hair, as well as the bridesmaids' and your mother's hair. You might also book a makeup artist for wedding day. (Be sure you have a trial makeup application by the artist before you hire him or her.)

• Shape unruly eyebrows now so any bare spots can grow in, redness can fade.

• Try any new hair removal methods, such as waxing, depilatory, electrolysis.

Two Weeks Before:

• Treat yourself to a day at a spa or salon: massage, facial, hair removal, manicure, pedicure, hair trim and styling, last-minute advice on wedding-day makeup. Or indulge in a soothing at-home facial, perhaps a home hot oil treatment to condition your hair.

• Buy necessary cosmetics and sunscreen for your honeymoon.

• Practice walking in shoes you will wear on wedding day—to improve your posture, break in shoes for comfort, and get soles somewhat roughened so you won't slip on polished floors.

• Get a wedding-day handbag organized. It should include lipstick, blush, translucent powder, fragrance, comb or brush, as well as safety pins, hair pins, miniature sewing kit, tissue, tampons, nail polish.

The Day Before:

• Plan to have (or give yourself) a manicure, pedicure.

• Tweeze stray eyebrow hairs. Remove hair from legs, arms, underarms, bikini line, face.

• Don't skip meals (you'll need fuel to combat stress), and try to get eight hours' sleep.

On Your Wedding Day:

• Soak in a warm, scented bath. Shampoo hair.

• Powder and moisturize all over. Use a deodorant. Mist on fragrance.

• Style hair or have someone else style it.

• Touch up manicure.

• Snack on a light meal.

• Relax: lie down for 30 minutes or so.

• Apply makeup: foundation, blusher, eye shadow, mascara, lip color. Finish with a dusting of translucent powder. Use makeup techniques you have practiced—this is not the time to try a new look!

• Step into your wedding dress and shoes. Adjust headpiece.

BRIDAL TROUSSEAU

Trousseau comes from the French word *trousse*, meaning "little bundle"; the clothes and linens a bride took with her to her new home. The idea expanded into a dowry—a larger collection of possessions that made the bride more attractive in the eyes of potential suitors.

In recent generations, *trousseau* has referred to the new clothes the bride bought before her wedding (as well as other possessions, such as linens, sheets, etc., she might bring to the marriage). Marriage was a rite of passage from the girl who lived with her parents to young matron with the responsibilities of home and community. For both her honeymoon and her new life, the bride needed an entire new wardrobe.

Although many brides today already have a

wardrobe that reflects their life-style, there are still reasons why buying new clothes at this time makes sense.

• You may be moving to a different climate.

• You may be changing careers.

• You may be traveling and entertaining more; therefore quality clothes—coats, suits, day and evening dresses—are a sound investment for the future.

• You will need new clothes for your honeymoon trip, or a special going-away outfit that you can wear later on.

• You'll want special lingerie, sexy nightgowns, for your honeymoon and after. Use this chart to determine what you need.

BRIDAL TROUSSEAU CHART

	COLOR ON HAND	COLOR TO BUY	COST
COATS			
Warm			$
Lightweight			
Raincoat			
Dressy coat			
SUITS			
1.			
2.			
3.			
4.			
Blouses			
1.			
2.			
Sweaters and short jackets			
1.			
2.			
3.			
WORK DRESSES			
1.			
2.			
3.			
4.			
DRESSY DRESSES			
1.			

DRESSY DRESSES, continued

2.			
3.			
4.			

SPORTSWEAR

Pantsuits

1.			
2.			

Jackets

1.			
2.			

Pants/jeans

1.			
2.			
3.			
4.			

Shorts

1.			
2.			
3.			

Skirts

1.			
2.			
3.			

Shirts

1.			
2.			

Shirts, continued

3.			
4.			

Sweaters

1.			
2.			
3.			

ACTIVE SPORTSWEAR

Tennis dress			

Swimsuits

1.			
2.			

Beach cover-ups

1.			
2.			

Ski pants

1.			
2.			

Parka

1.			
2.			

Leotard/Exerciseware

1.			
2.			

Other

1.			
2.			

LINGERIE

Bras

1.			
2.			
3.			
4.			
strapless			

other (camisole, garter belt, bustier, etc.)

1.			
2.			

Panties

1.			
2.			
3.			
4.			
5.			
6.			
7.			

Slips

1.			
2.			
3.			
4.			
full length			

half slips

1.			
2.			

LINGERIE, continued

Nightgowns

short			
short			
long			
long			

Robes

short			
long			

ACCESSORIES

Shoes

1.			
2.			
3.			
4.			
5.			

Boots

1.			
2.			

Sandals

1.			
2.			

Gloves/mittens

1.			
2.			
3.			
4.			

ACCESSORIES, continued

Hats

1.			
2.			
3.			

Belts

1.			
2.			
3.			

Scarves

1.			
2.			
3.			

Other

1.			
2.			
3.			

Hosiery

pantyhose			
knee-hi's			
sport socks			

Handbags

1.			
2.			
3.			

Luggage

large suitcase			

Luggage, continued			
wardrobe			
weekender			
cosmetic case and tote bag			
dress bag/hanging bag			
other			

TOTAL COST OF NEW TROUSSEAU CLOTHES $ _____

WHAT'S YOUR NAME?

As a bride, you have a choice. Once you're a married woman, you can use your husband's last name, retain your maiden name, hyphenate both names, or use combinations of these alternatives. Although you have a legal right to change your name when you marry—it's not required.

You can base your decision on many things—among them: ease of pronunciation and spelling, professional status, a desire to follow custom, a wish to carry on the family name. Here are the options and what they require.

Taking your husband's name. Start by signing the name you want to use on your marriage certificate, and begin using it on all documents thereafter. You will have to record the name change on all legal and official records, including:
- Social Security
- passport
- tax forms
- driver's license
- will
- checking and savings accounts
- voter registration
- stock and bond certificates
- employee ID
- post office address
- credit cards
- magazine subscriptions
- professional associations and clubs

Begin by changing the two most important documents—Social Security number and driver's license—which may require a visit to local offices and presentation of your marriage certificate. Thereafter, write in your new name on statements and bills, see your lawyer, banker, to update records.

Keeping your maiden name. If you plan to keep your maiden name, you don't have to notify any official agencies, just write your name as before. However, in Alabama, you must fill out a special form to keep your maiden name. In Hawaii, your official name is the one you sign on the marriage certificate.

Using your maiden name at work, your husband's name socially. This is a popular option, but can cause problems if you use two different names on legal documents, as well. For example, if you have a Social Security number in your maiden name, and then file taxes under your married name, the Internal Revenue Service (IRS) may request a notarized copy of your marriage license. You also may have to explain your identity when buying property jointly, when using your husband's credit card, and when attending parties that include your business associates *and* your husband's friends. Many women don't consider it an inconvenience, however. One prominent New York City lawyer kept her name professionally and legally, and only uses her husband's name when she calls her children's school. Friends of the couple know *both* her names.

Using your maiden name as a middle name. If your name is Mary Anne Jones and you marry Bill Smith, you might call yourself Mary Jones Smith (rather than Mary Anne Smith). This will enable you to use your maiden name *and* your married name, and preserve your independent credit rating. One traditional way to carry your family name into future generations is to make it the middle name of each child.

Hyphenate your names. Both husband and wife may decide to change their names: Mary Anne Jones-Smith and Bill Jones-Smith. Record the name change with the same agencies listed under "Taking your husband's name" (earlier in this section), or get it changed by court order. In most states, it's as easy for a man to change his name as it is for a woman. However, since state laws vary, check with your local county clerk. (Note: If your last names are long, hyphenating them may prove cumbersome when filling out standardized forms, or when making introductions.)

Alternate ideas: Today some grooms adopt their wife's family name after marriage. Or, together, the couple legally may adopt a completely new married name.

Informing others of your name. Here are some helpful ways to spread the news to family, friends, and business associates:

• Use the name you've chosen on personal stationery, letterhead, business cards, in all correspondence.

• Send at-home cards. These are printed cards listing your names and address, which can be enclosed with wedding invitations or announcements, or with thank-you notes.

• For business, you might want to send out announcement cards that read, for example, "Mary Anne Jones has taken the surname of Smith."

• Note in your newspaper wedding announcement, "The bride will keep her own name."

• If you are keeping your maiden name, introduce yourself as "Mary Anne Jones, Bill Smith's wife," at social gatherings.

• Have your husband use your last name when introducing you.

• Respond to misaddressed invitations in your maiden name: "Mary Ann Jones and Bill Smith will gladly attend."

• Take inevitable slipups in stride. Tactfully correct the person, or just let it pass at an informal gathering.

Give Yourself Some Credit!

Did you know that—single or married—it's important for a woman to establish credit in her own name? If all of her accounts read "Mr. and Mrs." a wife may have no identity of her own in the eyes of her creditors. A bank doesn't know that "Mrs. Jones" is the same person who paid off a college loan and managed five charge accounts as "Mary Smith." If a woman ever needs money (to start her own business, to put toward a house), it helps if she's earned her own credit rating. How do you do it?

Use one name in all your financial dealings. It might be Mary Smith or Mary Smith Jones. It should not be Mrs. John Jones.

Maintain your own bank and charge accounts. Expect to be treated as an individual. If a bank or card issuer wants to know about your husband's income or credit standing, tell them it's irrelevant since the account is yours, not his.

Insist that creditors keep separate files on each of you. If you open any kind of joint account—it's your legal right. Make sure a separate credit card is issued to you, not just an "authorized user" card for his account.

TIME TO TALK ABOUT . . .

While wedding planning may be taking up all your thoughts and time right now, it's important to remember that while the wedding will last only one day, the marriage should last a lifetime.

Many counselors agree that one major cause of trouble in marriage is unfulfilled expectations and disparate goals. We each have certain expectations about what married life will be like. Some of these expectations are spoken of, others are secret—even to ourselves. When an expectation is not met, there is bound to be disappointment, resentment, and the foundations of the marriage may be shaken.

For example, though Charles and Maggie set a goal of moving out of their small city apartment after the wedding, they had different ideas of what that meant. Charles assumed Maggie shared his dream of married life in a suburban house with a lawn; he thought a family would soon follow. Maggie thought they were saving for a two-bedroom condominium in the same city, convenient to their two busy careers. Babies were many years ahead in her future plans. Neither could understand why the new home search they'd agreed upon prompted the worst fights they'd ever had.

Tom and Angela thought they'd settled their style of living before the wedding. Both agreed that leisure time was very important and that they'd take wonderful vacations. However, they failed to discuss what each meant by "wonderful." Angela pictured European trips abroad that would take them far away from the everyday, and adventures they could recount to their future children. Tom's idea of wonderful was a small cabin at a nearby lake where he could read, fish, and contemplate nature in peace and quiet. When he suggested this idea, Angela was hurt that he seemed to be going back on their "wonderful vacation" agreement. Tom couldn't understand why she thought long plane trips and the stress of trying to get around in a foreign country were relaxing.

The questions in the following areas are starting points for a discussion on the important aspects of married life.

Money

• Will we pool our incomes into one fund?

• Will we have a joint checking account or separate ones?

• Should we each have money of our own?

• Will one of us be the chief bookkeeper, or will we share the responsibility?

• Do we have a budget? How much money should we set aside monthly for an emergency fund?

• Are we saving money for a major purchase such as a house?

• Do my partner's saving and spending habits bother me?

• What do we estimate our incomes to be in five years?

Career

- Will we both work full-time?
- Would either of us willingly move if the other was transferred or found a better job in another city?
- How many hours a day will we each work?
- Will we have many professional meetings outside regular business hours?
- Will we share housework? How?

Children

- Do we want children? If so, when?
- If not in the near future, do we plan to discuss our decision again?
- Are we content with our method of birth control?
- If we have children, who will take care of them?
- What maternity/paternity leave and child care benefits do our companies offer?
- Will one of us have more responsibility for day-to-day child raising?
- If we found we were infertile, would we consider adoption?

Sex

- Are we open with each other about sexual preferences and needs?
- Are we content with the frequency of sex?
- If a sexual problem developed, would we seek professional help?

Leisure Time

- Will we spend all of our free time together, or schedule time apart?
- What leisure activities do we plan to pursue in the coming years?
- What alternatives are there if one of us does not enjoy the other's favorite activity?
- Where will we take our vacations?
- How much money and time will we spend on leisure activities?
- If we have children, will they accompany us or will we take vacations without them?

Friends

- Will one partner be more responsible for social activities, such as party planning?
- Will we maintain close friendships outside the marriage, or do we expect to be each other's best friend?
- Is it acceptable to each of us that we allot time alone to be with friends?
- Will we share time with each other's friends, whether we like them or not?
- Do I object to my partner having a close friend of the opposite sex?

Relatives

- How often do we plan to see our respective families?
- Which family will we visit on which holidays? Will we visit both?
- Does one of us think the other spends too much time with parents or relatives?
- Do I think my partner is too influenced by his or her parents?
- Would we mind having a parent live with us someday?

Religion

- Will we attend religious services regularly? Together?
- Which religious traditions, if any, will we observe at home?
- Will we raise our children in a particular faith?
- Will we attend religious services more regularly, become more observant, after our children are born?

FAMILY PLANNING GUIDE

To find the right contraceptive for you, first study the chart below. Then consult your doctor.

Method	Availability	Reliability
HORMONE PILLS	Require a doctor's prescription. Yearly check-up, including Pap test, breast exam, and blood pressure test recommended. Fees for initial examination, regular checkups, and pills.	Combination pills virtually 100% effective when taken according to directions. Mini-pills (no estrogen) slightly less effective.
INTRAUTERINE DEVICE (IUD)	Available only through doctor. Fee for device insertion and follow-up visit. Annual check-ups are also necessary. Hormone-releasing device and IUDs using copper must be replaced periodically; check with doctor.	About as effective as mini-pills, as long as the device remains in place.
DIAPHRAGM	Requires a doctor's prescription and fitting. Besides the physician's fee, you pay for the diaphragm and the spermicidal jelly or cream used with it.	Very effective when used properly. (Jelly or cream protects if diaphragm is displaced during sex.) Must be refitted every year or so, after pregnancy, or with marked gain or loss of weight.
CERVICAL CAP	Requires a prescription and fitting from a specially trained doctor or clinician. Besides the examination fee there are costs for the cervical cap, the spermidical jelly or cream.	Very effective when properly fitted and used correctly. Since the cap can hold only a small amount of jelly or cream, these chemicals offer little added protection. Must be refitted every few years, especially after pregnancy.

How It Works	Advantages	Disadvantages
Most regimens require one pill taken orally for 21 consecutive days each month to suppress ovulation. During the next seven days, no pill (or an inert pill that maintains routine) is taken. Mini-pill is taken every day.	Pill taking not related to intercourse. Except for mini-pill, nearly 100% effective in preventing pregnancy. Fewer menstrual problems. Decreases risk of tubal infections—a common cause of infertility.	Possible nausea, headaches, weight gain, or breakthrough bleeding. There's a link between the pill and blood clots, heart attack, liver or gall bladder disease. Higher risk after 35, especially for smokers.
Presence of an IUD in the uterus prevents pregnancy—probably by interfering with fertilization.	Second most effective method. Once inserted, an IUD requires user to check occasionally to make sure device is in place. Does not affect pleasure of couple.	IUD may be expelled, cause discomfort, bleeding. Some risk of perforation of uterus, tubal pregnancy, spontaneous abortion, or pelvic infection that, in rare cases, may cause infertility.
A flexible rubber dome is inserted into the vagina prior to intercourse to cover the cervix and prevent sperm from entering the uterus. Sperm are immobilized by jelly or cream. Diaphragm must be left in place six hours after intercourse.	High level of protection with virtually no risk to health or interference with sexual pleasure of either partner during intercourse (insertion can be a bedtime routine).	Some women have pelvic conditions that rule out use. It may become dislodged if woman's on top during intercourse. The need to add more cream or jelly prior to repeated intercourse may inhibit spontaneity.
A thimble-shaped rubber cap with a firm rim is placed on the cervix to snugly cover the opening and prevent sperm from entering the uterus. The cap may be left in place for 48 hours. Not to be used when there is vaginal bleeding.	High level of protection, similar to that of the diaphragm, with virtually no risk to health or interference with sexual pleasure. Can be left in place for 48 hours. No need to add more cream or jelly prior to repeated intercourse.	Some women have cervical conditions that rule out use. More difficult than the diaphragm to fit, place, and remove, the cap also may become dislodged.

Method	Availability	Reliability
CONTRACEPTIVE SPONGE	No prescripton or examination necessary. Sponge, called Today, sold in drugstores and some super-markets.	Less effective than prescription methods, such as birth control pills, IUD. Thought to be about as effective as vaginal contraceptives or condom. Highly effective when used with condom.
CONDOM	No prescription necessary. Varies in cost. Available in drugstores, supermarkets.	About as effective as a diaphragm when used carefully, consistently. Some failures from slippage, puncture.
OTHER VAGINAL PRODUCTS	No prescription or examination necessary. Sold in drugstores.	Varies with type of product. Highly effective when used with condom.
FERTILITY AWARENESS METHODS (FAM)	Available to anyone at no cost (except for ovulation and temperature calendars, basal thermometer). Must learn to calculate fertile period. (Variations in cervical mucus, body temperature, will help.) Consultation with doctor advised.	Varies with system used and with accuracy and consistency of records kept; generally less effective than other methods mentioned above.

How It Works	*Advantages*	*Disadvantages*
The polyurethane sponge (with bottom loop for removal) contains spermicide. It is inserted into vagina prior to intercourse to block the cervix. Sperm are immobilized by spermicide in sponge. Must be in place at least six hours after intercourse.	Good degree of pregnancy prevention. Can be inserted several hours before intercourse. One sponge may be used for multiple acts of intercourse over a 24-hour period.	Sensitivity to chemicals sometimes causes irritation. Possible risk of Toxic Shock Syndrome when not used according to directions.
A thin sheath worn by the man during intercourse keeps sperm out of the vagina. A spermicidal barrier in the vagina can give extra protection.	High degree of protection against pregnancy. Latex condoms provide the best protection against sexually transmitted diseases.	Interrupts sexual foreplay for some. Less direct genital contact may interfere with sex. Allergy to rubber in rare cases.
Spermicidal jellies, creams, suppositories (including VCF, a film), or tablets are placed in the vagina shortly before intercourse to immobilize sperm.	Good to fair degree of pregnancy prevention without a prescription. Relatively low cost. No known health hazards to either partner. Because of better dispersion, foam may be more effective.	The need to use before each act of intercourse may inhibit spontaneity. Tablets and suppositories must dissolve in vagina before intercourse. Sensitivity to chemicals may cause irritation. Tends to be messy.
Couples abstain a certain number of days—before, during, and after a woman's ovulation—usually amounting to at least one week of cycle.	No health risks or side effects for either partner. Only birth control method offically sanctioned by Roman Catholic Church.	Continuous recording of dates of menstrual cycles, and/or mucus consistency, and temperature required. Must note conditions (stress, illness) that may change cycle regularity.

Method	Availability	Reliability
STERILIZATION	Male: Vasectomy is a minor operation, usually in doctor's office under a local anesthetic. Female: Tubal sterilization with hospital costs.	Male: Virtually fail-safe once the doctor has confirmed the absence of sperm in the ejaculate. Female: Virtually safe from pregnancy at all times.

Safe and legal abortion is available in all 50 states. Although abortion should not be considered a method of family planning, a pregnancy might pose a threat to a woman's health and she may elect termination. For a free copy of a birth control chart by the U.S. Food and Drug Administration, write: F. James, Dept. 544P, Consumer Information Center, Pueblo, CO 81009.

PRENUPTIAL AGREEMENTS

Do you need a prenuptial agreement? Prenuptial agreements or contracts have been drawn up primarily in instances where one or both partners are very wealthy or where children's estates must be protected. Today, however, couples in all income brackets are signing agreements that specify their goals and desires in important areas such as money, children, leisure time, even housework. To be sure, couples must *talk* about these things. But many couples and counselors feel that *writing out* a prenuptial contract is too much like negotiating for a divorce. Since every marriage has its rules (spoken and unspoken), you might want to summarize the results of your premarital discussions in writing. Provisions such as who will do housework are morally enforceable between the two of you, but probably can't be enforced by law. Only the financial aspects of a pre-wedding contract can stand up in court.

There are some circumstances when prenuptial agreements are useful:

• You have children from a previous marriage and want to protect their inheritances.

• You have property (such as family antiques) or income you want to keep separate.

• You would like to make sure your spouse will not accept a job transfer for a specified period of time, while you develop your career or finish school.

• You want to outline a unique arrangement—he will be a househusband, you will be the breadwinner.

• You want to specify that, in case of divorce, one or both partners will not seek alimony.

How do we create a prenuptial agreement? Start by discussing important marital concerns, especially finances. Determine if you both would feel more comfortable having your decisions and plans in writing. Will you need a legal contract, or will a personal agreement do? You can keep a contract as a personal document, but for any financial dealings, you should each have a lawyer. When you get married, the laws of your state automatically create certain contractual responsibilities on how property is divided—you may find that these laws already fit your needs. An enforceable agreement is gen-

	How It Works	*Advantages*	*Disadvantages*

How It Works
Male: The tubes (vas) which carry sperm are blocked. Female: Tubes through which egg travels to uterus are closed off. For both, there is no impairment of sexual functioning.

Advantages
Contraception is separated from the sexual act. The only method designed to provide permanent and complete birth control.

Disadvantages
Reversal of male or female operation is difficult, and fertility is often not restored. Female: Standard tubal ligation may be performed shortly after childbirth or abortion, or combined with other surgery, and must be arranged well in advance.

Consultant: Louise Tyrer, M.D., Planned Parenthood.

erally one that requires fair dealing between parties—in other words, disclosure of all assets.

Another person to consult with is a financial planner or accountant. Depending on your state's laws and tax regulations, it may make more sense to keep property in one person's name, put it in both your names, or even make a gift of property to your spouse. A financial planner can help you create a spending and saving strategy for your marriage, help smooth out economic differences.

Once you draw up your contract, it's a good idea to specify a time to review and revise if necessary (e.g., every two years).

YOUR MARRIAGE LICENSE

Every state has different regulations regarding the issuance of marriage licenses. Find out what yours requires at the town hall or town clerk's office in the county where you will marry.

Blood tests. Many (but not all) states require blood tests for venereal diseases; some may require counseling for genetic diseases such as sickle cell anemia, others mandate rubella tests for women. (Rubella can cause birth defects if contracted during pregnancy.)

At least 12 states require that couples receive information about AIDS (Acquired Immune Deficiency Syndrome) and/or are offered an HIV antibody blood test to determine if they have the virus. Check with your own state to find out if any requirements about AIDS and marriage licenses exist. Or contact the AIDS Policy Center Intergovernmental Health Policy Project at George Washington University in Washington, DC. (202-676-8144) for up-to-date information. If you both plan to have HIV antibody blood tests, do so at least three months in ad-

MARRIAGE LICENSE CHECKLIST

Date we go for the marriage license _____ Time _____

Office of City Clerk _____

      Building _____

      Address _____

      Phone _____ Fee $ _____

We both need

_____ Identification (Driver's license,   _____ Rubella, sickle cell anemia, or other
         birth certificate)   blood test

_____ Proof of age   _____ AIDS blood test

_____ Citizenship papers   _____ AIDS counseling

_____ Doctor's certificate   _____ Proof of divorce

_____ Venereal disease blood test

Waiting period _____ License is valid _____ days

---

vance of the wedding. Results do not come for six to eight weeks.

Your own doctor or a clinic in your neighborhood can perform standard blood tests for marriage licenses, or the marriage license bureau can recommend a doctor or clinic that specializes in processing these tests quickly. Find out how long the results are valid.

Other requirements. You will probably need to bring *proof of identification* (a birth certificate, passport, or driver's license) and *proof of parental consent* if you are under age (in most cases, 18). If you were not born in the United States, you will probably need *proof of citizenship*; and if you are divorced, you may need *proof of the divorce*. You will also have to pay a fee (costs vary, so check before you go); some bureaus accept only cash.

Remember that . . . A marriage license doesn't mean that you're married. A civil or religious official licensed by the state still has to sign the license for you two to be legally wed.

There is usually a "cooling-off" period—a few days between the issuing of the license and the time it becomes valid. The validity of blood test results also expires after a certain period. Take all these factors into account when you choose the time to get your license.

Getting your marriage license is a major step closer to marriage. Celebrate with a festive lunch for the two of you, a champagne dinner.

Section 8:

CEREMONY AND RECEPTION TIMETABLES

WEDDING REHEARSAL

How will everyone know where to go and what to do at the wedding ceremony? All wedding ceremony mysteries will be solved at the wedding rehearsal. The ceremony officiant is in charge: He or she walks everyone through the ceremony and explains each participant's role. (The actual marriage service is not read at the rehearsal, however.)

It would be preferable if everyone could gather a few days before the wedding to rehearse and enjoy a relaxed rehearsal dinner that same evening. But these days, participants often travel long distances and arrive only a day or two before the ceremony. It's more convenient if the rehearsal and traditional dinner are held the night before.

Other tips for a successful wedding rehearsal:
• Discuss ideas for personalizing your ceremony at premarriage meetings with your clergymember; don't wait until the rehearsal to suddenly get creative.
• Go over plans with parents and participants in advance, especially when there are spe-

cial variations. For example, if you would like your mother to participate in the "giving away," make sure she's comfortable with the idea early on, rather than surprising her at the rehearsal.
• Bring along a *faux* bouquet (made of gift ribbons from the shower) to practice handing to your honor attendant when you reach the altar.
• Anyone who has a unique role, such as lighting a Unity Candle, should attend the rehearsal and practice his or her part. Make sure the person knows exactly at what point in the ceremony he or she will perform.
• Brief ushers on seating instructions and special duties such as spreading an aisle runner. They should also know important facts about the facility—such as the location of rest rooms or coat racks—and have directions to the reception site.
• Before the rehearsal is over, repeat instructions, times and places participants should gather. Ask if there are any questions and answer them on the spot.
• Have clergymember check the marriage license.

WEDDING CEREMONY TIMETABLE

Wedding day is here! Use this schedule to make sure all last-minute details are covered, and that everyone does the right thing at the right time. It is based on a formal wedding that is 15 minutes away from the bride's home. Adjust it if you live more than 15 minutes away from the ceremony site.

Wedding Morning

• Reconfirm plans with caterer, florist, photographer, musicians. Double-check that they know correct times and locations.

• Finish last-minute packing.

• Give the bride's wedding ring to the best man to hold at the altar.

• Make sure the outfits you both will wear when leaving the reception are ready and are brought to the reception site, if you intend to change there.

• Eat a small meal. It may be many hours before a reception meal is served, and by then you may be too busy to eat much.

TWO HOURS TO GO The bride starts dressing with the help of her mother and honor attendants. If any bridesmaids are dressing at home, they put on their outfits now.

ONE HOUR TO GO Attendants who've gotten ready elsewhere join the bride at her home to have pictures taken and pick up flowers. Parents should finish dressing too, so family photos can be taken.

45 MINUTES TO GO Musician(s) starts playing introductory music in the church or synagogue. Meanwhile ushers escort guests to their seats, starting with the rows in the main aisle, behind those kept for family. Bridal attendants and mother leave home for the wedding.

20 MINUTES TO GO Groom and best man arrive and await the bridal party in the vestibule. Clergymember gives any last-minute instructions to the groom and ushers. Bride and her father leave for the wedding.

10 MINUTES TO GO Bridal attendants arrive, followed by bride's mother, groom's parents, other close family members. Wedding party and family wait in the vestibule. Relatives are shown to reserved seats.

5 MINUTES TO GO Groom's parents are seated in the front row on the right (left, if a Jewish ceremony) of the main aisle. Bride and her father arrive about this time, and join the wedding party. Any late-coming guests who are waiting are seated. The last person to take her place is the bride's mother. Musical solo begins.

ONE MINUTE TO GO Two ushers lay the aisle runner. The same two ushers should readjust the aisle ''ropes'' after the bride's mother is in her seat. They then return to the vestibule for the procession.

CEREMONY TIME Clergymember takes his or her position at the front of the church. Groom, accompanied by best man, stands ready. The processional music begins, and ''Here Comes *the Bride*!''

PROCESSIONAL AND RECESSIONAL DIAGRAMS

FORMAL PROCESSIONAL (CHRISTIAN) The priest/minister awaits the procession at the altar next to the best man, then the groom. The ushers begin the procession in pairs, followed by pairs of bridesmaids. The maid of honor walks down the aisle after them, followed by the flower girl and ring bearer, side by side (girl to left, boy to right). The bride comes down the aisle last, escorted by her father, to her right.

CHRISTIAN WEDDING (AT THE ALTAR) The bride (center, left) and groom (center, right) stand together facing the priest/minister with their honor attendants at their other sides. Left and slightly behind the bride stands her father. The flower girl stands in front of the row of bridesmaids. Behind the best man is the ring bearer, followed by a row of ushers.

CHRISTIAN WEDDING RECESSIONAL The bride, to her groom's right, begins the recessional, followed, in pairs, by the flower girl and ring bearer, maid of honor and best man, and bridesmaids and ushers, all women to the men's right.

A longer procession that includes the bride's and groom's parents and grandparents, if desired (a Jewish custom), lines up like this:

FORMAL FAMILY PROCESSIONAL (JEWISH) The cantor (left) and rabbi (right) await the procession at the altar. The bride's grandparents (woman on right, man on left) walk down the aisle first, followed by the groom's grandparents. Next are pairs of ushers followed by the best man. The groom is then escorted by his father on his left, his mother to his right. The bridesmaids follow in pairs, with the maid of honor behind them. Last is the bride, escorted by her parents, with her father to her left, her mother to her right.

JEWISH WEDDING (AT THE ALTAR, PARENTS INCLUDED) The bride (center, right) and groom (center, left) face the rabbi at the altar, with the maid of honor and best man at their immediate sides. Next in line, on either side, are their respective parents (mothers closest to couple), followed by the bridesmaids to the right and the ushers to the left.

DOUBLE WEDDING PROCESSIONAL Both sets of ushers begin the procession in pairs, followed by pairs of bridesmaids and the honor attendant of the first bride. The bride is escorted by her father on her right side. Following the first wedding party are the pairs of bridesmaids and honor attendant for the second bride, who is escorted by her father on her right side.

DOUBLE WEDDING RECESSIONAL *The two couples (bride to the groom's right) walk down the aisle followed by their attendants in pairs, with women to the men's right.*

PROCESSIONAL/RECESSIONAL VARIATIONS

If the bride's parents are divorced, her father can take his place in the third pew after walking her down the aisle, rather than sitting with her mother (his ex-wife). If the bride is closer to her stepfather, however, she might prefer to be escorted by him down the aisle. Or she might choose another relative, such as her brother or grandfather. In the Jewish procession, both parents walk the bride and groom down the aisle. If parents are divorced, it is usually the parent and stepparent who raised the bride or groom.

If the bride's father has died, her stepfather, brother, uncle, other close relative, family friend, or usher can escort her. The bride's mother may also "give her away." She can do this by remaining in her seat and nodding or saying, "I do," at the appropriate time in the ceremony. Or the best man can escort her to the bride's side at the right moment. Another option: The bride's mother can be the one to walk up the aisle with the bride and stand at the altar until the appropriate moment.

If yours is an informal wedding, guests will seat themselves. When it's time for the ceremony to begin, the bride and groom, the honor attendant, and the best man all take their appointed places in front of the judge or clergy. At the end of a short ceremony, the recessional is usually eliminated, and the couple turn to greet their guests.

THE RECEIVING LINE

Must we have a receiving line? A receiving line is a good idea at all but the smallest, most informal weddings. It provides one certain opportunity for greeting *all* guests—at a large reception you may not have time to talk to everyone. And it provides guests an opportunity to wish you and your new husband well, and to speak to other members of the wedding party.

Even at a large reception, the receiving line can be made to move faster by eliminating bridesmaids from the main line. (You can form a separate attendants' line nearby.) Urge participants to avoid long conversations. Although some waiting is unavoidable, guests can be made as comfortable as they would at any cocktail party. Have waiters serve drinks and hors d' oeuvres, provide seats, and set up musicians or other entertainment close by.

When and where should we have the receiving line? The receiving line is traditionally held near the entrance to the reception site, in an area where guests can move easily. There can also be a receiving line at the ceremony site for greeting guests as they file out of the church or synagogue. Assemble the line quickly. Many brides schedule photography sessions prior to the receiving line, which causes a tedious delay for guests eager to see the newlyweds. Take photographs before the ceremony, at a later point in the reception, or both. If you must have photographs taken before the receiving line, tell your photographer and participants ahead of time so they can be done as quickly as possible.

Who stands in the receiving line? Traditionally the receiving line starts with the bride's mother as hostess, followed by the groom's mother, the bride, the groom, the honor attendant(s), and finally the bridesmaids. If fathers join the line, each stands to the left of his wife. Fathers, however, as well as male attendants, traditionally mingle with guests rather than stand in the receiving line. Child attendants do not participate.

What if your parents are divorced? It's probably easiest to leave fathers out of the line. If you want to include your stepmother, as well as your mother, she could stand on the groom's left. Remember that each family situation is in-dividual—ask parents and stepparents what would make them feel most comfortable.

If the reception is hosted by persons other than the bride's parents, they would head the receiving line. The father and a grandmother, sister, or aunt could be first in line if she has no mother or stepmother.

What do we say in the receiving line? This

RECEPTION TIMETABLE

Here is a timetable for a three-hour buffet reception. Yours may be shorter or longer, so while the order of events will remain about the same, the time between them will vary. Fill in estimated times for your reception, then appoint a close friend or relative to oversee this schedule and make sure caterer, florist, musicians, photographer, are on track.

_____ You and all members of the wedding party arrive at the reception site.

The first half hour:

_____ Bridal party gathers for a few quick photos, while musicians start to play.

The second half hour:

_____ Bridal party forms the receiving line; guests begin to walk through it. Drinks are poured. Guests mingle, pick up table-seating cards, if any.

After one hour:

_____ Dinner is announced. Wedding party is seated. Guests line up for buffet. Wedding party is served. Best man proposes first toast. Musicians continue playing.

After one and one-half hours:

_____ First course is cleared from head ta-ble. Musicians strike up dance music; tradi-tional first dance begins. Main course is served.

After two hours:

_____ Tables are cleared. Musicians signal time for cake-cutting ceremony. Cake is cut. Dancing music resumes. Dessert is served.

The last half hour:

_____ Bride and groom throw the bouquet and garter.

_____ Bride and groom slip away to change, say good-bye to parents.

_____ Bride and groom run out to their car in a shower of rice. Honeymoon time!

_____ Parents signal musicians to stop play-ing, bar to close. Parents bid farewell to guests.

RECEIVING LINE ORDER <u>Left to right</u>: Bride's mother, groom's mother, groom's father, bride, groom, honor attendant, bridesmaids, (ushers, optional). (The bride's father, as the host, circulates among guests, but may stand to his wife's left in the line.)

is the time for guests to meet the whole wedding party, so introductions are in order. The bride's mother might say to the bride's new mother-in-law, "Martha, I'd like you to meet Jane's roommate, Mary Smith." The groom's mother would say a few words, then give the bride a chance to greet her friend and, if necessary, introduce her to her groom. To keep the line moving, limit your conversations—thank guests for coming, tell them how happy you are to see them, or comment on wedding events.

Here, receiving line tips:

• The two of you should go over the guest list with your parents, so all names will be fresh in your minds.

• Introduce yourself if you don't know a guest. The person will most likely offer his or her name in return.

• Leave gloves off. If you're worried about sweaty palms, lightly apply antiperspirant to them prior to receiving line formation.

• In addition to providing food and drink for guests waiting in line, consider entertainment, like music or a photo display of the bride and groom as children.

RECEPTION SEATING ARRANGEMENTS

At most receptions, the bride and groom sit at a head table in full view of the guests. A bridal table is optional, however; some couples prefer to mingle with guests and distribute wedding party participants as hosts at a number of "honor tables." Here is the seating order at a typical bride's table:

At a small wedding, the spouses of married attendants, parents of the bride and groom, and ceremony officiant and spouse may join the bride's table.

There is usually a parents' table or two (diagram below). You could create two parents' tables: one for the groom's parents and their relatives, and one for the bride's parents and their relatives. If parents are divorced, it's best to seat them at separate tables. Each parent is seated with his or her spouse, family, and friends.

Guests are usually happiest when seats are assigned. That way they know you have thought about them, and have seated them with people they would enjoy. Perhaps the bride's and groom's relatives will like sharing a table. You might also want to have a children's table (with games and toys) or a singles' table for unmarried guests. Married couples customarily sit at the same table, but not necessarily next to each other.

If you have arranged reception seating, you or a calligrapher will write the guest's name on a card with a table number. These "escort" cards are placed on a table near the entrance.

You might also have place cards at each guest's seat with names on both sides of the card, written legibly and large enough so others can read them across the table.

RECEPTION SEATING <u>At the head table:</u> *The bride and groom sit in the center. (Groom is at bride's left.) The best man is to the bride's right, the maid of honor to the groom's left. Bridesmaids and ushers alternate seating on either side of the table.*

At the parents' table: The bride's mother and father sit opposite each other (here, far left and right). The groom's mother, a guest of honor, sits on the father of the bride's right. On the mother of the bride's right, the clergymember or the groom's father is seated. If it is the clergymember, the groom's father is seated on the mother of the bride's left (shown here). In the remaining seats are the clergymember's spouse (to his/her right), grandparents, or special, out-of-town relatives.

RECEPTION SEATING WORKSHEET

Use this space to draw reception tables, determine who sits where.

THE GUEST BOOK

A guest book is a keepsake that records the names of your wedding guests. Available in stationery stores, a guest book should have space for guests to write sentimental messages, as well. One practical idea: Use a new address book as your guest book. Each guest will sign in—and provide an address and phone number!

You can place your guest book on a table near the entrance to your reception site or at the end of the receiving line (in which case, the last person in the receiving line can direct guests to the book). A friend or usher can circulate the book later in the reception to make sure everyone signs it.

THE FIRST DANCE

The traditional "first dance" is your first as husband and wife. But there's no reason why your guests shouldn't begin dancing as soon as the receiving line is over and the music starts playing. After you've caught your breath from greeting the guests, there is a pause in the music, the floor clears, and the bride and groom circle the floor alone. The bride is next claimed by her father, while the groom dances with his new mother-in-law. The best man and the father of the groom are the bride's next two partners, while the groom takes the maid of honor and his own mother around the floor. The order of these traditional dances is optional, but they are usually completed before the guests join in again. The bride will probably dance with each usher and the groom with each bridesmaid before the dancing ends. It's also customary for each man in the wedding party to dance with each bridesmaid and both mothers.

THE CAKE CUTTING

The wedding cake should be beautifully displayed on a lace-clothed table with decorations of flowers and ribbons. The bride and bridesmaids can also place their bouquets there. Position the table where guests can admire the arrangement, but far enough out of the way that it won't get toppled.

The wedding cake can be cut approximately an hour after the receiving line disbands at a tea or cocktail reception, or before dessert at a dinner reception. There are several ways to alert guests that the ritual is about to take place: The band might signal with "The Bride Cuts the Cake" or other song; the banquet manager, wedding consultant, or bandleader might invite guests to gather; or you might signal guests.

Hand over hand, the bride and groom cut the first piece of wedding cake from the bottom layer. Customarily the bride and groom feed a piece of the first slice to each other, then perhaps serve pieces to each of their parents. The rest of the cake is cut by a member of the catering staff, the baker, or a friend, and is served to all guests.

If there is a groom's cake, it is sliced by the catering staff, and then boxed for guests to take home.

TOASTS

Toasting can begin any time after the receiving line has ended and everyone has a glass of champagne or other celebratory beverage in hand. Toasts can be given just before a meal, between courses, after the meal . . . or several times throughout the reception.

The best man always begins the toasts by saluting the bride and groom. The groom usually responds by thanking the best man and toasting the bride, his new in-laws, and his parents. The bride may then add her own toast—honoring the groom and his family, and thanking her parents. Attendants and other guests may add short toasts. (Longer family anecdotes are best given at the rehearsal dinner.) After the toasts are completed, the best man reads aloud any congratulatory telegrams.

How do you make a toast? Refer to your relationship with the person being toasted and add a wish for their future good fortune. Be succinct, be sincere, and be loving. For example, you could say, "To my parents, for helping me put together this wonderful day, and for all their love and support over the years. May we have many more happy family gatherings."

THROWING THE BOUQUET AND GARTER

Just before the bride changes into her going-away clothes, word is passed to the bridesmaids and other single women to gather at the bottom of a stairway, under a balcony, or at some other convenient spot. If the going-away flowers are part of the bridal bouquet, the bride should remove them first. If she carried a prayer book instead of a bouquet, she can throw the flowers and/or ribbon streamers that decorate the book. The bride may keep her bouquet, and toss a smaller version, or a silk replica made by the florist. Some brides turn and toss the bouquet over a shoulder, but if you want to aim at a sister or dear friend, you should probably face the group as you throw. Tradition says that the woman who catches the bouquet will be the next bride.

The groom may remove the bride's garter and toss it, just as the bride tossed the bouquet, to the single men. Or the bride may toss her garter to the men. Whoever catches it will be the next to marry, according to tradition. To continue the fun, in some areas it is the custom for the bachelor who catches the garter to then place the garter on the leg of the woman who caught the bouquet.

Section 9.

YOUR HONEYMOON

HONEYMOON PLANNING

After the work, stress, and *joy* of planning a wedding, your honeymoon glistens and gleams like a coveted, long-awaited prize. Whether your trip will last a few days or a few weeks, this is your opportunity to unwind and spend time alone together. For many couples, a honeymoon isn't just the "trip of a lifetime." It is also the first major vacation they'll plan together. You may feel overwhelmed by the many choices—a whole world of destinations, hundreds of hotels in every price range, a jumble of airfares, package deals, and car rentals. Follow these tips, and you'll find that planning isn't just easy, it's fun!

Start planning early. You should start discussing your honeymoon when you begin your other wedding plans. The more time you have, the better your chance of getting exactly what you want. Low-cost airfares are best booked months ahead; the same is true for popular hotels and resorts—and their best rooms. Many inns book up a full year in advance in prime vacation (and honeymoon) season, so get your wheels in motion *now*.

Put your dreams on the table. Talk honestly about the type of honeymoon you both envision. Do you prefer lying on a tropical beach with nothing but books and each other?

Or would you enjoy exploring a foreign city? Perhaps you're looking forward to skiing, tennis, and golf—or maybe shopping and sightseeing are your favorite activities. At night, what has the most appeal—a quiet gourmet dinner, or a glittering nightclub show?

It's important to remember that you are bound to be tired after the wedding, and the planning and parties preceding it. You may prefer a laid-back vacation at a resort rather than one that involves long flights or full days of sightseeing. If your hearts are set on a foreign location, consider spending the first night in a nearby hotel, and leave for long-distance travel the next day, when you've had time to rest. And even on the most ambitious trips, build in plenty of time for simply relaxing and delighting in the start of a new life together.

Consider your budget. Preparing a budget means setting priorities. What's more important: stretching your money in order to fit in Paris, London, *and* Rome, no matter what; or enjoying non-stop gourmet meals and pampering in just one city, or in a place that's closer to home? If seeing Europe, Hawaii, or Australia is your number-one goal, you can investigate ways to save money on airfares, stay in modest hotels, eat at inexpensive restaurants. But if you prefer more elegant surroundings, consider a destination that won't cost as much to get to. San Francisco can be just as exciting as Sardinia, and you'll save thousands of dollars in airfare.

Other Budget Tips:

Investigate off-season rates—they are usually lower than those in the most popular "high season." In Europe, off-season months are winter and spring. Mid-April through late fall, rates drop as much as 30 percent at resorts in the Bahamas, Caribbean, and Mexico, and temperatures are generally more comfortable than those back home.

It's almost always less expensive to explore the countryside rather than cities. So if you're thinking England, don't plan for a whole week in London; arrange trips to some of the quaint nearby towns and villages. Besides discovering another part of British culture, you'll find considerable savings in hotel and restaurant prices.

At many resorts, the meal plan, which includes some meals in your room rate, can save some money.

Packaged trips—including hotel, some meals, sightseeing, etc.—are often less expensive than ones you arrange yourselves, and many of the time-consuming details, such as arranging transfers from airport to hotels, will be handled for you.

Allow for some extras such as laundry, telephone calls, bar bills, airport taxes (up to $10 per person), and tipping (which can represent as much as 15 percent of your hotel and restaurant budget).

Unless you're planning to pay for everything by credit card, carry most of your money in traveler's checks. They are accepted nearly everywhere, can be replaced if lost or stolen, and make it easier to track spending, particularly in foreign countries, where the exchange rate will vary.

Gather information. Consult friends and relatives, your travel agent, *BRIDE'S* travel section, and travel magazines for destination ideas. Once you have narrowed your selections, visit your local library and bookstore, and research the sites more thoroughly. To learn more about travel in foreign countries, consult government tourism offices. For travel facts about U.S. cities, contact the appropriate Convention & Visitors Bureau. Write to airline tour departments or call their ticket offices for timetables, fare information, package tour booklets. You also can call the major hotel chains (which often provide toll-free numbers), and a variety of companies that sponsor tours, such as American Express, Liberty Travel, GoGo Tours, Perillo Tours, Thomson Vacations, Islands in the Sun. Ask about honeymoon packages—they are geared to your needs and may be less expensive than regular packages. If you plan to travel to a foreign-speaking country, you may want to familiarize yourself with the language. Consider language classes, and purchase travel, vocabulary, menu and wine guides, tape and book guides with mini-dialogues.

Consult a travel agent. You can make reservations on your own, but a good travel agent makes planning easier. A travel agent can recommend the best place to stay, the least expensive transportation, can help you get the paperwork you need—tickets, passports, visas, reservations, and immunizations. Most agents offer their services to consumers for free or nominal charges. (Airlines and hotels pay travel agencies commissions for booking their services.) Visit your travel agent with a list of preferred destinations, your travel dates, and a realistic budget.

About 10 days before you leave, your travel agent should provide all the necessities—itinerary, tickets, transfer coupons, hotel confirmations, and sightseeing vouchers. And if something goes wrong on the trip (a hotel doesn't have

HONEYMOON TRAVEL CHECKLIST

Travel Agent _____

Address _____ Phone _____

Fax Number _____ Confirmation Number _____

Agent's representative at destination site _____

Address _____ Phone _____

Cable address _____

TRANSPORTATION

Air, Rail, or Ship Line _____

Ticketing Address _____ Phone _____

	Departure	*Return*
Date	_____	_____
Ticket Number	_____	_____
Airport or Station	_____	_____
Flight or Route Number	_____	_____
Class	_____	_____
Take-off Time	_____	_____
Arrival Time	_____	_____

Confirmation date _____ Transportation cost $ _____

Car Rental Agent _____

Address _____ Phone _____

Make and model of car reserved _____

Pick-up and Drop-off site _____

Terms of charges _____

Estimated car rental cost $ _____

YOUR ROOM

Hotel or motel _____

Address _____ Phone _____

Phone for reservations (800) _____

Fax number _____ Confirmation number _____

Manager, assistant manager, or reservations manager _____

Check-in Date _____ Time _____ Check-out Date _____ Time _____

Description of room _____

Daily rate _____ Total room cost $ _____

MEAL PLAN

European (none) _____ Continental (just a light breakfast) _____

Modified American (breakfast dinner) _____ American (breakfast, lunch, dinner) _____

Other _____

                                                    Total meal cost $ _____

POCKET MONEY

                                        $ _____ Amount or Limit

Bills (10 singles, 4 fives, and 1 ten is good) _____

Other cash _____

Traveler's checks _____

Personal checks _____

Credit and charge cards (American Express, Visa, Diner's Club,
   Master Charge, oil company cards) _____

Foreign currency, if any _____

                                            Total pocket money _____

                                            Total cost of honeymoon _____

TO CARRY

_____ Driver's licenses

_____ Proof of age, citizenship (birth certificates, voter registration cards)

_____ Marriage license

_____ Passports or visas, if needed

_____ Names, addresses, phone numbers of all parents, with notation of time difference between their homes and your honeymoon spot

_____ Hometown doctor's name, address, phone number

_____ Copies of any prescriptions (for eyeglasses, contraceptives, etc.)

_____ List of all credit card numbers

_____ List of all traveler's check numbers

_____ Checking account numbers

_____ Name, address, phone number, and fax number of home banker (in case you run out of money)

_____ Shopping and gift list with everyone's sizes

_____ Names, addresses, phone numbers of local friends, relatives to call

_____ List of recommended restaurants, sights, etc., in honeymoon area

_____ List of luggage contents (needed for claiming any losses)

your room, you miss a flight, etc.), the travel agent will know the best way to handle the situation for you.

How to find a good travel agent? Family and friends can often offer the best recommendations, or check the yellow pages. Make certain the agency is a member of the American Society of Travel Agents (ASTA), a national association that sets professional standards for the travel industry.

Obtain necessary documents. If you plan to travel to a foreign country (Mexico, Canada, and some parts of the Caribbean are the exceptions), you will need a passport. You can apply for a passport at a county clerk's office, authorized post office, or federal passport office—there are 13 nationwide. Bring proof of citizenship (birth or naturalization certificate), proof of identity (driver's licenses), two identical two-inch-by-two-inch head shots (black and white or color) for each of you, and $42 each, in cash. (You can also write a personal check.) Allow at least a month to receive your passport. (Same-day passports can be obtained, often by waiting in long lines and presenting proof of immediate departure, at any federal passport office.) Passports are valid for 10 years, and can be renewed by mail; fee is $35. Call your main post office for more information.

A passport cannot be obtained in your married name before you wed. Use your maiden name on it, and on international airline tickets, visas. You can use your married name for hotel reservations, and on airline tickets for travel within the United States. Traveler's checks should be in your maiden name to match the identification needed to cash them, typically your passport.

Your travel agent will tell you if you need a visa, immunizations, or other documents. Mexico and some Caribbean countries now require photo IDs, so bring your driver's license (also needed for renting a car), along with proof of U.S. citizenship: a notarized birth certificate or voter registration card. Check the list "To Carry" on page 193.

Review important details. Check your tickets and reservations for accuracy as soon as you receive them. Keep tickets in a safe place—they're as good as cash.

Make sure luggage is properly tagged—inside and out—with your name and address. Check with your travel agent about any restrictions on number, weight, size of bags and carry-on luggage.

Reconfirm overseas flight 72 hours in advance, 24 hours ahead for domestic flights.

When leaving a hotel, recheck the room to make sure you have all your belongings. Always open all drawers and closets for a last look; check the back of the bathroom door; and scan your terrace for bathing suits left to dry. Allow plenty of time for hotel check-out and travel to the airport.

HONEYMOON WARDROBES

You may know where you're going to honeymoon, but do you know what to take, and in what bags? Probably not. Begin by making two lists—what you're likely to be doing each day, then all the clothes you'd need for those activities. Next, rate each item. Is the fabric good for travel? Can you wear it more than once? Does it fit into a basic color plan? "Yes" votes go on your packing list. Here are sample lists for three different honeymoons.

For a Tennis Weekend

Her:
1 all-weather coat or jacket
1 sporty daytime outfit (jeans and T-shirt?)
1 evening outfit

1 slip (if needed)
2 pairs of pantyhose (if needed)
7 sets of underwear
1 evening bag
1 cardigan sweater
2 tennis outfits
1 tennis hat or visor
2 wrist bands
1 tennis racket
1 can of tennis balls
7 pairs of tennis socks
1 pair of tennis shoes or sneakers
1 pair of casual flats
1 pair of dress sandals
1 pair of slippers
1 nightgown
1 travel robe
1 bathing suit and cover-up (if needed)

For a Tennis Weekend

Him:
1 all-weather coat or jacket
1 sporty daytime outfit (jeans and T-shirt?)
1 pair of dress pants
1 button-down shirt (or sport shirt)
1 tie (optional)
1 blazer
1 cardigan sweater
2 tennis outfits
1 tennis hat or visor
2 wrist bands
1 tennis racket
1 can of tennis balls
7 sets of underwear
7 pairs of tennis socks
2 pairs of dress socks
1 pair of tennis shoes or sneakers
1 pair of sandals
1 pair of leisure shoes
1 pair of slippers
1 pair of pajamas
1 travel robe
1 bathing suit and cover-up (if needed)

For a Week in the Sun

Her:
1 blazer
1 cardigan sweater
2 pairs of casual pants
1 pair of dressy pants
2 pairs of shorts
5 washable tops
1 sun hat, visor, or cotton bandana
2 evening outfits
1 slip (if needed)
2 pairs of pantyhose (if needed)
1 evening bag
7 sets of underwear
7 pairs of sport socks
1 pair casual sandals
1 pair of dress sandals
1 pair of tennis shoes or sneakers
1 pair of slippers
1 nightgown
1 travel robe
2 bathing suits
1 beach cover-up

For a Week in the Sun

Him:
1 blazer
1 cardigan sweater
2 pairs of casual pants
2 pairs of dress slacks
2 pairs of shorts
5 sport shirts
1 visor
5 button-down shirts
7 pairs of sport socks
7 pairs of dress socks
7 sets of underwear
1 pair of tennis shoes or sneakers
1 pair of sandals
1 pair of slippers
1 pair of pajamas
1 travel robe
2 bathing suits
1 beach cover-up

For Two Weeks Abroad

Her:
1 all-weather coat
1 head scarf
1 collapsible umbrella
1 pair lightweight gloves
2 skirts (one casual, one city)
2 pants (one casual, one city)
1 jacket or blazer
6 washable T-shirts and/or blouses
1 cardigan sweater
2 evening outfits
1 evening bag
3 pairs of pantyhose

1 slip

7 sets of underwear (bring hand-wash detergent)

7 pairs of sport socks

2 pairs of sneakers or walking shoes

1 pair of dress shoes

1 pair of slippers

1 nightgown

1 travel robe

If summer, add: bathing suit, cover-up, sandals, shorts, sneakers.

If winter, add: boots, lined gloves, wool scarf, two wool sweaters.

For Two Weeks Abroad

Him:

1 all-weather coat

1 collapsible umbrella

1 pair lightweight gloves

2 sport pants

2 dress pants

6 casual and/or dress shirts

1 blazer

1 cardigan sweater

7 sets of underwear (bring hand-wash detergent)

7 pairs of sport and/or dress socks

2 pairs of sneakers or walking shoes

1 pair of dress shoes

1 pair of slippers

1 pair of pajamas

1 travel robe

If summer add: bathing suit, cover-up, shorts, sneakers.

If winter add: boots, lined gloves, wool scarf, two wool sweaters.

HONEYMOON PACKING

1. Pack all your bulky things first—shoes, blow dryer, travel iron. Lay shoes heel to toe against hinge side of bag; place the other items there, too. You want heavyweight things nearest the ground when you're carrying the bag, so lightweight items don't get crushed.

2. Make a layer of all no-wrinkle separates next—jeans, T-shirts, sweaters, underwear. Roll them up tightly. (This is especially smart if your bag is soft-sided—rolled-up clothes will move with the give and take, still neatly pressed.) Fill up all the empty spaces—put a padding of panties around blow dryer. Snugly packed clothes can't move around or rumple.

3. Now put in everything that requires careful folding—linen slacks, cotton jackets, silk dresses. The secret is to make as few folds as possible. Lay slacks out flat, lining up creases, then fold in half. Fold each dress at the waist and pack lengthwise, skirt on bottom. Alternate collars and waistbands at opposite sides of the suitcase. Put plastic between layers to act as a cushion against wrinkles. (Plastic dry cleaner bags are economical, but plastic trash bags also can be used to tote your dirty laundry and wet swimsuits later on.)

4. Find extra spaces for belts and fun jewelry inside your shoes.

5. Pack a collapsible suitcase you can fill later with mementos, gifts.

6. Save for packing *last* anything you want to get at *first*—your swimsuit and cover-up, or your nightgown.

7. Keep all crucial items (birth control, camera, traveler's checks, contact lens case, travel tickets, good jewelry) in a tote bag at your side—in case your suitcase gets lost or stolen.

HONEYMOON BEAUTY BAG

Check off which toiletries and beauty aids *below* (you won't need them all) to pack for your trip.

_____ contraceptives

_____ foundation makeup

_____ blusher

_____ powder

_____ under-eye cover-up

_____ eyeshadow

_____ mascara

_____ eyeliner

_____ eyebrow pencil

_____ lipstick

_____ lip gloss

_____ facial moisturizer

_____ toner or astringent

_____ blemish cream

_____ shampoo

_____ cream rinse/conditioner

_____ blow dryer

_____ hair clips or bobby pins

_____ hairbrush

_____ comb

_____ nail brush

_____ body moisturizer

_____ body powder

_____ deodorant

_____ disposable razor or depilatory

_____ razor blades

_____ toothbrush

_____ toothpaste

_____ purse-size breath freshener or mouthwash

_____ emery boards

_____ nail polish

_____ polish remover pads

_____ nail clippers or scissors

_____ tweezers

_____ cotton swabs

_____ prescription medicines

_____ aspirin

_____ first-aid kit

_____ extra contact lenses or glasses

_____ contact lens solution

_____ tampons/sanitary napkins

_____ sunscreen or tanning lotion

_____ needle and thread

_____ safety pins

_____ travel-size clothes detergent

_____ bottle opener/corkscrew

HONEYMOON TIPPING

Tips—how much, for what, and to whom—can be perplexing, if you're not sure what is appropriate.

1. Starting Out: Add 15 percent to the taxi meter fare, 50 cents for each bag the driver stows in the trunk.

2. At the Airport: Pay the sky cap $2 for up to four pieces of luggage. $1 for each extra bag. When checking luggage curbside, $1 a bag is usually expected.

3. Aboard Ship: $5 per day per couple to the cabin steward and the table steward. If you wish, tip the dining room captain a few dollars too. $5 a week for the deck steward if you take chairs. Pay each the day before the cruise ends by placing cash in an envelope marked with the steward's name and your cabin number.

4. On a Train: Give the sleeping car porter $2 each time he makes up your berths.

5. At a Resort: With the exception of the bellhop (50 cents per bag) and the doorman (50 cents to hail a cab), it's customary to tip personnel directly (in an envelope) at the end of your stay: Your waiter get $5 a day, chambermaid $1 a day. Check the assistant manager about who else to tip.

6. In a Restaurant: Tip 15 percent of the bill; add no less than $2 for the wine steward—if you consult him. In Europe, a service charge may be automatically added to your bill; if so, no tip is expected.

7. On a Package Tour: Though tips are often included, check your travel agent to make sure.

NOTE: A tip is a bonus for good service. If the service you get is poor, or superior, tip accordingly.

HONEYMOON CATASTROPHES THAT NEEDN'T BE

Even with the most careful planning, mishaps can occur when traveling. Read through these typical problems so that you will know what to do if they happen to you.

You lose your tickets. First, remember that tickets are as good as cash, so act quickly. If there's time, call your travel agent and he or she will give advice, and may even be able to get a new ticket delivered—even to your hotel if you're already on the road. In a last-minute situation, airlines will ask you to file a lost-ticket claim, buy new tickets, and—if no one finds and uses the originals—will refund your money within 90 days. Or, if you have proof of purchase—automatic if you charge your tickets on a credit card—they will simply reissue tickets when you sign a pledge of responsibility in case of fraud. If your cruise tickets are missing, locate the cruise company representative in charge

on the pier. There should be a minimum of hassle if you have proof of identity, since a stateroom has been set aside in your name. At the Amtrak station, the station manager will remake your tickets if you fill out a form; if you hold reserved space, the computer should have a record of your payment and other necessary information.

You miss the plane (boat, train). Phone ahead to release plane or train space or warn the ship line, if you possibly can. If you're traveling on full-fare tickets, an airline will rebook you on the next available flight (even another line's), accept the tickets you hold. With restricted tickets, there may be an extra charge. Amtrak will put you on the next train, charge five percent penalty (minimum $5 per ticket) if you haven't cancelled. The agent of the cruise line or the local port authority will advise you about chartering a launch (if the ship is in sight) or flying to meet it.

Your luggage doesn't show up after a flight. Hold on to your claim checks and notify an airline agent immediately. Do not leave the airport without filing a loss report (or your claim may not be honored later). The airlines will provide a "reasonable amount of expenses" for necessities if you are left in a strange city without luggage. Airlines have different policies for reimbursing you for lost luggage and its contents. Most provide you with $1,250 in liability insurance for luggage when you buy your ticket. But you must be able to provide proof of contents—that means receipts—before collecting money.

There's no room at the inn. Ask to speak to the senior hotel staff person on duty and show him or her your confirmation slip, letter, or any other written proof of your reservation. In most cases, hotels will find ways to accommodate you. If there are higher-priced rooms available, you will be upgraded. If there are no rooms at all for some reason, they should pay for your lodging at an equivalent hotel, and for transportation there. They may even provide a free long-distance call—so you can notify your parents or others about your new whereabouts—and may give you complimentary drinks or meals.

Your double bed is two twins. Reconfirm your reservation a week before your arrival and double-check the bed situation. If this mistake does occur, call the assistant manager or front desk. He or she can probably move you to another room; or join the twins and change to double sheets, and give you top priority for the next double-bedded room.

The room is rotten. Again, call the assistant manager or front desk and describe the problem. He or she will try to fix things, or give you another room.

You get sick. Call the front desk and tell them you need a doctor. Many hotels have phy-

sicians on call, or at least can get in touch with local doctors. Travelers with an American Express Card or Visa Gold Card can get quick help in locating a doctor, lawyer, or prescription replacement by calling numbers provided to card members. If you're going abroad and don't speak the language, an organization called the International Association for Medical Assistance to Travelers (IAMAT) puts its members in touch with local English-speaking physicians in 70 countries around the world. (Write to IAMAT, 417 Center Street, Lewiston, N.Y. 14092, for information.)

If you have a persistent or potential health problem—an unusual blood type, an allergy to penicillin, or a chronic disease like asthma or diabetes—you should know about the Medic Alert Foundation. It provides members with a bracelet or neck chain that identifies your condition, even when you're unable to make it known yourself. (Write to Medic Alert Foundation, Turlock, Calif. 95380, for information.)

You have problems with the sun, bugs, the food. Go prepared. Bring plenty of sunscreen lotion and use it often. You can get burned simply walking around a tropical town, not only when sunbathing. Vinegar can take the sizzle out of sunburn, and it's most likely available from the housekeeper or kitchen when drugstores are closed.

If you're allergic to insect stings, bring proper serums with you. Otherwise, pack repellent spray, lotion, or stick, and an anti-itch preparation such as calamine lotion, a cortisone cream, or an anesthetizing spray. Ammonia can take the sting out of bites, too.

Check with your travel agent about food and drink precautions you should take in foreign countries. When in doubt, drink bottled water; avoid milk, unpeeled fruit and vegetables, ice made from local water; make sure food is thoroughly cooked.

It rains . . . and rains . . . and rains. Hotels sometimes provide rainy day activities such as movies or scavenger hunts. Bring along a selection of paperback books, playing cards, miniature backgammon or chess set. Get into your rain gear and go for a walk—the fresh air will lift even the dampest spirits.

You lose your passports. Search thoroughly, then report the loss at once to the nearest U.S. Consulate. They will tell you what to do from there. Keep a record of your passport number, date, and place of issue with your list of traveler's check numbers in a safe place: your carry-on bag or zipped into the lining of your suitcase. You might even want to keep two copies of important papers: one in luggage that you check at the airport, one in a bag you carry with you at all times.

You run out of money. If it's a matter of paying the hotel bill, the manager may bill you at home for all or part of what you owe. If you see a shortage coming, call or cable home for an international draft in the currency of the country you're in; your hometown bank can arrange it. And if you should lose all your money, the U.S. Consulate will help out with modest emergency funds.

You wonder how you will get along. Even if you've spent a lot of time with each other, you may feel awkward or embarrassed about things like suddenly having to share a bathroom, registering as husband and wife. You

might be nervous about traveling abroad; exhausted from wedding planning. And you might worry that you won't have anything to talk about after a few days, or that your interests differ. (He wants to play tennis, you want to lie in the sun.) These tensions should disappear as the days and weeks go by. Don't pressure yourselves into trying to have a good time every minute. The clichéd view of a honeymoon is that it is nonstop romance and togetherness. In reality, there will be highs and lows, exciting times and relaxed times. No rule says you have to do everything together. Whatever you're doing—whether one of you is swimming, and the other taking a golf lesson—just relax and enjoy the moment.

They find out you're honeymooners. While you may feel embarrassed admitting this, remember that all over the world, there are standing orders to give honeymooners extra special treatment—complimentary champagne, flowers, even a day on a sailboat. Don't miss out!

You're too tired to make love. Even couples who have lived together find the post-wedding fatigue, the pressure to perform, too much. There's no reason why you can't put off lovemaking until the next few days—when you are both rested.

Section 10:

YOUR HOME

YOUR PRIVATE WORLD: FINDING A HOME

You will want your home to reflect your personalities and provide a welcoming refuge from a hectic world. Whether you are buying a house, a cooperative apartment (where residents own *shares* of a corporation, which owns the building), a condominium (where residents own individual *portions of space* in the building), or renting an apartment or house, follow these helpful steps:

Talk about your needs and budget. Ask yourselves the following questions:

How many bedrooms will you need? Do you want space for a child, a home office or two, guests?

How much can you afford in rent, mortgage, and maintenance payments?

Are the costs of gas, water, electricity, taxes, garbage pickup, parking, included in monthly payments? If not, take these additional expenses into account.

Do you want a furnished or unfurnished place to start?

Do you want a doorman, alarm system, or other security measures?

Are other features important to you—living in an elevator building, having access to a swimming pool or exercise facilities?

In what area do you want to live?

How will you commute to work? Is the home you're considering near enough to public transportation?

Do your research. Check newspaper ads to see what's available in your price range. Visit apartment buildings, and leave your name and telephone number so the landlord can call you if there are any openings. Ask friends and colleagues if they know of any homes on the market. You can also register with a real estate broker, but in some states you will have to pay him or her a fee (a percentage of the purchase price or the yearly rent) once he or she finds you a home.

If you're moving to a new city, order a subscription to the local newspaper. Contact the Chamber of Commerce or other community organization for maps and information on newcomers' clubs and real estate agencies.

If you're moving to an apartment, you may also want to look at local landlord-tenant laws, which specify what a landlord must provide (heat, hot water, appliances, window guards, smoke detectors). Local consumer groups can provide copies of these laws, or check the local library.

Telephone first. Before actually looking at a home, save time by asking important questions about the purchase price or rent, the size, the date it will be available, and, if applicable, the property taxes and when the city or town last reassessed the property. If the rent or purchase price seems too low, ask why; the house or apartment may be in particularly bad shape, in a bad area, or near a noisy highway.

Examine the home carefully. Try to visit during the day *and* at night. Visits made in bad weather will allow you to observe any leaks, flood damage, or erosion. Take a close look at the neighborhood: Does it have services you need, such as a grocery store, dry cleaner? Is it pleasant and safe? If you're buying a home, pay a professional inspector to examine plumbing, heating, paint condition, roof, electrical wiring, insulation, basement. Any problems? Renegotiate the purchase price, accounting for all repair costs.

Here are other points to consider:

• **Space.** Are the rooms spacious enough for your needs?

• **Condition.** Is it clean, newly painted? If not, will walls be painted and problems fixed before you move in?

• **View.** Is there adequate light? Do you like what you see when you look outside? Are there any known plans to erect any new buildings in your line of vision?

• **Noise.** Can you hear street noise, trains, people from next door?

• **Utilities.** If renting an apartment, are gas, electricity, and water included in monthly payments? Are there appliances (stove, refrigerator, washer/dryer)? Do they work? If there is no washer/dryer in the building, are there laundry facilities nearby?

• **Heat/air-conditioning.** Where are the heat controls? Are there vents or outlets in every room? Are they controlled centrally or individually? If air-conditioning is not included, can

you install your own window units? Make sure insulation is adequate. (Good insulation keeps down heat and cooling bills.)

• **Plumbing.** Check if the water from all faucets/tubs/showers runs clear and strong and is free from rust. Have faucets dripped and eroded porcelain sinks? Hot water should be hot; toilets should flush.

• **Wiring.** Are there adequate electrical outlets in every room? Is there a fuse box in the apartment? Is there a cable television outlet?

• **Children.** If renting an apartment or buying a condominium, are children allowed?

• **Pets.** Are dogs and cats allowed? Many rentals, in particular, forbid pets.

• **Windows.** Make sure they open easily. Are there storm windows, screens, shades, or blinds?

• **Landscaping.** Have the grounds been kept well? Will you have to spend a lot of money to re-seed or de-weed a lawn, blacktop the driveway, remove an eyesore, paint trim?

• **Storage.** Is there enough room for clothes, linens, sports equipment? Is additional, secure basement, attic, or garage storage available?

• **Pests.** Is there a regular program for exterminating roaches, ants, rodents? If buying a home, check for termite damage.

• **Security.** Are there any protective devices—door and window locks, burglar alarms, a doorman?

• **Services.** How are mail delivery, garbage pickup, handled? If you're looking at an apartment building, is there a full-time maintenance staff or superintendent? Are there other services such as a garage, laundry, or exercise room?

Here, major requirements for buying, renting:

Get a mortgage. If you decide to buy a home, you'll need a mortgage, which is a sum of money a bank loans out to allow a person to buy a home. The homeowner pays back the loan to the bank, with interest, over a period of years. The home is considered collateral. To qualify for a mortgage, you must demonstrate a good credit history or record of paying back loans. Banks look for prompt, regular payments on student, credit cards, or car loans in the past. Before requesting a mortgage, investigate your own credit history to clear or explain any damaging data. Ask your bank which credit agency they report to and contact that company to request a copy of your history. (There may be a nominal fee.)

Give a down payment. Home buyers must hand over a down payment (usually 10 percent of the purchase price, although some cooperative apartments require more) in a check or in cash at the time they sign the contract. Usually a mortgage does not cover the down payment. You must come up with the money for this on your own.

Add up other costs. Think ahead about the fees involved in purchasing an apartment or home: mortgage payments, property taxes, title and mortgage insurance, recording fees for the deed, home inspector's charges, attorney's fees, title search, credit report.

Pay a security deposit. If you decide to rent an apartment, the landlord will probably ask for a security deposit, usually equal to one month's rent. Some, however, require the first and last month's rent. This deposit reserves the apartment while the landlord checks your references. It is held as security against your breaking the lease or damaging the property. It should be returned (plus interest in many states) when you move out, if you haven't broken any lease agreements.

Sign a lease or contract. When renting, it's important that details of the rental agreement be in writing, in a lease. Otherwise, rent could be raised unexpectedly, you could be asked to leave, or you may discover that appliances or fixtures that you expected to be included are missing. Some renters, instead of getting the more common lease that runs for one, two, or three years, sign an agreement based on month-by-month tenancy. Before you sign a tenant's lease, make a list of items you want fixed, projects that should be done, such as plumbing, repairs, or painting. Send the list to the landlord by registered mail and keep a copy for yourself. If the problems are not fixed, this will serve as proof of previous damages—if the landlord should try to withhold your security deposit when you move out.

Before you sign any lease, read it carefully. If you don't understand the wording, take a copy home and bring it back. Contact your local housing department, district attorney's office, or consumer affairs bureau if you have any questions.

A lease should include:
• name of the landlord—owner, not just manager
• apartment address and number
• amount of rent and date it's due
• amount of security deposit; the conditions for its return
• length of lease; what happens if you vacate before it expires?
• how much advance notice must be given by either party wanting to terminate the lease?
• who pays utilities?
• repairs the landlord must make; steps the tenant can take if such repairs aren't made (can you complain to a city or state agency or withhold rent?)
• conditions under which the landlord may enter the apartment.
• rules regarding pets
• conditions for making alterations—hanging pictures, wallpaper (structural improvements may become the landlord's property)
• conditions regulating subletting (a clause that allows you to rent the place to someone else is helpful if you must move before the lease runs out)

APPLIANCES AND OTHER HOUSEWARES

If the house or apartment you move into does not already have major appliances, you will have to buy them. This includes a refrigerator, range, microwave, dishwasher, washer, and dryer. Here's how to decide what to buy:

Evaluate Your Budget, Space

• Determine how much you can spend. Then weigh the appliance's cost versus its energy consumption. Sometimes energy-saving features on a more expensive model will save money on operating costs in the long run.

• Measure the space intended for the appliance, adding additional inches for air circulation (if needed), clearance for width/height of doors and hallways.

• Contact local utility companies to make sure that you have the appropriate hookups: a gas or electric line for a range; adequate water pressure and drainage for a dishwasher, washer/dryer unit.

Guarantee a Wise Buy

• Inquire if the appliance is approved by a leading appliance organization, such as Underwriters Laboratory (electrical), American Gas Association (gas).

• Find out if delivery and installation are included in the price.

• Read the warranty carefully. What is its length? Does it cover *all* parts, labor? Who is responsible for arranging service?

Consider Size, Features

• Refrigerator—Allow six cubic feet per person (four feet in the freezer). Select a larger refrigerator capacity if you garden and freeze vegetables; more freezer space if you cook meals ahead; adjustable shelves if you buy large items; an automatic ice cube maker if you entertain often. Save energy with an insulated door.

• Range—The best space saver is a free-standing unit, about 30 inches wide, that combines oven and surface burners. A self-cleaning oven saves time, work; removable burners, drip pans, promote easy cleaning. Consider clock timers—to allow automatic start-stop cooking.

• Microwave—Save room with a model that's built into your range, or one that fits on the countertop. A programmed cooking feature changes the temperature level automatically. Timers set the unit at defrost, then cook while you're away.

• Dishwasher—Built-in models fit under a kitchen counter. Choose one with different washing cycles (light, normal, heavy) to save energy. A rinse-and-hold feature rinses food off a light load of dishes, until you're ready to run a full load.

• Washer/Dryer Unit—For limited space, opt for a front-loading washer with a dryer stacked above (about 2.3 cubic feet). Look for energy-saving cold cycles and adjustable water levels for washing smaller loads. Time controls, auto-drying features on a dryer cut energy costs.

FURNISHING YOUR HOME

When faced with empty rooms and an enormous selection in furniture, floor and wall coverings, decorating may seem like an overwhelming task. Here are some tips on getting started.

• **Determine your tastes.** Talk together

about your likes and dislikes. Window-shop and look at decorating magazines to get ideas about the colors and styles that please you both.

• **Draw up a floor plan.** Be sure the furniture you choose will fit into each room. Using graph paper, figure out a scale (for example, ¼ inch on paper equals one foot); then sketch the room, indicating location of windows, radiators, any other built-in features. Next, draw furniture shapes to scale on another piece of paper, cut them out, and arrange them to suit your needs and traffic patterns.

• **Work out a budget.** Calculate your monthly discretionary income—money available after all essentials (rent, utilities, loan payments, food, transportation) are paid. Each month, deposit a portion of these available funds in a separate "home furnishings" savings account. Let money accumulate until you're ready to buy. If you decide to buy on credit, be *sure* that the monthly payments will not strain your budget.

• **Work with what you have.** You both probably already own some furniture. Tie everything together with a strong color scheme. For example, use warm yellow for curtains, rug, walls. Re-cover sofas and chairs in a coordinating fabric.

• **Determine what to buy first.** Here is a list of must-have furnishings:

For sleeping: mattress and box spring, two sets of linens, blankets and comforter or bedspread, pillows, bedside tables

For sitting: sofa, chairs (at least two—these could double as dining room chairs), end tables

For light: one lamp on each side of the bed, several for the living and dining room, one for a desk; extra ceiling lighting for bathroom and kitchen, if necessary

For privacy: curtains, shutters, or shades for bedroom and bathroom; may also be necessary for other rooms

For eating: dining room table and at least two chairs (extra chairs can be fold-up style)

For storage: chest of drawers for bedroom, shelves for books and records; low cabinets can double as tables

• **Go shopping.** The better stores are not always the most expensive, and often provide free decorating help.

Here, some hints on buying different types of furniture:

Choosing wood furnishings. "Solid wood" means almost what it sounds like: All visible furniture surfaces are composed of top-grade wood. (Interior parts, however, may be a less expensive wood.) "Veneers" are surface sheets of a particular wood, covering a material like plywood or hardboard. Something described as having an "oak finish" has a surface stain the color of oak.

Whatever the construction, a quality piece of furniture should pass these tests:

• Operate all moving parts. Drawers should glide smoothly; automatic stops should keep them from falling out. Inset or glass panels in cabinets should not rattle when the door is opened or closed.

• Examine the joinery (the method by which the various parts are attached). Dovetailed joints are best on drawers; either double-dowel joints or interlocking mortise-and-tenon joints are preferred for other furniture parts. Wherever a leg joins a frame, there should be reinforcing corner blocks. (All joints should also be glued or screwed for extra strength.)

• Check the back panels on wall units or cabinets. They should be inset or screwed in place, with holes for electrical cords.

• Make sure the grain pattern is uniform; finishes shouldn't be streaked.

Selecting Upholstered Pieces. Buying upholstered furniture is tricky because you have to assess something you really can't see. Here are some of the more obvious ways to determine quality:

• Try to lift the piece from an end—it should not wobble or creak. Heavy frames are best—

DECORATING PLAN

LIVING ROOM

Square footage _____

Wall color _____ paint ☐   paper ☐

Floor covering color _____ carpet ☐ area rugs ☐ price _____

Drapery color _____ dimensions _____ fabric _____ price _____

Period or type of furniture _____ finish _____

Sofa _____ style _____ brand _____ color _____ price _____

Chair _____ style _____ brand _____ color _____ price _____

Chair _____ style _____ brand _____ color _____ price _____

Chair _____ style _____ brand _____ color _____ price _____

Tables _____ coffee _____ end _____ occasional _____

Television _____ brand _____ price _____

Stereo components _____ brand (s) _____ price(s) _____

Desk _____ price _____ Desk chair _____ price _____

Lamps _____ floor _____ table _____ wall _____ ceiling _____

Storage units (chest, etc.) _____

Paintings, prints, wall hangings, other accessories _____

_____

_____

DINING ROOM OR AREA

Square footage _____

Wall color _____ paint ☐   paper ☐

Floor covering color _____ area rugs ☐ carpet ☐ flooring ☐ price _____

Drapery color _____ dimensions _____ fabric _____ price _____

Table size _____ style _____ finish _____ brand _____ price _____

Chairs, number _____ style _____ finish _____ brand _____ price _____

Sideboard or chest _____ style _____ finish _____ brand _____ price _____

Serving cart _____ style _____ finish _____ brand _____ price _____

Lamps _____ floor _____ table _____ wall _____ ceiling _____

Paintings and other accessories _____

_____

_____

BEDROOM

Square footage _____

Wall color _____ paint ☐   paper ☐

Floor covering color _____ area rugs ☐ carpet ☐ price _____

Drapery color _____ dimensions _____ fabric _____ price _____

Bed size _____ headboard style _____ brand _____ price _____

Mattress/box spring _____ brand _____ price _____

Dresser/chests _____ style _____ finish _____ brand _____ price _____

Mirror _____ style _____ finish _____ brand _____ price _____

Chair _____ style _____ finish _____ brand _____ price _____

Vanity table or desk _____ style _____ finish _____ brand _____ price _____

Night table _____ style _____ finish _____ brand _____ price _____

Lamps _____ floor _____ table _____ wall _____ ceiling _____

Paintings and other accessories _____

_____

_____

they indicate thick hardwood stock that has been treated so it won't warp.

• Look for frame joints that are double-doweled, screwed, glued, and reinforced with corner blocks for greater strength.

• Push hard on the arms. They should feel sturdy, stable. (Arm caps will double fabric life.) Corners of arms, backs, and the front frame edge just below the cushion should not be lumpy. Hard frame edges mean padding is inadequate.

• Remove the seat cushions and examine the deck (base of the seat). Fabric should be coordinated; you shouldn't be able to feel any springs when you press down.

• Examine the tailoring. Patterns should line up, seams and trims should be straight, without puckering, loose threads.

• Ask your retailer to apply a soil- and stain-resistant coating to the fabric.

Ask about delivery time—it's often a minimum of four weeks. Find out if delivery personnel will help set up furniture. You may not have to pay in full until the furniture is delivered. Whatever payment plan you work out, keep copies of contracts, warranties, receipts.

Ways to save: Comb tag sales or thrift shops—occasionally one comes across a real "find" that needs refurbishing to bring it back to life. Build bookshelves or other furniture (some companies produce kits), or buy one-of-a-kind pieces by craftsmen.

BUYING A MATTRESS

Here are some important points to consider when selecting a mattress:

Firmness. One manufacturer's "firm" may equal another's "extra-firm," so don't rely on descriptions. Try them all together and see what's comfortable for you both. Your body should be supported at all points, especially the hips, shoulders, and lower back. If one likes "extra-firm" and the other doesn't, order two different twin-size mattresses and push them together behind a single headboard to make a dual-king bed. Or custom order a mattress that's hard on one side, soft on the other; a firm mattress with thick padding on top.

Size. Consider comfort, leg and arm room. If one of you is tall, order an extra-long king-size bed. Snugglers can sleep in a queen or even a *double* bed, while thrashers need at least a king-size in order to get a good night's sleep. Even if you end up putting your clothes somewhere else, nothing is more important in the bedroom than a bed.

Innerspring vs. foam. Solid foam bedding is lightweight and may be used on a platform base with drawers underneath for storage. The new plastic foams come in different firmnesses and won't crumble or powder.

Innerspring mattresses have heavy steel coils padded with upholstery fabric inside. Look for reinforced edges to save wear and tear, strong handles for easy turning, plastic or metal mesh ventilators to help air circulate inside. A good innerspring should be guaranteed for approximately 15 years.

Box spring. A box spring prolongs the life of the mattress by acting as a shock absorber. Mattresses and box springs are designed to work well together.

Frame. A frame holds the mattress and box spring off the floor. Order casters (wheels) to make moving and cleaning behind and beneath the bed easier.

Care. To prolong the life of your mattress, protect it from dust by using a protective covering, vacuuming it regularly. Alternate turning your mattress over side to side, then end to end every two weeks at first, later every few months. Reverse your box spring once a year so it wears evenly.

Water beds. A water bed, in which the mattress contours to your own body curves, is an alternative you may want to consider. The thermostat-controlled water bed heater can provide just the warmth you need to soothe body aches and ensure a relaxing sleep. There are many styles and options in choosing water bed mattresses. A hard-sided water mattress is a vinyl bag enclosed in a wooden frame, requiring special sheets and quilt. A soft-sided water mattress has a foam perimeter and designer ticking—to combine the look of a conventional bed with the benefits of sleeping on water. Also, be sure to ask your water bed dealer to show you a mattress with your choice of motion—from full motion, to semi-motionless, to motionless—depending on how accustomed you are to being lulled to sleep.

Sofa beds. A sofa bed provides necessary sleeping space if you live in a one-room apartment or you have a one bedroom and want an extra place for guests to sleep. Test a sofa bed carefully. The bed should glide out easily, upholstery should be lump-free, and the mattress should be comfortable. Hardware on the bed frame should have no protrusions that might scratch a leg or tear a sheet. Make sure the mattress is protected against mildew, bacteria, odor, and that the upholstery fabric is stain-resistant.

YOUR BUDGET

Good budgeting will give you control over your bills. It can provide a way of life that both of you will find rewarding. Here, are some steps to follow:

Set goals. Discuss how you both will be living in the next year, in five years, in ten years. Record your goals on paper and estimate how much money you will need to achieve them.

Size up weekly income. Write down what each of you makes after taxes, Social Security, and other deductions from your paycheck. Include any other income such as bonuses, or stock dividends.

Calculate fixed expenses. Fixed expenses are the ones that remain unchanged on a monthly, quarterly, or annual basis. They usually include rent or mortgage, insurance, loan payments, savings. (Note: saving is as important as other fixed payments.)

Estimate flexible expenses. These are items that change from month to month: food, telephone, clothing, entertainment, transportation. The only way to accurately determine these expenses is to keep a record of *everything* you spend for about three months.

Draw up a weekly budget. Use the following worksheet to record your estimated income and expenses. If expenses exceed your income, or there is not enough left for savings toward your goal, cut back on flexible expenses—the easiest to control. If that's not enough, consider whether it's possible to cut back on fixed expenses. (Maybe move into a less expensive home, look for a higher-paying job or extra work.) If what you make is more than you spend, save a set amount each paycheck, perhaps consult a financial planner or your accountant to inquire about investments.

Review your budget. Go over it at least every six months. Your lives are changing—so should your budget.

SUPERMARKET CHECKLIST

You can make copies of this list, check off your needs as they arise during the week, and take this list with you.

STAPLES
_____ Tea
_____ Coffee
_____ Granulated sugar/ sugar substitute
_____ Confectioner's sugar
_____ Brown sugar
_____ All-purpose flour
_____ Baking soda
_____ Baking powder
_____ Yeast
_____ Cornstarch
_____ Vegetable shortening
_____ Vegetable oil
_____ Unsweetened chocolate/cocoa
_____ Spaghetti/noodles
_____ Rice
_____ Cereals

CONDIMENTS
_____ Prepared mustard
_____ Mayonnaise
_____ Catsup/chili sauce
_____ Relishes/olives/pickles
_____ Olive oil
_____ Vinegar
_____ Worchestershire sauce
_____ Hot pepper sauce
_____ Peanut butter
_____ Jams/jellies
_____ Pancake syrups
_____ Vanilla extract
_____ Spices
_____ Herbs
_____ Salt/pepper
_____ Garlic

SHORT-CUT FOODS
_____ Sauce mixes
_____ Bouillon cubes
_____ Pudding mixes
_____ Flavored/unflavored gelatins
_____ Spaghetti sauce
_____ Salad dressings
_____ Biscuit/piecrust mix
_____ Bread crumbs
_____ Pancake mix
_____ Canned/powdered milk

WEEKLY NEEDS
_____ Milk
_____ Cream sweet/sour
_____ Eggs
_____ Butter/margarine
_____ Ice cream
_____ Cheese
_____ Dinner meats/fish/ poultry
_____ Lunch meat/ frankfurters
_____ Bacon/sausage
_____ Potatoes
_____ Onions
_____ Fresh fruits
_____ Salad vegetables
_____ Baked goods/bread/ rolls
_____ Cocktail nibbles
_____ Crackers/cookies
_____ Alcoholic beverages/ wine/liquor

DRUG ITEMS
_____ Toothpaste
_____ Adhesive bandages
_____ Aspirin
_____ Cotton
_____ Shampoo
_____ Razor blades
_____ Tampons/sanitary napkins
_____ Shaving cream
_____ Deodorant
_____ Mouthwash

CANNED AND FROZEN FOODS
_____ Soda
_____ Beer
_____ Fruit juices
_____ Vegetables
_____ Fruits
_____ Tomato sauce/paste
_____ Tuna/salmon
_____ Concentrated soups

HOUSEHOLD NEEDS
_____ Paper napkins
_____ Plastic wrap
_____ Plastic bags
_____ Aluminum foil
_____ Waxed paper
_____ Toilet paper
_____ Facial tissues
_____ Matches
_____ Light bulbs
_____ Bars of soap
_____ Household cleaners/ soaps/detergents

WEEKLY BUDGET CHART

	WEEKLY TOTALS
INCOME	
Add: His weekly income $_____	
Her weekly income $_____	
Total $_____ $_____	

EXPENSES

Fixed: Monthly housing expenses

Rent/Mortgage payment $_____
Water $_____
Gas $_____
Electricity $_____
Telephone $_____
Total $_____

Convert to weekly estimate:

$_____ × 3 = $_____ ÷ 13 $_____

Periodic fixed expenses
(Figure each annually)

Loan payments $_____
Insurance premiums $_____
Medical check-ups $_____
Other (Tuition) $_____
Total $_____

Convert to weekly estimate:

$_____ ÷ 52 = $_____

	WEEKLY TOTALS
Periodic flexible expenses	
(Estimate annually)	
Her Clothing $_____	
His Clothing $_____	
Other (Vacations) $_____	
Total $_____	

Convert to weekly estimate

$_____ ÷ 52 = $_____

Flexible: Weekly living expense
Food/Beverage $_____
Transportation $_____
Household (Upkeep, etc.) $_____
Laundry/Dry Cleaning $_____
Entertainment $_____
Gifts/Donations $_____
His Personal $_____
Her Personal $_____
Total $_____ $_____

Planned savings/Emergencies $_____

_____

Add total weekly expenses $_____

Compare to total weekly income $_____